GOD SPEAKS OF RETURN

AND BANNERED

ANTHONY A EDDY

Front and Rear Covers

Joy, Freedom, and Exuberance— Celebrating The Rewards of Life

Instances wherein a crown is mentioned: *Pages*

1. My Spirit shall place a victor's crown on each who so deserves.   8

2. The sanctity of life carries a crown of preservation.   207

3. Isa 28:5 In that day The Lord of hosts will be For a crown of Glory and a diadem of beauty To the remnant of His people,   226

4. In these things lie the victor's crown: ...   249

5. The Crown Jewel of Creation has an image beyond compare,   261

6. ... regally before the crowns;   274

7. The Martyrs of The Crown.   379

Plus several other places in conjunction with these.

GOD Speaks of Return

For His Bride
And of the Impact of this Event
Upon the Peoples of The Earth

and Bannered

Introduces
His Banner – His Flag – His Standard

A Sign of The Kingdom of God
An Emblem of The Holy Spirit

Anthony A Eddy
(Scribe)

Copyright and Publishing

© 2019 by BookWhip Publishing.

All rights reserved. No part of this publication may be reproduced, stored in a retrieval system or transmitted in any way by any means, electronic, mechanical, photocopy, recording or otherwise without the prior permission of the author except as provided by USA copyright law.

Printed in the United States of America

Soft Cover ISBN: 978-1-950580-98-9
Hard Cover ISBN: 978-1-951469-58-0
Ebook ISBN: 978-1-951469-46-7

1. "GOD Speaks of Return and Bannered"

Cover design, Manuscript Content and Layout, Conceptual Related Imagery and titling texts, ©® Copyright 2010, 2012, 2015, 2017, 2018, 2019 by The Advent Charitable Trust, CC45056, Hamilton, New Zealand. All rights reserved worldwide.

www.thewebsiteofthelord.org.nz

Prepared on a 27in iMac™© with the use of Nisus®© Writer Pro. All trademarks™ and intellectual rights remain the property of their respective owners.

To order additional copies of this book, contact:
Bookwhip
1-855-339-3589
https://www.bookwhip.com

Dedication

To our God of Love,

of Justice,

of Redemption—

who is very interested in all we do

and in our achieving our return home.

For He alone is worthy of the devotion of Man.

The Divinely Dictated Parts of The End-time Psalms of God are—

	Pages	Total Words
1. GOD Speaks of Return and Bannered	416	90,840
2. GOD Speaks to Man on The Internet	498	122,349
3. GOD Speaks as His Spirit Empowers	272	65,494
4. GOD Speaks to Man in The End-time	166	38,920
5. GOD Speaks in Letters of Eternity	202	48,073
6. GOD Speaks to His Bridal Presence	326	78,183
7. GOD Speaks to His Edifice	512	122,516
8. GOD Speaks of Loving His Creation	280	67,234
9. GOD Speaks Now of a Seal Revealed	124	23,260

Acknowledgements

My especial thanks and appreciation both to my Pastor (and also in his callings both as a prophet and an apostle) and to his wife. They have invited me to their home on numerous occasions.

Without his support and counsel (sometimes with the wisdom of silence!) this collection of divine leading would not have come to be. The items, as they have been received, have been handed regularly to him over the past eighteen months. Our fellowship also has been kept informed.

My thanks also to those who had several words from God and were faithful enough to bring them before our fellowship prior to their significance being known to them.

My thanks, as well, to those many forbearing folk who have taught our family and have encouraged us in the ways of God over the last many years.

Contents— Order Received

(2, 3, 4 ...) Denotes following items with a similar or same name as earlier ones

(Title) GOD Speaks of Return and Bannered	I
About The Cover	II
GOD Speaks of Return and Bannered	III
Copyright and Publishing	IV
Dedication	V
Acknowledgements	VI
Contents— Ordered Index	VII
Contents— Alphabetical Index	X
Contents— Category Index	XIII
Appeal of Jesus (Excerpt Bk 9)	XVI
Testimony of The Day of The Lord	XVII
Prelude	XIX
History of The Book	XX
Introduction	XXIV

001. Vision	1
002. Vision Scriptures	2
003. Banner Named, Introduced	7
004. Banner Comes Forth	8
005. Banner Affirmed as His Will	10
006. Banner of Design	14
006a. Red Cross	14
006b. White Cross	14
006c. Star and its Positioning	14
006d. Blue on The Banner	14
007. Character of Man	15
008. Banner Defined	17
009. Divine Scriptural Revelations	18
010. Divine Commentary	19
011. Banner Speaks of Unity	36
012. Banner of The Protocols	37
013. Slaughter of The Innocent	39
014. I Love My People	44
015. Roar of The Lion of Judah	46
016. Churches in The Mountains	47
016a. ROAR of The Lion	48
017. Responsibility of Freewill	51
018. Lion Offers All, His Ways	53
019. Lioness and The Lion	54
020. Sin Beneath The Veil	57
021. In Love	58
022. New Signs in Use	59
023. New Signs of The Kingdom	61
024. Justice in Judgement	63
025. Intent of The Lord	64
026. Servants of The Lord	66
027. Return of The Shepherd	67
028. Hurdles of Man	68
029. Book of Life	70
030. Battlements of The Mind	72
031. Mystery of Life	75
032. Turning Points in Life	76
033. Fickleness of Man	78
034. Message of Compassion	80
035. Journey of Man	81
036. Butterflies of Heaven	83
037. Lion of Judah in Readiness	86
038. Lion of Judah	87
039. Glory of The Kingdom	88
040. New Day	89
041. Edifice of God	91
042. Spectacles of Heaven	93
043. Transgressors of The Soul	94
044. Healing of Man	95
045. Death of Man	99
046. Birth of Man	102
047. Pathways of The Rain	103
048. Tenants of The Mind	105
049. Message of Healing	107
050. Effects of The Fall on Man	109
051. Wrath of God	111
052. Frustrations of God	112
053. Entrance to Heaven	114
054. Temple of The Body	116
055. Guidance of God	118
056. Handshake of Creation	120
057. Silence of God	122
058. Pathway of The Son	123
059. Fall of a House of Hell	125
060. Miracle of Christmas	127
061. Body of Man 1— Designed	129

062. Gathering of The Bride	131	107. Garden of The Lord	221
063. Sequencing of Time	133	108. Coming of The Spirit	223
064. Body of Man 2— A House	135	109. Coming of The Trumpet Call	224
065. Body of Man 3— A Temple	139	110. Coming of The Turmoil	225
066. Body of Man 4— Protected	142	111. Precept upon Precept	226
067. Variety of Choice	144	112. Carriers of God's Wisdom	228
068. Chains of Choice	146	113. Footpaths of The Lord	230
069. Abilities of Man	148	114. Distractions of Man	232
070. Fiefdom of The Lord	150	115. Confines of The Spirit	234
071. Plunder of The Soul	153	116. Polishing of The Soul	235
072. Christmas Day	155	117. Stepping-Stones of The Lord	237
073. Banner Prepared	156	118. Attendants of The Bride	239
074. Wings of Heaven	157	119. Tongue of Fire	241
075. Bones of The Earth	160	120. Mission of My People	244
076. Waters of Life	161	121. Mark of The Beast	245
077. Earth of God	162	122. Way Home	248
078. Messages of Life	164	123. Defilement of The Spirit	250
079. Banner of Effects	166	124. Needs of Life	251
080. I, The Lord	167	125. Utterance of A Promise	253
081. Banner of Destiny	169	126. Visitation of The Earth	255
082. Fire and The Tribulation	171	127. Power of The Spirit of Man	257
083. Banner Brings Response	175	128. Preparedness of Man	259
084. Banner in The Role	177	129. Crown Jewel of Creation	261
085. Banner as A Signpost	179	130. Survival of The Flock	263
086. Banner of The Battle	181	131. Feast of The Incarnation	265
087. Keys of The Kingdom	183	132. Comfort of The Lord (1)	267
088. Banner Setting Forth	185	133. Temperature of The Soul	269
089. Banner on The Way	186	134. Wealth of Man	272
090. Rising of The Son	187	135. Lion of Judah Reigns	274
091. Banner of Assails	189	136. Trinkets of The Heart	275
092. Banner in its Presence	191	137. Morality of God	278
093. Banner at Home (Pottage of Stew)	193	138. Gospel of The Lord	280
094. Land of Plenty	196	139. Dispelling of The Shadows	283
095. Favour of The Lord	198	140. Cup of Fruit of The Vine	285
096. Race of The Righteous	200	141. Feeding of The Sheep	288
097. Beauty of The Earth	202	142. Attacks Upon The Heart of Man	291
098. Troops of The Lord	204	143. Exorcizing of Demons	294
099. Candles of The Lord	206	144. Visitors to The Garden	295
100. Sanctity of Life	207	145. Lick of The Lion	299
101. Plank of A Nation	209	146. Victors of The Soul	301
102. Galleons of Service	211	147. Power of The Holy Spirit	303
103. Vapours of The Earth	213	148. Mustering of The Bride	306
104. Coming of The Son	216	149. Rise of Ashkelon	313
105. Commitments of Man	218	150. Hackers of The Body	316
106. Birthday of A Saint	220	151. Pets of The Earth	318

152. Arms of The Lord	320
153. Wherewithal of Man	322
154. Goliaths of Man	324
155. Coming of The Kingdom	326
156. Portals of The Kingdom	328
157. Purring of The Lion	331
158. Righteous in Preparation	332
159. Trickle of The Foe	334
160. Promises of God	336
161. Census of God	339
162. Age of Grace	342
163. Ways of God	345
164. Advent of The Lord	349
165. Inheritance of Man	351
166. Fear of God	352
167. Profanity of Man	354
168. Comfort of The Lord (2)	356
169. Roar of Zion	358
170. Tears of The Lord	360
171. Strength of The Lord	362
172. Window of Wonder	364
172a. Window of Wonder— A Parable	366
173. Replevin of The Lord	368
174. Dungeons of The Heart	370
175. Extraction of Man	372
176. Measure of A Man	374
177. Foretaste of Heaven	376
178. Glory of God	378

Appendix—	*381*
Flag and Standard in Use	382
Banner of The Kingdom in Use	383
Emblem of The Spirit in Use	383
Emblem of The Kingdom in Use	384
Anthem of The King	385
About the Scribe	*387*
Journaling and Notes (1)	*388*
Journaling and Notes (2)	*389*
Book 4 Reviews (2)	*390*
Book 8 Review (1)	*391*

Contents— Alphabetical

(2, 3, 4 ...) Denotes following items with a similar or same name as earlier ones

(Title) GOD SPEAKS OF RETURN AND BANNERED	I
About The Cover	II
GOD Speaks of Return and Bannered	III
Copyright and Publishing	IV
Dedication	V
Acknowledgements	VI
Contents— Ordered Index	VII
Contents— Alphabetical Index	X
Contents— Category Index	XIII
Appeal of Jesus (Excerpt Bk 9)	XVI
Testimony of The Day of The Lord	XVII
Prelude	XIX
History of The Book	XX
Introduction	XXIV

A

Abilities of Man	148
About the Scribe	398
Advent of The Lord	349
Age of Grace	342
Appendix—	381
Arms of The Lord	320
Attacks Upon The Heart of Man	291
Attendants of The Bride	239

B

Banner Affirmed as His Will	10
Banner as A Signpost	179
Banner at Home (Pottage of Stew)	193
Banner Brings Response	175
Banner Comes Forth	8
Banner Defined	17
Banner in its Presence	191
Banner in The Role	177
Banner Named, Introduced	7
Banner of Assails	189
Banner of Design	14
Banner of Destiny	169
Banner of Effects	166
Banner of The Battle	181
Banner of The Protocols	37
Banner on The Way	186
Banner Prepared	156
Banner Setting Forth	185
Banner Speaks of Unity	36
Battlements of The Mind	72
Beauty of The Earth	202
Birth of Man	102
Birthday of A Saint	220
Blue on The Banner	14
Body of Man 1— Designed	129
Body of Man 2— A House	135
Body of Man 3— A Temple	139
Body of Man 4— Protected	142
Bones of The Earth	160
Book of Life	70
Butterflies of Heaven	83

C

Candles of The Lord	206
Carriers of God's Wisdom	228
Census of God	339
Chains of Choice	146
Character of Man	15
Christmas Day	155
Churches in The Mountains	46
Comfort of The Lord (1)	267
Comfort of The Lord (2)	356
Coming of The Kingdom	326
Coming of The Son	216
Coming of The Spirit	223
Coming of The Trumpet Call	224
Coming of The Turmoil	225
Commitments of Man	218
Confines of The Spirit	234
Crown Jewel of Creation	261
Cup of The Fruit of The Vine	285

D

Death of Man	99
Defilement of The Spirit	250
Dispelling of The Shadows	283
Distractions of Man	232
Divine Commentary	19

Divine Scriptural Revelations	18
Dungeons of The Heart	370

E

Earth of God	162
Edifice of God	91
Effects of The Fall on Man	109
Emblem of The Spirit	22
Entrance to Heaven	114
Exorcizing of Demons	294
Extraction of Man	372

F

Fall of a House of Hell	125
Favour of The Lord	198
Fear of God	352
Feast of The Incarnation	265
Feeding of The Sheep	288
Fickleness of Man	78
Fiefdom of The Lord	150
Fire and The Tribulation	171
Foretaste of Heaven	376
Footpaths of The Lord	230
Frustrations of God	112

G

Galleons of Service	211
Garden of The Lord	221
Gathering of The Bride	131
Glory of God	378
Glory of The Kingdom	88
Goliaths of Man	324
Gospel of The Lord	280
Guidance of God	118

H

Hackers of The Body	316
Handshake of Creation	120
Healing of Man	95
Hurdles of Man	68

I

I Love My People	44
I, The Lord	167
In Love	58
Inheritance of Man	351
Intent of The Lord	64

J

Journey of Man	81
Justice in Judgement	63

K

Keys of The Kingdom	183

L

Land of Plenty	196
Lick of The Lion	299
Lion of Judah	87
Lion of Judah in Readiness	86
Lion of Judah Reigns	274
Lion Offers All, His Ways	53
Lioness and The Lion	54

(Also see 3 others as 'Roar', 1 as 'Purring')

M

Mark of The Beast	245
Measure of A Man	374
Message of Compassion	80
Message of Healing	107
Messages of Life	164
Miracle of Christmas	127
Mission of My People	244
Morality of God	278
Mustering of The Bride	306
Mystery of Life	75

N

Needs of Life	251
New Day	89
New Signs in Use	59
New Signs of The Kingdom	61

P

Pathway of The Son	123
Pathways of The Rain	103
Pets of The Earth	318
Plank of A Nation	209
Plunder of The Soul	153
Polishing of The Soul	235
Portals of The Kingdom	328
Power of The Holy Spirit	303
Power of The Spirit of Man	257
Precept upon Precept	226
Preparedness of Man	259
Profanity of Man	354

Promises of God	336
Purring of The Lion	331

R

Race of The Righteous	200
Red Cross	14
Replevin of The Lord	368
Responsibility of Freewill	51
Return of The Shepherd	67
Righteous in Preparation	332
Rise of Ashkelon	313
Rising of The Son	187
Roar of The Lion	48
Roar of The Lion of Judah	46
Roar of Zion	358

S

Sanctity of Life	207
Sequencing of Time	133
Servants of The Lord	66
Silence of God	122
Sin Beneath The Veil	57
Slaughter of The Innocent	39
Spectacles of Heaven	93
Star and its Positioning	14
Stepping-Stones of The Lord	237
Strength of The Lord	362
Survival of The Flock	263

T

Tears of The Lord	360
Temperature of The Soul	269
Temple of The Body	116
Tenants of The Mind	105
Tongue of Fire	241
Transgressors of The Soul	94
Trickle of The Foe	334
Trinkets of The Heart	275
Troops of The Lord	204
Turning Points in Life	76

U

Utterance of A Promise	253

V

Vapours of The Earth	213
Variety of Choice	144
Victors of The Soul	301
Vision	1
Vision Scriptures	2
Visitation of The Earth	255
Visitors to The Garden	295

W

Waters of Life	161
Way Home	248
Ways of God	345
Wealth of Man	272
Wherewithal of Man	322
White Cross	14
Window of Wonder	364
Window of Wonder— Parable	366
Wings of Heaven	157
Wrath of God	111

Appendix—	381
Flag and Standard in Use	382
Banner of The Kingdom in Use	383
Emblem of The Spirit in Use	383
Emblem of The Kingdom in Use	384
Anthem of The King	385
About the Scribe	*387*
Journaling and Notes (1)	*388*
Journaling and Notes (2)	*389*
Book 4 Reviews (2)	*390*
Book 8 Review (1)	*391*

Contents— Category

(2, 3, 4 ...) Denotes following items with a similar or same name as earlier ones

(Title) GOD SPEAKS OF RETURN AND BANNERED	I
About The Cover	II
GOD Speaks of Return and Bannered	III
Copyright and Publishing	IV
Dedication	V
Acknowledgements	VI
Contents— Ordered Index	VII
Contents— Alphabetical Index	X
Contents— Category Index	XIII
Appeal of Jesus (Excerpt Bk 9)	XVI
Testimony of The Day of The Lord	XVII
Prelude	XIX
History of The Book	XX
Introduction	XXIV

Communication (20)

057. Silence of God	122
067. Variety of Choice	144
078. Messages of Life	164
082. Fire and The Tribulation	171
094. Land of Plenty	196
101. Plank of A Nation	209
103. Vapours of The Earth	213
106. Birthday of A Saint	220
111. Precept upon Precept	226
115. Confines of The Spirit	234
126. Visitation of The Earth	255
127. Power of The Spirit of Man	257
140. Cup of Fruit of The Vine	285
146. Victors of The Soul	301
151. Pets of The Earth	318
153. Wherewithal of Man	322
154. Goliaths of Man	324
163. Ways of God	345
167. Profanity of Man	354
168. Comfort of The Lord (2)	356

Edicts of The Lord (1)

100. Sanctity of Life	207

Edifice of God (5)

041. Edifice of God	91
063. Sequencing of Time	133
074. Wings of Heaven	157
098. Troops of The Lord	204
119. Tongue of Fire	241

Eternity Beckoning (10)

029. Book of Life	70
045. Death of Man	99
046. Birth of Man	102
096. Race of The Righteous	200
122. Way Home	248
129. Crown Jewel of Creation	261
130. Survival of The Flock	263
160. Promises of God	336
165. Inheritance of Man	351
176. Measure of A Man	374

Fear of God (1)

166. Fear of God	352

Freewill of Man (5)

017. Responsibility of Freewill	51
050. Effects of The Fall on Man	109
056. Handshake of Creation	120
069. Abilities of Man	148
072. Christmas Day	155

Good News (11)

027. Return of The Shepherd	67
040. New Day	89
044. Healing of Man	95
049. Message of Healing	107
061. Body of Man 1— Designed	129
064. Body of Man 2— A House	135
065. Body of Man 3— A Temple	139
066. Body of Man 4— Protected	142
113. Footpaths of The Lord	230
117. Stepping-Stones of The Lord	237
156. Portals of The Kingdom	328

My Banner (23)

003. Banner Named, Introduced	7
004. Banner Comes Forth	8
005. Banner Affirmed as His Will	10
006. Banner of Design	14
008. Banner Defined	17
009. Divine Scriptural Revelations	18
010. Divine Commentary	19
011. Banner Speaks of Unity	36
012. Banner of The Protocols	37
022. New Signs in Use	59
023. New Signs of The Kingdom	61
073. Banner Prepared	156
079. Banner of Effects	166
081. Banner of Destiny	169
083. Banner Brings Response	175
084. Banner in The Role	177
085. Banner as A Signpost	179
086. Banner of The Battle	181
088. Banner Setting Forth	185
089. Banner on The Way	186
091. Banner of Assails	189
092. Banner in its Presence	191
093. Banner at Home (Pottage of Stew)	193

My Counsel (30)

013. Slaughter of The Innocent	39
024. Justice in Judgement	63
030. Battlements of The Mind	72
031. Mystery of Life	75
032. Turning Points in Life	76
033. Fickleness of Man	78
043. Transgressors of The Soul	94
047. Pathways of The Rain	103
051. Wrath of God	111
052. Frustrations of God	112
059. Fall of a House of Hell	125
068. Chains of Choice	146
071. Plunder of The Soul	153
097. Beauty of The Earth	202
102. Galleons of Service	211
105. Commitments of Man	218
114. Distractions of Man	232
121. Mark of The Beast	245
124. Needs of Life	251
125. Utterance of A Promise	253
136. Trinkets of The Heart	275
141. Feeding of The Sheep	288
142. Attacks Upon The Heart of Man	291
143. Exorcizing of Demons	294
149. Rise of Ashkelon	313
150. Hackers of The Body	316
159. Trickle of The Foe	334
173. Replevin of The Lord	368
174. Dungeons of The Heart	370
175. Extraction of Man	372

My Garden (2)

107. Garden of The Lord	221
144. Visitors to The Garden	295

My Grace (4)

048. Tenants of The Mind	105
058. Pathway of The Son	123
123. Defilement of The Spirit	250
162. Age of Grace	342

My Harvest (5)

036. Butterflies of Heaven	83
120. Mission of My People	244
128. Preparedness of Man	259
148. Mustering of The Bride	306
161. Census of God	339

My Kingdom on The Earth (5)

062. Gathering of The Bride	131
080. I, The Lord	167
087. Keys of The Kingdom	183
090. Rising of The Son	187
099. Candles of The Lord	206

My Love (9)

014. I Love My People	44
021. In Love	58
025. Intent of The Lord	64
034. Message of Compassion	80
060. Miracle of Christmas	127
118. Attendants of The Bride	239
131. Feast of The Incarnation	265
139. Dispelling of The Shadows	283
152. Arms of The Lord	320

My Return (9)

039. Glory of The Kingdom	88
042. Spectacles of Heaven	93
053. Entrance to Heaven	114
054. Temple of The Body	116
070. Fiefdom of The Lord	150
075. Bones of The Earth	160
104. Coming of The Son	216
155. Coming of The Kingdom	326
164. Advent of The Lord	349

Preparation (13)

020. Sin Beneath The Veil	57
025. Intent of The Lord	64
028. Hurdles of Man	68
035. Journey of Man	81
055. Guidance of God	118
076. Waters of Life	161
095. Favour of The Lord	198
108. Coming of The Spirit	223
116. Polishing of The Soul	235
132. Comfort of The Lord (1)	267
133. Temperature of The Soul	269
134. Wealth of Man	272
158. Righteous in Preparation	332

The Cross (1)

170. Tears of The Lord	360

The End-time (13)

007. Character of Man	15
015. Roar of The Lion of Judah	46
016. Churches in The Mountains	47
018. Lion Offers All, His Ways	53
019. Lioness and The Lion	54
037. Lion of Judah in Readiness	86
038. Lion of Judah	87
109. Coming of The Trumpet Call	224
110. Coming of The Turmoil	225
135. Lion of Judah Reigns	274
145. Lick of The Lion	299
157. Purring of The Lion	331
169. Roar of Zion	358

The Trinity (5)

077. Earth of God	162
137. Morality of God	278
147. Power of The Holy Spirit	303
171. Strength of The Lord	362
178. Glory of God	378

Vision & The Dream (5)

001. Vision	1
002. Vision Scriptures	2
138. Gospel of The Lord	280
172. Window of Wonder	364
172a. Window of Wonder— Parable	366

Wisdom of God (1)

112. Carriers of God's Wisdom	228

Appendix—	381
Flag and Standard in Use	382
Banner of The Kingdom in Use	383
Emblem of The Spirit in Use	383
Emblem of The Kingdom in Use	384
Anthem of The King	385
About the Scribe	387
Journaling and Notes (1)	388
Journaling and Notes (2)	389
Book 4 Reviews (2)	390
Book 8 Review (1)	391

The Appeal of Jesus (2)

"These End-time Books,
 these parts of The End-time Psalms of God,
  I,
   the Lord Jesus,
    have dictated to My willing servant,
                 Anthony.

These End-time Psalms of God highlight the behaviour of man,
                highlight the streaming ways of Heaven,
                highlight the testing of man,

        highlight the call for man,
        highlight the eternities of man,
        highlight the preparation of man,

        highlight the protocols of Heaven,
        highlight The Love of God for man,
        highlight the adoption of man into The Family of God.

These End-time Psalms of God accompany My word of ages,
            My scriptures recorded for the advantaging of man,
            My inter-relationship with man in his development
                    upon The Earth. ..."

Scribal Note: *An excerpt from* 'The Appeal of Jesus (2)',
                from Part Nine of these End-time Psalms of God.
                    Used here with His permission.

My Content Study Aid

_____
_____
_____
_____
_____
_____
_____
_____
_____
_____

Testimony of The Day of The Lord

"I,
   The Lord,
      this day speak to the peoples of The Earth in confirmation of the effort of
                                                                    My servant,
      Anthony,
         in bringing forth this book which he now lays before you.

      This book in which I speak of My Return,
                and of the preparation of those who would participate in
                                                 a journey for the jubilant,
         is of significance to all.

      This book is of My Will,
         is of The Spirit of God,
         is the introduction of My Banner into the environment of man.

      This book proclaims the words of My mouth,
         discloses My intent,
         brings forth the word for today.

      Anthony has overcome the attacks of the Disqualifier and stands with his
                                                                      integrity intact,
         has persevered in the face of adversity,
         has honoured his calling,
         has bound demonic forces for his walk with Me,
         is My scribe with ears attuned to hear.

              His ears are accurate.
              His ears are fortified by The Fear of God.
              His soul is in harmony with his spirit.

      By My Spirit and by determination has Anthony set a table for eternity from
                                                  which man is invited to partake.

I,
   The Lord,
      have garnished the table with the fare of fêtes,
              with the fare of festivities,
              with the fare of fanfares.

      Anthony has validated the accuracy of his actions prior to each disclosure of My
                                                            intent received.

      This book in which I,
            The Lord,

speak of My Return,
has My Blessing,
is under My Authority,
discloses My Banner as therein revealed.

This book is a tug of encouragement at man's freewill in pre-emption of the later fitting of the shackles.

Today is in The Age of Grace.

Wait not for tomorrow which the grave may claim.

Foolish are they who wait as their life-blood seeps away,
who lack the will to act,
who discourage a commitment to a gown of life,
who remain within the grips of demons with destruction,
who let pride get in the way of an onward journey in The Temple of The Spirit.

I,
   The Lord,
      say to the peoples of The Earth,
      'Read My Word.

      I change not.

      From times past My Word has been preserved for all generations to this day.'

I,
   The Lord,
      say,
      'Read My book here placed before you.

      Study My book for your redemption.

      Take into each heart this saying of The Lord while it is today,
         for this book is as a golden scroll.' "

Scribal Note: *Gracefully received from The Lord for use in this, His book.*

The above Testimony, with the title also supplied by The Lord, was His response to my request for His assistance with the history (the 'History of The Book') which is now placed in the Appendix so the front of the book is not unduly extended when an ebook.

I was very very surprised when He dictated the above. And all I can say is, "Wow!"

I sincerely trust there will be as many 'Wows!' for each of you in this book as there have been for me. And in all those which followed: of which I was completely unaware of what was laying in wait when this one and the rest all started to appear.

Agapé,

Anthony,

Hamilton, New Zealand.

Prelude

Now, after 9 to 10 years of listening to Our Lord Jesus, via The Holy Spirit, and typing, with their layouts, these nine books, the volumes, or the parts, of 'The End-time Psalms of God' - some 1100+ different dictated items together with His Divine Commentaries on His selected Chapters and Verses within the Biblical Books of Daniel, Revelation, and Ezekiel, the time has come for heraldic activity to declare their presence and availability to all upon The Earth.

May the Lord truly speed His End-time Psalms of God on their journey, and bless all the hands which hold them.

With the declaration of love, and certainty of purpose, to accompany them, The End-time Psalms of God, know the winged hosts of His Spirit going before to opens doors— for His word is fruitful and travels as an arrow to each heart with His message of Grace in determining a freewill destiny of choice— to be either honoured or respected on The Lord's return or, alternatively, from within the grave of man. So be it, Lord.

May the blessings of The Lord follow in strengthening all who seek to read and to discover The Will of The Loving Living God— for each life so touched and upheld.

The purpose of these books is not to entertain per se but rather to impart wisdom with knowledge. There are no opinions, except the counselling of God, in their pages and a very great many truth statements which will greatly reward when seriously considered for the truth therein. For an insight refer to 'Testimony of The Day of The Lord' in the Front Indexing area. They have all been waiting for this moment in time.

Also it is worth noting that Book 8 "GOD Speaks of Loving His Creation" also has a thirteen page Alphabetical listing of some eleven hundred plus items from all nine books— where a lookup of the item's title yields the book in which it occurs. While on the preceding page the nine books have all their categories listed with the number of the items in each category for when a study is proposed.

Agapé,

Anthony Eddy

Scribe, Officer, and Trustee,

The Advent Charitable Trust.
Hamilton, New Zealand

www.thewebsiteofthelord.org.nz

History of The Book

A Dream, A Vision, A Reality

In the late 1980's I awoke one morning from a vivid dream of a flag with a Cross that I could immediately draw but didn't know for what it was intended. I initially believed it was a new flag for our country, but it had some design elements that lingered from the existing flag and I was never completely happy with this although I had had twenty made, of which two were sold.

I did very little about this flag over the intervening twenty odd years until the early part of 2006 when a vision developed quickly in just a few days for a fully designed flag that I just knew was to be for The Kingdom of God.

Also about this time (2006) Dr Myles Munroe had a second Kingdom Book, 'Kingdom Principles™', published and therein on page twenty four, he said:

*'This book is about another Kingdom **whose flag we should hold** and another King to whom we should sing praises.' (emphasis added.)*

I could scarcely restrain myself from jumping up and down and shouting 'It's here! It's here!'

Mid to late 2007 I started to receive the words to a number of songs (six - seven) and later some prose items, together with confirmatory answers to prayers. I started taking particular note of dates and times.

22nd July 2007 6.00am. I had been receiving conflicting words of design that were critical to the banner's appearance for several weeks.

This morning I knew I MUST bring this to a head one way or the other so I prayed early in the morning about 6.45am that He, The Lord, or The Holy Spirit, show me clearly what His will was or I would throw everything out and not touch it again. I was NOT going to do the work of Satan if there were any chance of it. I was emphatic that it was better to do nothing rather than entertain the possibility, however remote, that this was the devil's work. So I prayed both in The Spirit and with understanding that the Lord make his will known to me in an absolutely unambiguous manner. I needed to KNOW within my own spirit that this was from God.

Sunday 22nd July 2007 And so I went to church at 8.20am to straighten any chairs, that may have been recently used in the auditorium, ready for the 10am morning service. With hindsight, my prayers were about to be answered within a few hours!

During the Service, one of the service leaders (GW) opened it to those present with an invitation to come to the front and share their favourite scriptures. I thought about what mine would be and was directed to the inside flyleaf of my Bible where I must have written many years ago Habakkuk 2:1— 3 which was annotated as 'Holding to a vision/ revelation'. I opened it at the scripture, as people commenced coming forward to share, and pondered the words in my heart as the nervousness increased. "Will I" "Won't I's" were going through my mind as scriptures were being read out. Suddenly, I heard it being read out! A lady had gone forward and was reading out the exact scripture over which I had been prevaricating! This I thankfully accepted as a very prompt confirmation.

Two design elements are very important: The Star must be level with the horizontal arm of The Cross, and the Star must have seven points. These were the two questions I was struggling with early yesterday morning: the positioning of the Star and its number of points in an alternate version of The Banner where I was under the impression that the Star was the Pole Star and simply indicating the domain where The Holy Spirit was moving i.e. the area of The Earth *(Northern Hemisphere) from where the Pole Star was visible. I knew there was something wrong with the design but could not hear clearly enough to be absolutely sure. There has been a very real battle going on to prevent this design being completed correctly.*

Monday 23rd July 2007 I had a web site go live. I also ordered the production of twenty five Kingdom Flags 1800 x 900mm as He had made known.

Three days later I became convinced this flag was incorrect (the single seven pointed star should have been five pointed and was in the wrong position— aesthetically it should have been slightly lower and I cancelled the order just as they were about to start printing them with all the inks mixed and about to proceed. And I ordered production of the five pointed star in a lower position instead— the 'False' one had been born!

On 29.9.2007 I was pondering a single line I had received (I had received a number of them, usually a day or so apart, and I referred to them as 'one liners'— "The Fire of Heaven is the Torch of The Spirit." I prayed that I might know for a certainty that this was from God.

On 30.9.2007 The very next day in the morning service one of the folk (SD) present brought a word about a flaming torch and it was immediately obvious to me that this was to be the basis of the seventh verse in a song ('Igniting The Fire!') for which I had already received six verses.

11th November 2007 Then this text was brought in the morning service at church, by a lady (CG):

I had been having pictures and dreams of people standing on the roofs of their houses waving large standards or flags so that all people could see. After enquiring of the Lord I felt that this is what He was saying:

The Lord is raising up a standard across the land. It is to be shouted from the roof tops and proclaimed across the city so that all can hear. There is a shift and move of The Spirit across this land. God is looking for a people who will now boldly declare truth.

A Cornerstone has been laid; a plumb line and a measuring line have been put in place. All men will be judged by these. No longer will the precepts of men have their way and sow a web of confusion and lies into the heart of this nation. God is dismantling the lies and precepts of men and raising His standard. There is an opening in The Spirit as if the veil and scales are lifting off people's eyes so that they can see and understand truth. People are longing for truth in their inner beings.

The people of NZ are like sheep lost without a shepherd. God is looking for a people who will boldly stand up for truth and the precepts of God; who will gladly wave a standard from the roof tops and declare "Here is truth!" God is raising an army across the nation.

There will be forerunners. There are people here today that have harboured a frustration in their hearts that they have not been able to speak out more openly, but God is calling you today to be forerunners on the frontline to declare truth. It is a costly call, but God is releasing an extra measure of His Spirit over you for courage and determination to speak out. As you step out, you will begin to break the stronghold that the precepts of men have held in this nation.

Others in the Body of Christ will follow you. It is as if they are watching you to make the first move. The Lord is calling us to step out into our communities, families, workplaces, media; wherever we are called to speak. This move requires more than being salt and light. It is being proactive in the things of God.

(and later typed by the Church and distributed to those then present)

This, I also took as further confirmation of the flag as being from God.

Then for the next twelve months (Approximately Aug 07— Jul 08) I went down the path of producing 'False' ones galore— a series of really false flags with a varying right hand half of the flag whose content was dependent on each country's flag. (Also a single five pointed star in a more centred position!) I produced artwork for about twenty different nations and trademarked designs of physical flags and produced clothing items and decals for each of about five or six different nations and put them up on a website and then sat still for about nine months leaving everything completely un-promoted. I did not have any queries or interest whatsoever. I was not surprised. None of this has been, in any way, at the expense of the church.

On 10th July 2008, I was to receive my own personal call from God. And later, on 3rd August 2008, in the morning church service, I was to receive a personal public prophecy from Apostle and Prophet Leon Walters, Indiana, U.S.A., that was confirmatory in its content.

Since late July 2007, I knew something wasn't right and, although I didn't want to admit it initially, I was continuing to be conscious of checks to my spirit each time I considered this 'False' design's future. I knew in my heart, and had confirmed many times during this time, the original design, in its inherent simplicity, was indeed the one from the Lord. It was to be world wide and 'national' variants weren't from Him. I had fallen for a 'False' deception when I was just hours away from having the original printed twelve months earlier.

So I re-ordered production of the correct original design in August 2008 (the two cartons were received on 29th August) and the current range of items in the months that followed prior to Christmas.

I knew I had also to destroy all the 'False' variants (twelve very large, full, and heavy cardboard cartons). It also had to be by fire and not by cutting out emblems etc or by trying to recoup costs by disposing of them cheaply. This was in order to make a new beginning.

Wednesday 31st December 2008 I burnt them on a funeral pyre, soaking some initial ones in petrol, over a period of three and a half hours ready for the new year. This seemed to be a significant act in the spiritual sense— I knew something had changed, and for the better.

The Banner of The Kingdom was first flown as a Flag at
10.30am on Monday, 1st September 2008
in Hamilton, New Zealand.

Jan/Feb 2009 Since then the Lord has been speaking very clearly to me about The Banner of The Kingdom again both in the number of texts and in their frequency and has now asked me to declare its history.

Mar/Oct 2009 Further texts have continued to be received and handed to my Pastor. I ordered and received a new replacement stock of items now with the correct design on flags, banners, standards, T-shirts, caps and vinyl stickers. Some A4 'concept' copies of texts relating just to The Banner were circulated within our fellowship - with very little feedback.

A further website www.thebannerofthekingdom.com went 'live' intended solely for the Revelatory items, further additional texts (if any), downloads, related aspects and the general progress of The Banner of The Kingdom and my walk with God. This has not been promoted, but has lain in readiness for the last six months.

Nov/Dec 2009 There was the strong indication and counselling of a book as being in The Will of God. So a cover was designed, a dictionary compiled (but now not included), and eighteen copies were printed in an A5 format of which eight were submitted to selected folk to read. There was little feedback except for the need to change the text layout because of the requirement for improved ease of reading. Several folk, I believe, didn't make it to the end of the book. There are also intended to be weekly newspaper columns across our country - so far with success as a very small beginning, which 'mustn't be despised'.

Divine texts have continued to be received, and handed to my Pastor, through Nov 09 to early March 2010 when the final text for the book was indicated and received, together with 'The Testimony of the Day of The Lord' which has been placed in the introductory part of the book for which it was supplied.

Feb/March 2010 All the texts were recast, within the A5 metric book format, to simplify ease of reading, personal study and review, and text referencing. It also provided an added benefit of providing room on each page for personal annotations as desired. The texts themselves remained textually unchanged - the change being that now every punctuation mark generates a new line so a vertical alignment can be imposed on phrases identified within a sentence.

Introduction

These Divine texts mostly consist of Truth Statements intermixed with counselling and are presented for serious contemplation as to their ramifications and how we approach them in the conclusions we may draw. For they are filled with great significance for these present times.

I testify here to one and all that these texts are not of my writing nor instigation. These texts do not stand alone but smoothly build on the preceding ones as if designed as an unfolding story with an establishing foundation. On the original individual documents the scribe has begun each Divine call with the words: 'And I hear The Lord Jesus saying,' "...". It does not appear necessary to have this phrase repetitively introducing each call in this book. Please take it, therefore, as a 'given' as to the stated origin both by testimony and by claim.

The style of the book preserves the scribal comments in italics; while double quotation marks " " denote and enclose text of a Divine origin. British spelling is used for reasons of national culture. Layout simplifies ease of reading and personal study. Each call itself may be accurately searched from within His website. A concordance or a thesaurus has not been used at any stage prior to, during, or after the receiving of these texts. A dictionary (Oxford Concise™) has sometimes been used to comprehend fully, the words of the Divine voice used in expressing His intent. Because the texts have been received via dictation spoken by the Divine voice directly into the mind, the punctuation is subject to human interpretation. Occasionally however, when required for clarity or emphasis, the capitalisation of words, together with the paragraphing, have also been indicated by the Divine. Minor spelling 'typos' are scribal and the punctuation, together with the titles, usually are, but not always. Multiple subject matters sometimes occur in a particular call which precludes the call's naming being entirely appropriate with respect to descriptive accuracy.

Attached to the end of most items is 'My Content Study Aid' inserted at the request of The Lord Jesus to enhance the benefits found in meditating on and understanding the 'Hows' and 'Whys' of the truth statements and His counselling as found herein. If no such Study Aid exists at the end of an item then there are additional Journaling & Notes pages provided in the Appendix. Please remember this is your book to use in the way which best serves your growth within the discipleship of God.

Great care has been taken to ensure scribal accuracy in hearing and transcribing what are now these printed pages of Divinely originated texts. Every word is as received without later omissions, additions, substitutions or edits.

May The Holy Spirit so testify as such to every enquiring soul.

The Vision

The Coming Forth of The Kingdom Flag— later, He named it.

"Habakkuk 2:1–3, Joel 2:28–32, Acts 2:17, Isaiah 60:1–2, Daniel 7:13, 8:17, 11:33–35, Psalm 27:14, Matthew 13:24–30, 36–43, Ezekiel 12:24–28, Malachi 4:1, Revelation 6:15–16, Psalm 49:14, Malachi 4:2, Romans 13:11–12, Proverbs 4:18, Job 22:18, Revelation 1:7–8, 22:16, 2:28–29, 14:20, 20:4–6, 8:8–9, 16:15, 22:19, Psalm 60:4, Isaiah 5:26, 11:12, 18:3, Psalm 21:5"

He who has eyes let him see,
    has Faith let him seek,
    has a tongue let him speak,
    has ears let him hear.

He who has understanding let him act,
        let him watch,
        let him be at peace.

It is so sealed by The Lord.

Only this can be said—
    The Lord Jesus,
    The Christ,
    The Lamb of God,
     now knows the time of His coming."

My Content Study Aid

_____

_____

The Vision Scriptures

The Lord dictated these consecutive scriptural references in the order just as they appear on the previous page, repeated left to right below, as quickly as they could be written down with NT intermingled with the OT. There was no use of a concordance.

"Habakkuk 2:1–3, Joel 2:28–32, Acts 2:17, Isaiah 60:1–2, Daniel 7:13, 8:17, 11:33–35, Psalm 27:14, Matthew 13:24–30, 36–43, Ezekiel 12:24–28, Malachi 4:1, Revelation 6:15–16, Psalm 49:14, Malachi 4:2, Romans 13:11–12, Proverbs 4:18, Job 22:18, Revelation 1:7–8, 22:16, 2:28–29, 14:20, 20:4–6, 8:8–9, 16:15, 22:19, Psalm 60:4, Isaiah 5:26, 11:12, 18:3, Psalm 21:5"

There follows the above scriptural references in the New King James Version text.

Habakkuk 2:1—3

I will stand my watch And set myself on the rampart, And watch to see what He will say to me, And what I will answer when I am corrected. Then The Lord answered me and said: "Write the vision And make [it] plain on tablets, That he may run who reads it. For the vision [is] yet for an appointed time; But at the end it will speak, and it will not lie. Though it tarries, wait for it; Because it will surely come, It will not tarry."

Joel 2:28—32

"And it shall come to pass afterward That I will pour out My Spirit on all flesh; Your sons and your daughters shall prophesy, Your old men shall dream dreams, Your young men shall see visions. And also on [My] menservants and on [My] maidservants I will pour out My Spirit in those days. And I will show wonders in the heavens and in the earth: Blood and fire and pillars of smoke. The sun shall be turned into darkness, And the moon into blood, Before the coming of the great and awesome day of The Lord. And it shall come to pass [That] whoever calls on the name of The Lord Shall be saved. For in Mount Zion and in Jerusalem there shall be deliverance, As The Lord has said, Among the remnant whom The Lord calls."

Acts 2:17—21

" 'And it shall come to pass in the last days, says God, That I will pour out of My Spirit on all flesh; Your sons and your daughters shall prophesy, Your young men shall see visions, Your old men shall dream dreams. And on My menservants and on My maidservants I will pour out My Spirit in those days; And they shall prophesy. I will show wonders in heaven above And signs in the earth beneath: Blood and fire and vapour of smoke. The sun shall be turned into darkness, And the moon into blood, Before the coming of the great and awesome day of The Lord. And it shall come to pass [That] whoever calls on the name of The Lord Shall be saved.' "

Isaiah 60:1—2

"Arise, shine; For your light has come! And the glory of The Lord is risen upon you. For behold, the darkness shall cover the earth, And deep darkness the people; But The Lord will arise over you, And His glory will be seen upon you."

Daniel 7:13

"I was watching in the night visions, And behold, [One] like the Son of Man, Coming with the clouds of heaven! He came to the Ancient of Days, And they brought Him near before Him."

Daniel 8:17

So he came near where I stood, and when he came I was afraid and fell on my face; but he said to me, "Understand, son of man, that the vision [refers] to the time of the end."

Daniel 11:33—35

And those of the people who understand shall instruct many; yet [for many] days they shall fall by sword and flame, by captivity and plundering. Now when they fall, they shall be aided with a little help; but many shall join with them by intrigue. And [some] of those of understanding shall fall, to refine them, purify [them], and make [them] white, [until] the time of the end; because [it is] still for the appointed time.

Psalm 27:14

Wait on The Lord; Be of good courage, And He shall strengthen your heart; Wait, I say, on The Lord!

Matthew 13:24—30

Another parable He put forth to them, saying: "The kingdom of heaven is like a man who sowed good seed in his field; but while men slept, his enemy came and sowed tares among the wheat and went his way. But when the grain had sprouted and produced a crop, then the tares also appeared. So the servants of the owner came and said to him, 'Sir, did you not sow good seed in your field? How then does it have tares?'
He said to them, 'An enemy has done this.' The servants said to him, 'Do you want us then to go and gather them up?'
But he said, 'No, lest while you gather up the tares you also uproot the wheat with them. Let both grow together until the harvest, and at the time of harvest I will say to the reapers, "First gather together the tares and bind them in bundles to burn them, but gather the wheat into my barn." ' "

Matthew 13:36—43

Then Jesus sent the multitude away and went into the house. And His disciples came to Him, saying, "Explain to us the parable of the tares of the field."

He answered and said to them: "He who sows the good seed is the Son of Man. The field is the world, the good seeds are the sons of the kingdom, but the tares are the sons of the wicked [one]. The enemy who sowed them is the devil, the harvest is the end of the age, and the reapers are the angels. Therefore as the tares are gathered and burned in the fire, so it will be at the end of this age. The Son of Man will send out His angels, and they will gather out of His kingdom all things that offend, and those who practice lawlessness, and will cast them into the furnace of fire. There will be wailing and gnashing of teeth. Then the righteous will shine forth as the sun in the kingdom of their Father. He who has ears to hear, let him hear!

Ezekiel 12:24—28

For no more shall there be any false vision or flattering divination within the house of Israel. For I [am] The Lord. I speak, and the word which I speak will come to pass; it will no more be postponed; for in your days, O rebellious house, I will say the word and perform it," says The Lord GOD.' " Again the word of The Lord came to me, saying, "Son of man, look, the house of Israel is saying, 'The vision that he sees [is] for many days [from now], and he prophesies of times far off.' Therefore say to them, 'Thus says The Lord GOD: "None of My words will be postponed any more, but the word which I speak will be done," says The Lord GOD.' "

Malachi 4:1

"For behold, the day is coming, Burning like an oven, And all the proud, yes, all who do wickedly will be stubble. And the day which is coming shall burn them up," Says The Lord of hosts, "That will leave them neither root nor branch.

Revelation 6:15—16

And the kings of the earth, the great men, the rich men, the commanders, the mighty men, every slave and every free man, hid themselves in the caves and in the rocks of the mountains, and said to the mountains and rocks, "Fall on us and hide us from the face of Him who sits on the throne and from the wrath of the Lamb!

Psalm 49:14

Like sheep they are laid in the grave; Death shall feed on them; The upright shall have dominion over them in the morning; And their beauty shall be consumed in the grave, far from their dwelling.

Malachi 4:2

But to you who fear My name The Sun of Righteousness shall arise With healing in His wings; And you shall go out And grow fat like stall-fed calves.

Romans 13:11—12

And [do] this, knowing the time, that now [it is] high time to awake out of sleep; for now our salvation [is] nearer than when we [first] believed. The night is far spent, the day is at hand. Therefore let us cast off the works of darkness, and let us put on the armour of light.

Proverbs 4:18

But the path of the just [is] like the shining sun, That shines ever brighter unto the perfect day.

Job 22:18

Yet He filled their houses with good [things]; But the counsel of the wicked is far from me.

Revelation 1:7— 8
Behold, He is coming with clouds, and every eye will see Him, even they who pierced Him. And all the tribes of the earth will mourn because of Him. Even so, Amen.
"I am the Alpha and the Omega, [the] Beginning and [the] End," says The Lord, "who is and who was and who is to come, the Almighty."

Revelation 22:16
"I, Jesus, have sent My angel to testify to you these things in the churches. I am the Root and the Offspring of David, the Bright and Morning Star."

Revelation 2:28— 29
and I will give him the morning star. "He who has an ear, let him hear what The Spirit says to the churches." '

Revelation 14:20
And the winepress was trampled outside the city, and blood came out of the winepress, up to the horses' bridles, for one thousand six hundred furlongs.

Revelation 20:4— 6
And I saw thrones, and they sat on them, and judgement was committed to them. Then [I saw] the souls of those who had been beheaded for their witness to Jesus and for the word of God, who had not worshipped the beast or his image, and had not received [his] mark on their foreheads or on their hands. And they lived and reigned with Christ for a thousand years. But the rest of the dead did not live again until the thousand years were finished. This [is] the first resurrection. Blessed and holy [is] he who has part in the first resurrection. Over such the second death has no power, but they shall be priests of God and of Christ, and shall reign with Him a thousand years.

Revelation 8:8— 9
Then the second angel sounded: And [something] like a great mountain burning with fire was thrown into the sea, and a third of the sea became blood. And a third of the living creatures in the sea died, and a third of the ships were destroyed.

Revelation 16:15
"Behold, I am coming as a thief. Blessed [is] he who watches, and keeps his garments, lest he walk naked and they see his shame."

Revelation 22:19
and if anyone takes away from the words of the book of this prophecy, God shall take away his part from the Book of Life, from the holy city, and [from] the things which are written in this book.

Psalm 60:4
You have given a banner to those who fear You, That it may be displayed because of the truth. Selah

Isaiah 5:26
He will lift up a banner to the nations from afar, And will whistle to them from the end of the earth; Surely they shall come with speed, swiftly.

Isaiah 11:12

He will set up a banner for the nations, And will assemble the outcasts of Israel, And gather together the dispersed of Judah From the four corners of the earth.

Isaiah 18:3

All inhabitants of the world and dwellers on the earth: When he lifts up a banner on the mountains, you see [it]; And when he blows a trumpet, you hear [it].

Psalm 21:5

His glory [is] great in Your salvation; Honour and majesty You have placed upon him.

My Content Study Aid

The Banner Named, Introduced

"By these this banner will be known by man:

    The Banner of The Kingdom—
            For by it each will know My servants.

    The Banner of Grace—
            For by it the world will witness My love.

    The Banner of Justice—
            For by it all will receive My judgement.

It's presence will bring repentance and love and it will bring peace.

    My angels will go with it,
            wherever it goes.

    Their charge will be to uplift the downtrodden,
            the poor and the oppressed and to overthrow the mighty,
            the proud and the vain and all who work iniquity.

The righteous will be blessed and My Disciples are to be numbered before the world and
            then My Banner will mark a seat of judgement.

Woe to all who use My Banner without My authority for great will be their darkness,
            but to My Disciples My Banner will be a blessing and an assurance,
                  written on their hearts,
                      of their eternal life of light."

The Banner Comes Forth

"I AM.

I love My prophets that bring forth My Word in due season;
        that encourage My people;
        that chide the souls of man;
        that speak to authorities in nations,
                in cities,
                      and in gatherings of the people of The Lord.

I,
  The Lord,
    now bring forth My Banner,
            of The Kingdom,
            of Grace,
            of Justice,
    to inspire as The Holy Spirit guides My people in the coming times of trial.

Before the eyes of enslaved nations this unfurled Banner held high in honour,
    in praise and in Glory will cast down the battlements of Beelzebub.

Demons will flee;
    for dominions,
    long held in bondage,
    will be free.

My Spirit shall place a victor's crown on each who so deserves.

    For the battle shall be fierce.

    And few there be among the sons of men who will join it.

But fear not!
    Do I not command The Hosts of Heaven?

    For I do The Father's will.

    And I shall prevail over all the powers of the enemy until the end of time.

Touch not My Prophets,
    those chosen by The Lord,
    those anointed by My Spirit.

Behold the deception in My house,
        laid bare for all to see across the nations.

Behold,
    the very ether of The Earth reels in disbelief at what the mind of man conceives to
        carry on the winds:

> to the four corners of The Earth,
> even unto all the islands of the seas.

Great in wrath shall be the judgement of The Father,
> against these workers in defilement that debauch The Kingdom of The Son.

I shall receive My own to Myself,
> those for whom I long.

> Those whose names I hold close to My heart.

> Those whose places I am now preparing.

To the others,
> to those who never knew Me,
> I,
>> The Lord,
>>> say,
>>>> 'Behold,
>>>>> the wine press is prepared.
>>>>
>>>> Repent,
>>>>> and turn from your evil ways while it is yet today.' "

My Content Study Aid

The Banner Affirmed as His Will

"It is My Will that this Banner flies over My Domain,
                              My Kingdom,
                              My Estate from this day forth.

This Banner,
this Flag,
this Standard,
    denotes gathering points of My people who know Me by name and through My Spirit.

    This Banner shall arise before the Muslim nations of The Earth,
            not in confrontation but in love and hope and salvation.

    This Banner shall uplift the poor,
                    the downtrodden and the oppressed.

    This Banner shall go with My servants,
            shall be in the vanguard of the harvest of the lost,
            is upheld and protected by The Hosts of Heaven.

    This Banner determines the survival of nations,
            dispels darkness,
                iniquity and famine,
            provides a hedge of protection around My people.

    This Banner will speak,
        will see,
        will hear the cries of those in anguish.

I shall gather My people.

In this,
    My time,
        I shall number My people as they stand before Me.

    Not one shall be lost,
        shall go astray,
        shall be unaccounted for.

    I shall gather My sheep to Me and only My sheep shall I gather.

Throughout The Earth My servants have laboured,
            My Spirit has moved,
                the whole of creation has borne witness of Me.

Throughout the whole of the heavens that man can see and will see the testimony of Me
                                              is true and consistent through all ages.

Man is left without excuse,

is left with wilful disobedience,
uses up his period of Grace.

Man will soon be left with judgement.

Man will seek mercy before The Throne of The Father,
 those whom are not named in The Lamb's Book of Life.

The Father's wrath will fall on those not covered by The Blood of The Sacrifice of
 The Father.

Their robes will be filthy and their hearts will be black.

Each will have denied Me and I will deny them before The Father.

This Banner shall be the last thing they recall.

For these have ignored My apostles,
 these have ignored My prophets,
 these have ignored My evangelists,
 these have ignored My pastoral ministers,
 these have ignored My teachers,
 these have ignored both My written and spoken Word.

These have ignored My Spirit even with signs,
 wonders and miracles.

These are the lost generation for they have fallen into idolatry,
 they lie and they cheat,
 they plunder and they rob.

Even the poor,
 the widows and the orphans are not safe from them.

I,
 The Lord,
 will bring to pass all that I have decreed.

All that I require,
 the prophets have proclaimed,
 My Word establishes.

For who is man to deny The Sacrifice of The Father?

Who is man that he can blaspheme and curse God with impunity?

The angels shout in dread and are silenced when the blasphemy of man echoes
 in Heaven.

All The Hosts of Heaven hear the blasphemy of man,
 hear the blasphemy of every soul,
 witness the blasphemy of man.

My sheep know Me and they return to My fold before the darkness of the
night overtakes.

> Great will be their homecoming,
> > the rejoicing,
> > > the joy of The Lord.

Prepare My Bride.

> Let no lamb be blemished,
> > be spotted,
> > > disqualify itself for I will not revisit The Cross.

> Let My Bride be spotless,
> > be beautiful,
> > > be beyond compare when dressed in the garden of My Father.

Purify My Bride.
Purify My Bride.
Purify My Bride."

The Father says, "Purify The Bride of The Lamb.
Purify The Bride of The Lamb.
Purify The Bride of The Lamb."

"And The Holy Spirit announced the Great Amen," *the Heavens say.*

"I,
  The Father,
    uphold My Son before the nations of the world.

> I will shake the nations of the world.
> > tear down the structures that defile My Son.
> > lay waste structures in which iniquity is practised.

> > Do not attend where iniquity is rampant,
> > for I will not suffer the guile of man that breaks My Word.

Where are the men of righteousness who will save their cities?
> who know not to sleep?

Awake!
Awake!
Awake to the harvest of My Son!

To all the men of righteousness,
  now is the time to stand your watch.

  Do not be found sleeping on your watch.

    But,

rather,
> learn to fast in holiness;
>> to pray in strength;
>> to act in Faith:
>>> that My Word shall kindle and ignite the flame within the harvest due
>>>> My Son.

I love My Son,
> The Comforter,
> all the creation of My Son.

> The Word of The Lord stands;
>> will surely come to be;
>> remains.

> For I have given My Word and it shall be upheld throughout all eternity."

And the Heavenly Hosts are in awe as The Father declares a thunderous "Amen."

My Content Study Aid

The Banner of Design

The Red Cross

"The Red Cross points man to My sacrifice of love within an agony of sin,
           and My Father's grief at My Blood that was shed.

    Shed,
        that man,
           in believing on Me,
               may now have eternal life."

The White Cross

"The White Cross decrees the purity of The Father standing behind His Son.

      He who has seen The Father has seen The Son.

      He who recognizes The Father will recognize The Son.

      He who knows The Father will know The Son.

He who is known by The Son is welcomed into The Household of The Father."

The Star and its Positioning

"It is the Star of the New Covenant.

It is the Star of Bethlehem.

It is the Bright and Morning Star of which John writes.

    And for the gentiles of the nations of the world in the new covenant,
    it is the Bright and Morning Star in all the fullness of Glory.

The position marks the meeting of the boundaries of man and the boundaries of Heaven.

      Let those who have wisdom,
           understand."

The Blue on The Banner

"It portrays the Curtain of Eternity.

The Curtain of Eternity is blue.

The Curtain of Eternity ensures the eyes of the flesh cannot penetrate the secrets of The
                              Kingdom of Heaven.

    The eyes of the flesh can only view as My Spirit so reveals.

My Spirit moves the Curtain of Eternity in the presence of The Father."

The Character of Man

"I am changing the ether of The Earth,
I am changing the very ether that is the breath of man,
     that the mettle of man shall be tested before Me.

 And the mettle of man shall be sharpened as an axe on the grinding wheel.

 The mettle of man shall be honed as the axe on the whetstone.

The whetstone of life shall test the character of man.
    shall mark the character of men.

The whetstone of life shall number the characters of My Kingdom,
     the characters of life,
     the characters of The Father.

Prepare for the characters of men to meet the whetstone of The Lord.

 For the whetstone of Earth,
 the whetstone of life,
 is the oilstone of Heaven.

Prepare for the oilstone of Heaven that carries The Anointing of The Father,
      The Holiness of The Father,
      The Presence of The Father.

Those who know The Whetstone of Life know The Oilstone of Heaven.

 They know My Holy Spirit that both whets and oils.

Each day of The Earth shall be lengthened in the minds of man.

The minds of man shall become weary,
 the flesh of man shall become tired,
 the voices of man shall cry out.

The steps of man shall stumble and the shadows of man shall fall to The Earth.

Verily,
  shall the soul of man be filled with woe.

For the rain will be withheld from the harvest and poured out at planting.

The seas will rise up,
  will tower,
  will teeter,
  will fall and boil and clean The Earth of footprints that contaminate.

The Land will move in desolation.

The wind will bend the boughs,

> break the boughs,
> scatter where it wills.

The heat of the sun will be preserved on The Earth,
> will parch The Earth,
> will whet The Earth;
> will bring forth the curses of man.

For the mettle of man shall be sharpened;
> shall be honed,
> shall be tested as to character.

For the world will see the heart of man as the character of man will speak.

The mettle of man is the foundation block of character.
> is formed from the conscience of man;
> grows as and when righteousness is established in the heart.

The mettle of man presages character.
> And character becomes part of the spirit of man and accompanies man beyond the realm of time.

My Content Study Aid

_____
_____
_____
_____
_____
_____
_____
_____
_____
_____
_____
_____
_____
_____
_____
_____
_____

The Banner Defined

"It is The Banner of The Kingdom when lifted high and fully extended with a pole at either end placed in sleeves of white material each carefully sewn with white thread.

It is The Standard of The Kingdom when a pole is used at the edge of The Cross only, in order to hold the sleeved Banner upright, but self-draping.

And it is The Flag of The Kingdom when held upright by cords, whether with toggles or clips, that enables it to fly freely in the winds of change, the closest to the heavens.

The pole or the cord can be either part of creation or manufactured, so long as either is chosen to do its task with excellence.

Truly does The Banner of The Kingdom proclaim over;
and truly does The Standard of The Kingdom mark asunder;
and truly does The Flag of The Kingdom establish claim to:
the territories of man;
whether held by kings or queens,
rulers of the people or despots who seize.

For The Banner of The Kingdom,
The Standard of The Kingdom,
The Flag of The Kingdom will become The Sign of The Kingdom,
The Sign of Grace,
The Sign of Justice.

This Sign will become The Emblem of My Spirit before the eyes of man."

My Content Study Aid

_____
_____
_____
_____
_____
_____
_____

The Divine Scriptural Revelations

Then, The Lord requested a diligent search of the scriptures for all references to "banners", "signs" and "standards", both in the plural and the singular, and to preserve the reference and to type out the text.

This appeared to be a huge task and some 3 weeks passed while considering it. Then someone (RVH) mentioned, in passing, the 'Blue Bible' website and this simplified the task tremendously.

Results summary—

Searched for:	Found:	Divinely selected:
Banner	13	7
Banners	4	2
Sign	83	20
Signs	72	8
Standard	18	7
Standards	3	0

Some, surprisingly, were also later used twice and also chosen in the order of use as well.

The scripture relating to each found reference was obscured, by the scribe, from the scribe's vision while they were being divinely selected so that human bias could not occur during the process of selecting as to inclusion and then, later, also as to order. These selection documents have been preserved (17,5,4 pages in three groups totalling 26 x A4 single-sided pages).

My Content Study Aid

_____
_____
_____
_____
_____
_____
_____
_____
_____
_____
_____
_____

The Divine Commentary

The Emblem of The Spirit

"Isaiah 11:12 For it is written **'He will set up a banner for the nations ...'**
Divine Commentary—

"That they may know the presence of The Lord within their midst,
> the presence of The Lord that soon comes forth from The Father,
> the presence of The Lord preceded by My Spirit."

Jeremiah 51:27 As it is written **'Set up a banner in the land ...'**,
Divine Commentary—

"So it shall be for each nation,
> for each territory,
> for each plot of land inhabited by man:
>> that all who know may so declare their feasance to The Lord.

For no man may claim,
> by ignorance,
> he did not know of his God:
>> if he had not heard The Word,
>> if he had not seen The Emblem,
>> if he had not walked The Earth in all its finery,
>> if he had not viewed the heavens in all their majesty;
> even so he could not deny the promptings of his spirit that suffered the suppression
>> of his soul."

Psalms 60:4 It is written **'You have given a banner to those who fear You, that it may be displayed because of the truth. ...'**
Divine Commentary—

"And the hearts of those who fear Me will rejoice at the coming of My Banner,
> will excitedly prepare their clothes and lay them
>> close to hand,
> will watch and wait,
> anticipating the announcing of The Lord:
>> The Anthem of The Lord that will resound throughout The Earth
>>> within the sanctuaries of The Lord."

Isaiah 7:11 So it is written **'Ask a sign for yourself from The LORD your God; ask it either in the depth or in the height above.'**
Divine Commentary—

"And I,

> The Lord,
>> will answer you in these days for it was for these days that it was written and it is in these days that it will be understood by those with wisdom and with The Fear of The Lord."

Isaiah 20:3 And it is written **'Then The LORD said, "Just as My servant Isaiah has walked naked and barefoot three years [for] a sign and a wonder against Egypt and Ethiopia,'**
Divine Commentary—

> "So shall the children of the promise and the children of the new covenant—
>> for the benefit of both My peoples,
>>> all My children—
>>>> the years of final gathering will total as sevenfold three years to walk thereunder the sign of The Kingdom.

> For the blessings of The Lord will be upon those whose steps are made under the sign of The Kingdom;
>> those who have sought out the sign of The Kingdom;
>> those who have run to the sign of The Kingdom.

> For the sign of The Kingdom proclaims the way to life,
>> declares the sovereignty of The Lamb,
>> institutes safety for the sheltered.

> The Flag of The Kingdom heralds the dominion of God."

Isaiah 11:12 And again it is written **'He will set up a banner for the nations, and will assemble the outcasts of Israel, and gather together the dispersed of Judah from the four corners of the earth.'**
Divine Commentary—

> "And even so will it be done;
>> for My outcasts I will assemble and the dispersed I will gather together all within the sanctuaries of The Lord.

> And I,
>> The Lord,
>>> decree that everyone who thirsts,
>>>> everyone who seeks,
>>>> everyone who hungers,
>>>> everyone who listens as My Spirit speaks,
>>>>> will be rescued from their plight in these days of Grace.

>> The sanctuaries of The Lord will be marked as to the dominion of God."

Psalms 74:4 It is written **'Your enemies roar in the midst of Your meeting place; they set up their banners [for] signs.'**
Divine Commentary—

"Set a watch on your meeting place.

Set the guards about and within fitted with the armour of God;
>> empower the guards with weapons they can use,
>> empower the guards with boldness to overcome,
>> empower the guards to stop the roar of your enemies,
>>> to pull down banners that would
>>>> mark their claims to territories
>>>> they must relinquish.

Reclaim your meeting place,
> cast down unrighteous banners,
>> banners that have no right to be within your meeting place,
>> banners that bring idolatry into the place of meeting."

Psalms 20:5 And it is written '**… And in the name of our God we will set up [our] banners! …**'
Divine Commentary—

"Set up your banners above the roar of the enemies.

Set up standards in proximity to those of the enemies.

Set up flags in pre-eminence over the flags of both enemies and nations for
>> all are subject to,
>> all owe homage to,
>> all are in subjugation to The Emblem of The Kingdom.

Mark well The Emblem of The Kingdom for it dips and bows in deference only before
>> the altars of God."

Isaiah 5:26 Know it is written for these days '**He will lift up a banner to the nations from afar, and will whistle to them from the end of the earth; surely they shall come with speed, swiftly.**'
Divine Commentary—

"My Banner is unfurled and lifted up from a distant place,
> from afar,
>> from an island in the seas to the nations of
>>> The Earth.

Behold what appears!
Behold what I say!
Behold who is to come!"

Mark 8:12 Remember it is written '**But He sighed deeply in His spirit, and said, "Why does this generation seek a sign? Assuredly, I say to you, no sign shall be given to this generation."**'
Divine Commentary—

"For as it was stated,

so it was upheld.

Now to this present generation a sign is being given,
    its intent made known,
        its message not requiring the tongue of man to speak,
            but only eyes that see,
                for understanding to be reached by those who
                      read The Word."

Isaiah 31:9 And it is written, 'He shall cross over to his stronghold for fear, and his princes shall be afraid of the banner," says the LORD, whose fire [is] in Zion And whose furnace [is] in Jerusalem.'
Divine Commentary—

"The ability of His people to rout the enemy shall lie in their understanding of the Flame
        of The Spirit and The Banner of The Kingdom—
    the sign now being given—
      which in unison shall stand in defiance against the enemies of the land,
        the enemies of God,
          the enemies that incur the wrath
            of God as it falls."

Isaiah 13:2 'Lift up a banner on the high mountain, …'
Divine Commentary—

"As it is written,
  let it be done.

Let The Banner proclaim from a place of conquest,
      from a place that is redeemed,
      from a place that is restored,
          that all may see the move of God across the land.

For The Spirit will move in company with the clarion call that goes forth notifying all
        who hear of the intent of The Lord to
        establish His Presence over all the land."

Isaiah 62:10 'Go through, go through the gates! Prepare the way for the people; build up, build up the highway! Take out the stones, lift up a banner for the peoples!'
Divine Commentary—

"As it was written of long ago so it will now be fulfilled.

      The people of The Lord are to be welcomed.
      The people of The Lord are to be greeted.
      The people of The Lord are to be loved.
          restored,
          reclaimed—

to be set free to rejoice in purity of heart."

Isaiah 37:30 'This [shall be] a sign to you: You shall eat this year such as grows of itself, And the second year what springs from the same; Also in the third year sow and reap, Plant vineyards and eat the fruit of them.'
Divine Commentary—

"Thence it was written now it comes to pass.

This year shall My Church reach out to its own,
        teach its own,
        purify the body of Disciples,
        prepare the spirits,
        hone the characters with the whetstone,
                the oilstone,
                      of Heaven.

        Set My Ecclesia,
            My Governance,
                in places where My Spirit leads.

In the second year,
        accept all who come that have been called—
        all who know The Saints.

        Marshall the servants to set apart the streams of living water that will water
                and refresh the vineyards of The Lord.

Also in the third year sow My Governances in the places decreed by My Spirit and send
        My servants two by two to reap the fruit that is now bunched,
                full grown and ripe,
        that now accepts the labourers sent forth.

Tarry not with fruit still green but dust your shoes and move on to the next vineyard—
        that all fruit now ripe be gathered before the coming of the storm.

Quickly separate and sort the fruit and send it forth in twos again to gather like with like
        in vineyards still not stripped of fruit belonging to The Lord,
        to places not yet visited by the labourers in the fields."

Ezekiel 20:12 'Moreover I also gave them My Sabbaths, to be a sign between them and Me, that they might know that I [am] the LORD who sanctifies them.'
Divine Commentary—

"As it is written so it is sustained.

        Every seventh day is still reserved as Holy unto The Lord,
        and this sign shall be upheld in honour by My servants,
                My labourers—
                all those professing,
                with The Spirit on their lips,

> and,
> with their tongues,
> declaring that Jesus is LORD."

Ezekiel 24:24 'Thus Ezekiel is a sign to you; according to all that he has done you shall do; and when this comes, you shall know that I [am] the Lord GOD.'
Divine Commentary—

"As it has been written now henceforth it comes,
> now to be fulfilled,
> now to confirm the preparation of,
> > the witness to,
> > The Lord."

Ezekiel 24:27 'on that day your mouth will be opened to him who has escaped; you shall speak and no longer be mute. Thus you will be a sign to them, and they shall know that I [am] the LORD.'
Divine Commentary—

"In that day it was written for a day such as this.

The Flame of Heaven will counsel those who labour in the vineyards,
> empowering with boldness those in The Kingdom of God:
> that they may go forth declaring The Kingdom of God is nigh and
> with power and with authority and with signs and with wonders and with miracles:
> > declaring The Word of The Lord—
> > with a certainty beyond their years and
> > with an impact beyond their present understanding."

Mark 8:11 'Then the Pharisees came out and began to dispute with Him, seeking from Him a sign from heaven, testing Him.'
Divine Commentary—

"Yet as it is recorded,
> so shall it be again.

> For new generations of Pharisees and their Gentile ilk now abound,
> > repeating the mistakes of the past to the detriment of the present."

Mark 8:12 'But He sighed deeply in His spirit, and said, "Why does this generation seek a sign? Assuredly, I say to you, no sign shall be given to this generation.'
Divine Commentary—

"As it is recorded so shall it be repeated.

And again the first shall be last and the last shall be first."

Romans 4:11 'And he received the sign of circumcision, a seal of the righteousness of the faith which [he had while still] uncircumcised, that he might be the father of all those who believe, though they are uncircumcised, that righteousness might be imputed to them also,'

Divine Commentary—

"As it has been recorded so it shall be.

The sign of circumcision both bestows by seal and imputes by Faith righteousness to all those who believe."

1 Corinthians 1:22 'For Jews request a sign, and Greeks seek after wisdom;'
Divine Commentary—

"As it is written so it was experienced.

The wisdom of the Greeks served them well;
> for the wisdom of the Greeks led them to salvation,
>> to belief in,
>> to acceptance of,
>>> The Son of God."

Revelation 12:3 'And another sign appeared in heaven: behold, a great, fiery red dragon having seven heads and ten horns, and seven diadems on his heads.'
Divine Commentary—

"As it is written,
> so it will come to be,
> so it will expand.

The passing of the dragon should be noted;
> for it carries the heads of the eldership of churches,
>> it carries the means of self-defence,
>> it carries the diadems of churches:
>>> the bodies of believers,
>>> the accolades of eldership entrusted to their care.

Behold,
> and Elders would be wise to emulate,
> the dragon that is neither lukewarm nor cold.

For the dragon will not cool,
> the dragon fights to defend,
> the dragon adds to what he has,
> the dragon parades through Heaven all he has acquired."

1 Corinthians 14:22 'Therefore tongues are for a sign, not to those who believe but to unbelievers; …'
Divine Commentary—

"As it has been written,
> so it states a purpose.

Tongues are encouraged to be spoken by all,
>> who report the harvest ripe,

when labouring in the vineyards.

Hence the harvest will perceive a wonder of The Kingdom as a sign of God's anointing presence within the lives of all who reap."

Revelation 12:1 'Now a great sign appeared in heaven: a woman clothed with the sun, with the moon under her feet, and on her head a garland of twelve stars.'
Divine Commentary—

"As it is written so it now is.

This sign still appears in Heaven.

The sun lights the woman with tendrils of fire that reach out to all the heavens throughout all ages and all time.

The woman moves her feet and the moon is gathered in her arms.

The woman claps her hands and the moon encircles her head.

The woman continues on her way and the moon draws her near—
she who has a garland of twelve stars upon her head.

Twelve stars that explode into fragments that envelop and develop like for like.

Twelve stars now become a multitude that stretches from her head right to her feet.

The multitude of stars is now gathered and conjoined:
each to the cluster star that gave each a birthright presence to exist."

Joshua 24:17 'for the LORD our God [is] He who brought us and our fathers up out of the land of Egypt, from the house of bondage, who did those great signs in our sight, …'
Divine Commentary—

"As it is written so it was done.

The Egyptians harried and harassed the children of Israel in denial of their word as uttered by their king.

Thus were tribulations heaped upon their heads;
as they suffered and incurred the wrath of God for the plight they so readily inflicted upon all those retained in bondage at The King's decrees.

Hence their final freedom was jealously protected by their God who with signs of awe and marvelling and within the view of multitudes,
cared for and protected them,
supplied and met their needs,
as they endured and they wandered on their extended journey to their promised land."

Psalms 65:8 'They also who dwell in the farthest parts are afraid of Your signs; …'
Divine Commentary—

"As it is written so it was reported.

Signs encourage The Fear of The Lord within the hearts of man.

Signs reveal My presence,
>My interest in creation,
>My caring and concern."

Numbers 10:14 'The standard of the camp of the children of Judah set out first according to their armies; …'
Divine Commentary—

"As it is written so it was the order.

>The standard of the camp was the battle flag of Judah,
>>but now the standard of the camp is The Standard of The Kingdom.

As it is declared so it is the order."

Revelation 13:13 '… so that he even makes fire come down from heaven on the earth in the sight of men.'
Divine Commentary—

"As it is written so it was witnessed.

>The fire will fall again from Heaven on The Earth and witnessed by multitudes
>>of men.

>The fire will fall according to the direction of The Lord.

>The fire will vanquish foes in the twinkling of an eye.

>The fire will set the boundary past which no foe shall cross.

>The fire will protect the land within the boundary of The Lord.

>The fire will establish A Kingdom that shall not be overthrown.

>The fire will secure the right of entry across the boundary of the land.

>The fire will obey the prompting of The Spirit.

>The fire will not retreat.

>The fire will advance against the foes.

Great is the sign of fire before the eyes of men."

Jeremiah 10:2 'Thus says the LORD: "Do not learn the way of the Gentiles; Do not be dismayed at the signs of heaven, For the Gentiles are dismayed at them.'
Divine Commentary—

"As it is written so it was instructed.
As it is written so it is.
As it is written so shall it be observed.
As it is written so shall it come to pass."

Revelation 16:14 'For they are spirits of demons, performing signs, [which] go out to the kings of the earth and of the whole world, to gather them to the battle of that great day of God Almighty.'
Divine Commentary—

"As it is written so it is foretold.

As it is written so that great day approaches.

As it is written The Kings are about to be gathered."

Isaiah 49:22 'Thus says the Lord GOD: "Behold, I will lift My hand in an oath to the nations, And set up My standard for the peoples; They shall bring your sons in [their] arms, And your daughters shall be carried on [their] shoulders;'
Divine Commentary—

"As it is written so it is committed.

As it is written so shall the children be carried.

As it is written My Standard of The Kingdom is now set up.

As it is written so My hand is lifted."

Isaiah 59:19 'So shall they fear The name of the LORD from the west, And His glory from the rising of the sun; When the enemy comes in like a flood, The Spirit of the LORD will lift up a standard against him.'
Divine Commentary—

"As it is written so shall it be.

As it is written so shall The Fear of the name of The Lord spread from the west.

As it is written so shall The Fear of His Glory spread from the rising of the sun.

As it is written so shall The Standard of The Kingdom be lifted up.

As it is written so shall the battle be resolved."

Revelation 13:13 'He performs great signs, ...'
Divine Commentary—

"As it is written so it is fulfilled.

As it is written so may all be forewarned.

As it is written great signs will be performed."

Jeremiah 4:21 'How long will I see the standard, [And] hear the sound of the trumpet?'
Divine Commentary—

"As it is written the answer is awaited.

As it is written the answer is delayed.

    The Standard of The Kingdom now stands within The Kingdom,
              will not fall,
                    accepts the surrender of the foes.

The surrender of the foes brings silence to the trumpet.

The gathering of the foe brings voice to the trumpet.

The trumpet that will sound across the network of The Earth.

The trumpet has a voice,
> the clarion call of God,
>> that awakens and alerts those with their clothes beside their beds.

Those who are now dressed should flee to the sanctuaries of God without delay.

Those who do not know the sanctuaries of God will perish,
> at that very hour,
> for lack of wisdom,
> lack of action,
> lack of belief in what has been foretold.

The fate of nations will be decided by their reaction to the clarion call of God."

Matthew 12:39 '… "An evil and adulterous generation seeks after a sign, and no sign will be given to it except the sign of the prophet Jonah." '
Divine Commentary—

"As it is written so it was declared.

Those who seek a sign should fear it as a gift of God;
> as a treasure of The Spirit,
> as a witness that I AM.

All those who seek,
> not fearing,
> and trample on the gift of God—
>> so it shall be done to them.

As they receive so shall they be rewarded.

The sign of the prophet Jonah is a precursor of a coming,
> is upheld in its validity,
> is applicable to every generation.

> Surrendered to be engulfed in darkness for three days and then released to live—
>> so did The Son of Man become the template via a Cross.

The sign of the prophet Jesus,
> The Messiah,
>> has fulfilled,
>> with vindication,
>> the sign of the prophet Jonah."

Psalms 86:17 'Show me a sign for good, That those who hate me may see [it] and be ashamed, Because You, LORD, have helped me and comforted me.'
Divine Commentary—

"As it is written so it shall be known.

As it is requested so it shall be granted.

The praises of lips and the meditations of pure hearts are a delight unto The Lord,
>> are a joy unto The Spirit,
>> are a celebration unto The Father."

Isaiah 37:30 ' "This [shall be] a sign to you: '
Divine Commentary—

"As it is written so it ascribes intent.

The Spirit of the Risen Lord will rest upon your shoulders.

The Spirit of the Risen Lord will hover over your family even unto the third generation.

The Spirit of the Risen Lord will bring the Fire of The Spirit,
>> that flames but does not scorch,
>> to each one of your family through all
>> these generations.

The Spirit of the Risen Lord will allocate three angels to each and all so blessed by fire
>> that each and all will surely know—
>> they walk their days on Earth in the
>> favour of The Lord.

  And this shall be a sign to you as you walk in and with the blessings,
>> as a prophet,
>> of The Lord."

Jeremiah 50:2 As it is written so it is apparent. "Declare among the nations, Proclaim, and set up a standard; Proclaim— do not conceal [it]— Say, ...'
Divine Commentary—

"'The Banner of The Kingdom is at hand;
  The Standard of The Kingdom stands alone on territory so marked;
  The Flag of The Kingdom flies nearest to the heavens and proclaims The Kingdom of
>> God's return upon The Earth.'

As it is proclaimed so it is declaimed."

Isaiah 66:19 'I will set a sign among them; and those among them who escape I will send to the nations: [to] the coastlands afar off who have not heard My fame nor seen My glory. And they shall declare My glory among the Gentiles.'
Divine Commentary—

"As it is written so it proceeds."

Jeremiah 4:6 'Set up the standard toward Zion. Take refuge! Do not delay! For I

will bring disaster from the north, And great destruction.'"
Divine Commentary—

"As it is written so it still forewarns.

As it is written requires The Wisdom of God.

As it is written the wisdom of man changes his understanding with the season.

As it is written The Standard of The Kingdom will mark the way to Zion.

Watchmen in the towers:
> seek The Wisdom of God.

It is with wisdom you should watch and count what musters in the north.

What musters in the north believes in vengeance for past battles,
> has not forgotten its loss of pride,
>> its loss of face,
>> its loss of standing:
>>> its humiliation witnessed by the nations of
>>>> the world.

Vengeance is mine and mine alone and so it is written 'For I will bring disaster from
> the north'.

Foolish unto death are those who act in vengeance;
> for the wrath of God will fall on all who commandeer the property
>> of God."

Jeremiah 51:12 'Set up the standard on the walls of Babylon; Make the guard strong, Set up the watchmen, Prepare the ambushes. ...'
Divine Commentary—

"As it is written so it must be done.

Set up The Standard of Justice,
> The Standard of Grace,
> The Standard of The Kingdom on the walls of the city like unto Babylon
>> now fallen:
>>> the city of vengeance,
>>> the city ignorant of God,
>>> the city without temples,
>>> the city where deception breeds the
>>>> iniquity of man.

And great destruction will befall the city like unto Babylon whose walls are
> marked and claimed by The Standard of The Kingdom."

Mark 13:4 "Tell us, when will these things be? And what [will be] the sign when all these things will be fulfilled?"
Divine Commentary—

"As it is written so will it be answered.

> These things will be when hornets can fly encased in metal and answer calls from man. These things will be fulfilled when the sun of man is charged by man to burn The Earth according to his will."

1 Corinthians 14:22 '… but prophesying is not for unbelievers but for those who believe.'
Divine Commentary—

"As it is written so it shall be followed.

> Those believers,
> > with the blessing of The Spirit,
> > > who continue prophesying with unbelievers in their midst no longer walk in the favour of The Lord.

> Let My prophets speak,
> > when moved,
> > > if unbelievers dwell among The Saints."

Isaiah 19:20 '… and He will send them a Saviour and a Mighty One, and He will deliver them.'
Divine Commentary—

"As it is written so He came to deliver."

Isaiah 7:14 'Therefore the Lord Himself will give you a sign: …'
Divine Commentary—

"As it is written so it is received.

I,
> The Lord,
> > declare to My people of all nations—
> > > 'Hearken to The Word of The Lord spoken through My prophets.

> > > > Let the prophets test according to My Spirit.
> > > > Acquaint yourselves with truth now so revealed.
> > > > Believe and adapt as counselled by My Spirit and The Word of God.'"

Psalms 74:4 'Your enemies roar in the midst of Your meeting place; They set up their banners [for] signs.'
Divine Commentary—

"As it is written so it must not be.

Do not recoil from the call to decontaminate The Bride.

For The Saints must purify:
> > > The Bride within the meeting place,
> > > The Bride that awaits The Groom,

The Bride to be dressed in white linen for the wedding of The Lamb.

Array all the white linen that it may be inspected and found spotless and thereby worthy to enrobe The Bride."

Revelation 13:14 'And he deceives those who dwell on the earth by those signs which he was granted to do in the sight of the beast, telling those who dwell on the earth to make an image to the beast who was wounded by the sword and lived.'
Divine Commentary—

"As it is written so it discloses.

As it is written the beast who deceives is made known.

The beast who deceives is the exceeding great company of false prophets,
                    each one known and numbered,
                    in the record of The Lamb.

This company of false prophets by their teaching and their leading will capture the hearts
                    and souls of those who listen in acceptance and,
                    taking note,
            thereby inscribe within their minds the mark that can be read
                    on foreheads by The Spirit of The Lord.

The image to the beast is composed of flaunted wealth—
        ignoble wealth not granted presence within The Throne-room of God—
        wealth that appeals to man,
                is clutched and not released,
        wealth that far exceeds the needs or generosity of man—
        wealth that fuels and feeds the building of the towers of Babel.

Those,
    in reaching to the heavens in the on-going quest for more:
                        of admiration,
                        lust and envy,
                    to thereby achieve each his attempted
                            domination of another.

'Enslave and rob the poor',
'Conquer and dispossess',
    are the catch-cries of the beast that grab the attention of the lost—
                        all those who will follow the beast
                            seen seeking land,
            the beast who was wounded and survived,
            the beast who granted all those signs designed so
                            to deceive:
    even so Satan cast down to The Earth and seen emerging from the sea;
        Satan wounded as he fought and warred,
                    with others,

> against the very Hosts of Heaven;
> Satan gifting signs of deception to those in his sight who willingly bend
> the knee.
>
> For in these images are the battle lines portrayed and drawn.
>
> For in these images is the kingdom of Satan desolated as territory is retaken;
> kingdom of Satan destroyed as its citizens are redeemed;
> kingdom of Satan thrown down as its ruler loses his throne,
> his lands,
> his people,
> and is captured in dismay."

Revelation 19:20 'Then the beast was captured, and with him the false prophet who worked signs in his presence, by which he deceived those who received the mark of the beast and those who worshipped his image. These two were cast alive into the lake of fire burning with brimstone.'
Divine Commentary—

> "As it is written so it is decided,
> so will the outcome be,
> so destinies are determined.
>
> Let it be known,
> the deceived will be judged with justice for the records will be available:
> those records that contain all thoughts and deeds and signs that resulted in the
> embedding of the mark of Satan and even
> idolatry within each soul that was deceived.
>
> The great company of false prophets shall accompany Satan into the lake of fire.
>
> The lake of fire will not consume.
>
> The lake of fire has extreme heat.
>
> The lake of fire affects the senses of the soul and of the spirit.
>
> The lake of fire with brimstone may purge a soul of intent and prejudice.
>
> Failing an objection,
> the lake of fire may bring about the redemption of those with both soul and spirit."

Revelation 15:1 'Then I saw another sign in heaven, great and marvellous: seven angels having the seven last plagues, for in them the wrath of God is complete.'
Divine Commentary—

> "As it is written so it was seen by My beloved.
>
> The angels carry the last plagues.
>
> The angels move with care.
>
> The angels form a circle round The Throne.
>
> The angels guard their plagues.

The angels process.

The angels worship.

The angels prepare to leave The Throne-room of God,
                              each angel with a plague.

As it was witnessed,
    so will it appear;
for the wrath of God soon blends within each bowl."

My Content Study Aid

The Banner Speaks of Unity

"The Banner of The Kingdom speaks of the unity of man in fulfilled and perfect
completion as the single and complete Bride of Christ:
all His saints now united and one with Him in the
Bright and Morning Star
ready for The Father's Blessing."

My Content Study Aid

The Banner of The Protocols

"It is My desire that The Banner of The Kingdom should not fly at night during the hours
of darkness.

Nor should it fly on a seventh day,
for The Seventh Day is the consecrated day of rest.

Only upon My Return shall The Banner of The Kingdom fly continuously denoting the
end of The Age of My Grace and ushering in the Time
of Justice—
as the seat of Judgement is established throughout all the realms of
The Earth.

Nevertheless,
until this time,
The Banner of The Kingdom,
The Sign of The Kingdom may be flown at the will of man and at the will of My
servants as they are moved by The Holy Spirit in wisdom
and understanding.

Great are the ramifications for man,
great are the portents for man,
great are the instructions in Heaven:
when the eyes of man behold The Sign of The Kingdom;
when the minds of man encounter The Standard of The Kingdom;
when the flesh of man turns away from The Blood of The Lamb
without appeal.

For then the tears of man will avail them little as the wrath of The Father mounts in the
heavens and the Time of Judgement is established on
The Earth.

At that time,
there will not be a cave on The Earth in which shelter is not sought from the seat of
My judgement.

All The Earth who shed tears of distress,
tears of woe,
tears of dismay will be brought before Me with tear-stained faces
dried with the dust of The Earth.

Woe to any servant whose face carries the dust of The Earth;
for the dust of The Earth will condemn all who wear it.

The dust of The Earth will mark the downfall of man;
will be put under My footstool,
will not be lifted up.

The demands of justice as decreed by The Father will be upheld by The Son.

    And the tears of man will wet The Earth in recompense for the tears of The Son and the tears of man will justify the absence of names from The Lamb's Book of Life.

    And the tears of man will mark the end of The Age of Grace.

The works of man shall be examined,
        shall be tested by fire,
        shall be aligned with the intent of the heart.

  For the intent of the heart will not be hidden,
    the intent of the heart is recorded;
    the intent of each heart will determine the judgement of The Lord at the seat of justice.

The cry for mercy will only be heard by The Father.

The decree of The Father who measures the works and the intent of the heart determines a call for mercy only when there is no call for justice.

The absence of a call for justice bestows a measure of Grace.

Upheld sustained calls for justice will bring retribution so all who call are satisfied.

Calls for justice will be heard,
    will be answered,
    will be resolved according to the record."

My Content Study Aid

_____
_____
_____
_____
_____
_____
_____
_____
_____
_____
_____

The Slaughter of The Innocent

"From the beginning of creation we have held to our dictum that the life of man
                                                     has purpose;
        that The Spirit of life has significance beyond the understanding
                                                     of man,
                that the soul of life,
                    the soul of man,
                        must grow to maturity.

We have held to our dictum that we will withhold our power of compliance in the life
                                                                     of man.

We have held to our dictum to warn man through the ages,
                              through our servants the prophets,
                                  of the consequences of the actions of man.

We shall hold to our dictum that man shall be held accountable in this age,
                                                         The Age of Grace,
      before the seats of justice for the treatment of his brothers;
                              the treatment of his children;
                              the treatment of the sons and daughters of man:
                              the treatment of the very sons and daughters of God.

The sons and daughters of God placed within the womb of woman:
                                              a sacred trust;
    where they may all be nurtured until their appointed time to come forth and there to
                                                              choose a destiny.

The age of Grace carries the new covenant,
                carries new testimony of The Word,
                        imparts wisdom and knowledge and calls for righteousness in the life
                                                             of man;
              is the era of the accountability of man.

Foolish are they who ignore the accountability of man.

Foolish,
    indeed,
        are they who ignore the time of appeal in The Age of Grace.

Foolish,
    in the extreme,
        are those who do not approach the evangelists of the cross,
             who do not call out for their redemption within The Age of Grace.

Foolish,
    even unto death,

                are those who will perish in their sins,
                                    their iniquities—
                        The Blood of the sons and daughters of God—
                                                    on their hands.

For the waters of The Earth cannot forgive,
                    cannot cleanse,
                        hands stained with The Blood of The Innocent.

Hands still stained with blood that reach for,
                            and grasp,
                                their repulsive pieces of silver:
                                the wealth of man.

I,
    The Lord,
        see The Blood-stained hands of those who wreck destruction within the womb
                                                    of woman.

            The bloodied perverted hands of man,
                                    that should caress and love,
                        maim,
                        disfigure,
                        mutilate and,
                            without mercy,
                        render asunder in dismemberment:
        the innocence of The Glory of man in The Likeness of His God.

Truly,
    I,
        The Lord,
            say,
                'The Holy Spirit of The Lord sees through your eyes all that you
                                                    have done;
                    each action of your hand;
                    each tool that you select;
                    each defensive move of the child of God you would destroy.'

I,
    The Lord,
        hear the call for justice that arises from each spirit denied the promise of the flesh.

        Recorded is the scream for justice from each soul denied maturity.

        Retribution will be exacted for each life that is cut short.

It would be better for those with blood-stained hands if they had not been born
                                                    of woman.

For as they have done,

so shall it be meted out to them—
>> cut for cut,
>> blow for blow,
>> agony for agony:
even to a seven-fold retribution shall a call for justice be resolved.

Each recorded call for justice shall stand alone;
>> according to the record,
>> according to the testimony,
>> according to the actions of those who stand before.

The mind of man cannot imagine the torture that awaits all those held accountable for destroying The Glory of man in the likeness of His God.

The chain of accountability will be followed for each call for justice.

The chain with all the links is locked.

All the links partake equally in the depravity so practised.

Even to those who would hide the evidence;
>> remove The Blood;
>> keep the records;
>> approve the action;
>> own the premises;
>> supply the products of The Earth and all kinds of efforts
>>>> of man;
>> hide in supposed anonymity behind doors of grandeur or
>>>> of wood.

As it is established,
> to those who plead ignorance of the affairs of man;
>> who rule and enable with authority they do not have—
>>> with the authority born of the ignorance of man;
>> who rule but do not listen to the counsel of Heaven;
>> who receive the proceeds of silver,
>>> the wealth of man,
>>> in whole or in part;
> all those who feed,
> all those who care,
> all those who love—
> these workers of atrocity.

None shall be excused when the uncircumcised heart of each link is laid bare with
>> knowledge for all to see.

In justice,
> the locked chain of accountability,
> that is so established,

reveals the hidden shameful images that befell The Innocent with the agreement
of the links.

For all those who forsake The Glory of their calling to enhance the life of man,
and choose thereby to bring destruction to the destiny of man,
shall themselves be cursed,
forsaken,
by their God they did not know.

Repent.
Repent.
Repent.

And turn from,
forsake,
your wicked ways,
while it is still today;
for the mind of man does not know the time of his accounting for this vast and
terrible abomination here laid before him at his door.

Else surely you will stand at the gates of Hell as they open.

And the horror of your harvest will fill your eyes.

And the scream from your throat will echo in your soul for ever,
as your feet are forced,
unwillingly,
through the gates of Hell.

For your destiny,
that concerned you not,
has verily come to be,
bringing full fear of understanding to your soul.

And the wrath of God will fall as the Gates of Hell slam shut:
imprisoning the dammed beyond the ears of He
who holds the keys.

So will it be with all found wanting,
when called before the seat of justice,
for lies will not avail,
deception will not assail,
all will be opened and prevail:
the heavens will applaud the brightness of the light.

For there,
in the brightness of the light,
will the deprived be rendered justice on the depraved of heart,
of soul,

of spirit.

Awake,
    this land of plenty,
    this people with power.

Now is the time to stop the slaughter of The Innocent that I,
    The Lord,
        may again bless this land,
            this nation,
            this people.

    Else I,
        The Lord,
            will continue to speak to this land in indignation at its complacency;
                at what the people of the land,
                  in degradation,
                  now permit,
              bereft of The Fear of The Lord.

Repent.
    Seek The Keys of The Kingdom.

Repent.
    Be taught and learn The Fear of The Lord.

Repent,
    that your land may again be watered in season according to its needs."

My Content Study Aid

_____
_____
_____
_____
_____
_____
_____
_____
_____
_____
_____
_____
_____

I Love My People

"I,
   The Lord Jesus,
      speak to My people with love and understanding that they may prosper
                in all they do,
                in all that they attempt,
                in all that they dream of achieving in their lives.

For My desire is that they live in joy,
                in happiness and with My Spirit in their time on Earth.

I would have them know Me,
      speak with Me and tell Me of their troubles,
      the troubles that beset their hearts.

And I will comfort them;
   I will enfold them in My arms.

   They can know that they may rest their heads upon My breast and I will bless them,
               their families and their homes.

They can be My children and I will be their God.

They can overcome all things and rejoice in the friendship of My Spirit as they can speak
                with Me and I will speak with them.

I love My children.

I adore My children.

I value My children above all the imaginings of man.

   More than the grandest aspirations of man;
      much greater than the greatest love man knows within his family.

My love for My children is so gentle and so true and I still shed My tears,
                in secret now,
                   away from the eyes of man.

Come to Me,
   My children,
      let Me wrap My arms around you,
      call you each by name:
      for I would bless you,
      and would know you,
      on that wonderful day,
      as sons and daughters of The Living God.

And I,
    and all the heavens,
        would rejoice as I install you as members of God's household in the company of
                                          the faithful.

    God's household where I would fellowship with you and you would fellowship
        with Me as we sup together at the table I have prepared and I say,
                with all My love,
                to you,
                'Welcome home'."

My Content Study Aid

The Roar of The Lion of Judah

"The Lion Roars to get attention,
        to gather the witnesses,
        in defiance of the darkness.

The Roar of The Lion precedes His Presence,
        brings consternation,
        causes flight.

The Roar of The Lion settles disputes,
        announces intent to rule,
        is supreme.

  Listen for,
        run to,
        shelter in,
        the Roar of The Lion of Judah.

The Lion Roars,
    offering protection.

The Lion Roars,
    declaring His territory.

The Lion Roars,
    assembling his pride."

My Content Study Aid

The Churches in The Mountains

"I speak to the churches in the mountains of the islands of the seas,
        the isolated islands of the seas,
        the uttermost islands of the seas,
        the islands that I have blessed in the presence of The Father,
        the islands that are prepared for battle,
                the battle that is Mine.

I know make known,
    by My prophet,
        to the churches that love Me,
        the churches that I acknowledge before The Father,
        the churches in which My Spirit rains,
        the churches with open doors,
        the churches that cry out to Me,
        the churches where My Spirit builds:
                a new thing.

A new thing prepared in the heavens for this time and now declared before the face
                              of man.

I,
  The Lord,
    speak and declare,
        I now unfurl The Banner of My Kingdom over the Islands of the Seas,
                          over the Lands both near and far,
                          over the very Nations of The Earth.

    And now I so declare that this Banner be established by My servants,
        for all with eyes to see;
        that they may,
        with seeking,
        understand and ponder on their destiny.

So My Banner will descend from the mountains of this land as it covers,
                          with Grace and,
                          later,
                          Justice,
                          the strivings of man.

    My Banner will signify,
        will usher,
        will mark,
        will spread,
        will concern,

will frighten,
will welcome.

All those with contrite spirits will run to The Banner of The Kingdom,
The Banner of Grace,
The Banner of Justice.

Turn them not away,
   for I would have them free:
taught by My servants,
baptized by water and The Spirit,
sent forth commissioned in their callings,
en-armoured and equipped—
to stand and not to fall,
to reap and to report,
the harvest of The Kingdom to be reclaimed from Hell.

For My servants in the mountains,
with wisdom and with care,
shall shepherd all My flock that is established there.

With prayer and praise,
in penitence,
shall be the building of the flock;
and as the whiteness of My sheep are seen,
as so shall be the gathering of this stock.

Prepare for the Roar of The Lion.

The ROAR of The Lion shall be heard in the mountains,
shall scatter the darkness,
shall go forth from the rock.

The ROAR of the Lion protects the pride,
summons the pride,
announces the pride.

All who answer the Roar,
the Call of the Lion,
are garnered as His pride;
for the Pride of The Lion prepares the way.

The pride of the Lion descends as the footsteps of the Lion.

Mark the way of the Lion.

Blaze a trail through the forests of man.

Mark the trail of the Lion.

Follow the scent of the Lion.

For the scent of the Lion invades the darkness,
    the scent of the Lion pervades all His territory,
           is recognized by His pride,
           indicates His Presence.

The scent of the Lion guides His pride,
        directs His pride,
        marks the path for the pride of the Lion.

Seek the scent of the Lion.

Find the scent of the Lion.

    The pride of the Lion knows His scent,
        loves His scent,
        runs into His scent.

Acknowledge the presence of the Scent of the Lion.

And I,
    The Lord,
        will bless My people,
        will watch over them both by day and by night and I will accompany each of them
            as they place their footsteps on My mountains,
            whether the valleys or the heights,
            carrying My Gospel with their armour and My Banner that both heralds
                      and proclaims.

Use My Banner,
    uphold it,
    recognize it,
    look for it in the byways and the cities of this land,
        for there will be found a refuge and a welcome from My Spirit as each extends
                      a hand.

For by it My servants will be known to one another as they travel,
        and in welcome greet,
        and in love a meal may share,
        and with interest hear of places near and far away and of successes there.

The Sign of The Kingdom may proclaim within the marketplace of man:
    all those who fear The Lord,
        who do not cheat,
        have honest scales,
        and do not bring dishonour to the dignity of man.

According to each will,
    all who love The Lord,
    all who fear The Lord,
    all who serve The Lord:

may fly,
> on high,
> The Flag of The Kingdom;

may mark,
> by pole,
> The Standard of The Kingdom;

may,
> on items,
> wear and use The Emblem of The Kingdom;

may,
> in hand,
> proclaim,
> celebrate,
> wave,
> rejoice with The Banner of The Kingdom and The Spirit of The Lord."

My Content Study Aid

The Responsibility of Freewill

"The Glory of The Lord,
  The Spirit of The Lord,
    the Revelation of The Lord bestows,
          declares,
             foretells the actions of The Lord.

For The Spirit of The Lord esteems The Freewill of man that man may love and serve
          with honour and not with the compulsiveness of a bound soul.

The freewill of man is the diadem of his creation,
      sets man apart from the animals,
      enables man to worship God,
      validates his sin,
      implants a voyage of discovery,
      takes him either to Heaven or to Hell.

It is wisdom for man:
    to honour the tribute of his diadem;
    to be bound by his word;
    to purify his heart;
    to be aware of the agency of man;
    to establish his walk in righteousness;
    to guard with fearful wisdom,
        and in like understanding use,
        and by like action turn,
            the very Key to his eternity
            embedded within his soul.

For The Key within the soul is turned,
        either to the left or to the right,
        according to the inclination of his heart.

The heart that loves My Spirit,
      accepts My counsel,
      seeks The Keys to My Kingdom—
    such a heart will know The Fear of The Lord,
        have reverence for The Lord,
        have embedded in it the record of The Lord:
          the record of all that man is choosing as he exercises his Freewill.

Thereby accepting or denying the presence,
        the indwelling,
        the counselling of The Spirit,
            The Comforter,

> the Gift of God to man.

Man shows his lack of wisdom and of understanding when he leaves his spirit
> unprotected and uncounselled and declines the Gifts of God;
> for the Key turns to the left and shows the misery of man.

Man then struggles all his life:
> for health,
> for wealth,
> for pleasure;
> and takes them to the grave,
>> a pauper in his soul."

My Content Study Aid

The Lion Offers All, His Ways

"The Lion banners His Kingdom,
    welcomes at the gate,
    has no debt.

The Lion encourages the disenfranchised,
    lifts up the injured,
    proclaims The Innocent,
    restores transgressors,
    lingers with the lost,
    redeems the pledging of the heart.

The Lion of Judah hears the heart-cry,
    calls the wanderer,
    defends the vulnerable.

The Lion leads by example,
    foresees potential,
    offers all,
        His ways."

My Content Study Aid

_____
_____
_____
_____
_____
_____
_____
_____
_____
_____
_____
_____
_____
_____
_____
_____
_____

The Lioness and The Lion

"The will of the lioness is to protect her cubs,
>   to nurture her cubs,
>   to prepare them for an enduring life as they mature.

The lioness is at the centre of the pride of the lion;
>   is the mantle of the lion;
>   declares,
>   by her presence,
>   the majesty of the lion.

The lioness receives protection,
>   receives comfort,
>   receives counsel from the scent of the lion.

The lioness recognizes the roar of the lion,
>   recognizes the Scent of the Lion.

The scent of the lion is to be followed.

The scent of the lion brings wisdom,
>   brings understanding,
>   brings unity of intent to both the lioness and the lion.

When the needs of the lioness are made known to the lion they will all be fully met.

Then she will know the scent of the lion signifies the presence of the lion,
>   the caring of the lion,
>   the protection of the lion.

The lioness will expand the pride with confidence supported by the lion,
>   approved by the lion,
>   encouraged by the lion.

At the calling of the lioness the lion roars,
>   as needed,
>   to dispel the darkness.

The lion roars,
>   counting with authority,
>   to the approaching dawn.

The lioness without the roar of the lion is fearful of all that she encounters,
>   cautious in the raising of her cubs,
>   with trepidation moves across the territory she surveys.

The lioness without the roar of the lion is defensive of her lair,
>   remains within her lair,

is moved by force of circumstance to protect its full extent.

The lioness that attempts to roar,
        usurps,
        decries the mantle of the lion;
the lioness that denigrates the roaring of the lion is both lonely and distraught
        in the wilderness of night.

The lioness will curl up in loneliness,
        as the pride diminishes,
        as the scent of the lion no longer pervades the lair.

The lion roars establishing His Kingdom,
        His territory,
        with The Standard where he governs.

Listen to the roar of the lion that calls the pride to order,
        that declares His authority,
        that brings all things within His lair under His control.

The Scent of the Lion calls the pride that seeks.

The scent of the lion leads the way to safety,
        protects from perils that would beset and from effort that is
        both wasteful and unnecessary.

The scent of the lion honours the lineage of the lion,
        the record of the lion,
        the journey of the lion.

The presence of the pride will accompany the lion to the new location of the lair.

Do not frustrate the roar of the lion.

The roar of the lion is for the benefit of the pride,
        the benefit of the lioness,
        the benefit of the cubs.

When the lion roars there is peace in the lair,
        contentment in the lair,
        security in the lair;
        into the silence His roar is heard throughout the pride;
        His will is actioned by the pride.

The roar of the lion beseeches attentiveness from all the pride.

As the scent of the lion conveys the will of the lion so the scent of the lioness brings
        comfort to the lion.

The scent of the lioness speaks of acceptance,
        of trust,
        in truth,

>   in love,
>   with paws that are not crossed.

For the scent,
> both of the lion and of the lioness,
> speaks in one accord the language of each spirit:
> that each soul may be protected and harmony prevail within the pride."

My Content Study Aid

The Sin Beneath The Veil

"As I,
   The Lord,
      spoke to My people through the prophets in times past,
         so I still speak to My prophets—
            My prophets whom I call,
            My prophets to whom I entrust My written and
                          My spoken word.

      Great is their responsibility within the confines of their calls,
         reward within the gates of Heaven,
         dominion within the earshot of The Lord.

I,
   The Lord,
      know what I have said,
      know what I am saying,
      know what I shall say.

The future of man approaches to the veil.

   So I charge My prophets slowly to lift the veil from the heart,
                   the face,
            the mind of My Bride and then to study carefully what
                              they perceive to be.

For hidden sin is to be disclosed and purged before the coming of The Throne.

The Bride is in her purity when hidden sin is no longer found beneath the veil.

My Bride that truly loves Me will rejoice with an open heart as the veil is fully lifted and
                                    her Glory is revealed.

The curtain of eternity is held in hands full of anticipation;
                    the presence of The Father is awaited:
                    for the curtain of eternity is about to rise."

My Content Study Aid

_____

_____

_____

_____

_____

In Love

"I,
  The Lord,
    love My people,
    everyone,
      no exceptions on any basis.

I love them each individually.

I know each by name.

I know their strengths and their weaknesses as they each walk their path on Earth.

I know both their loves and their hates—
  the choices they either select or reject.

In love,
  man was created for an eternal destiny in the presence of his God.

In love,
  man is bestowed a gift of agency—
    a gift of freedom to act according to his will,
      to choose and not be forced,
        without appeal,
          to a fate he would not want.

In love,
  man is not left alone;
  for I have unlocked the door.

In love,
  I have sent a comforter to counsel and advise and within the guidelines of His leading
    the way is ascertained.

In love,
  I have ensured the cross has sanctified and man is free to choose.

In love,
  I have assured all those who call to Me will not be left within the grave of man.

In love,
in truth,
in Glory,
  lies the destiny of man,
  for that he was created by his God:
    so he may dwell for ever in surroundings fit for kings,
    so he may be welcomed home at the end of his mortality,
    so he may see and live and witness what a loving God has planned."

The New Signs in Use

"The Banner of The Kingdom is to be used by those who know My Spirit,
                      promoted by those who know My Spirit,
                      appreciated by those who know My Spirit:
            for then will the use of My Banner spread throughout The Earth.

The Emblem of The Kingdom,
The Emblem of The Spirit,
      may be worn on clothing of the Saints:
                      with integrity,
                      and in honour,
                      of what is so displayed.

This Emblem,
    as acknowledged,
        may be used on stationery,
        may be used commercially,
        so long as the objective is to bring honour and recognition to The Kingdom here
                                  established on The Earth.

There is no shame in using,
              in purity,
              the markets of man to build The Kingdom of God.

The marketplace of man,
    where ever it is found,
        whether buildings built from labour or networks that criss-cross the globe of
                            The Earth:
        all aspects of the marketplace will know the jurisdiction of The Lord.

All networks designed to hear voices or to carry letters or to portray images from afar,
                      whether built from metal,
                              the power of light,
                              or the very ether of The Earth:
    so they shall be used to establish the visibility of the presence of My Spirit that
                      awaits with anticipation The Coming of My Return.

The Age of Grace draws to a close as the coming of My Return approaches and impacts
                                  upon My Bride,
        and even more so on those not present at the Wedding Feast.

The Banner of The Kingdom is to stand throughout The Earth.

The Standard of The Kingdom denotes dominion that has been established by those who
                                  have so marked.

The Standard of The Kingdom marks The Triumph of The Lord.

The Standard of The Kingdom leads the vanguard of The Lord,
  all those sent forth in twos to reap as they are asked,
  and the very Hosts of Heaven as they have been so marshalled,
  and now await intently for their words of command that issue from the lips of
                                                                    The Saints.

All The Saints of The Earth should be encouraged via the networks of The Earth to seek
  and then display The Banner,
    The Standard,
    The Flag of The Kingdom of God:
  where and when and as so established across The Earth and before the face of man."

My Content Study Aid

The New Signs of The Kingdom

"The Banner of The Kingdom will withstand the attacks of man,
                is defended by The Hosts of Heaven,
                stands from this time.

The Standard of The Kingdom stretches across the heavens,
                marches across the heavens,
                reveals The Love of God to all who are beneath.

The Flag of The Kingdom speaks of victory achieved,
                will speak of a site of Justice,
                speaks of the rallying of man.

The Emblem of The Kingdom is mixed among the throngs,
                raises awareness within the spirit,
                brings rejoicing to the soul.

These signs of The Kingdom will prevail,
                as needed,
                at the coming of The Lord.

These signs of The Kingdom speak of the heart-beat of The Lord,
                speak of The Lamb beside the Throne,
                speak of the new beginning about to be proclaimed.

Foolish are they who ignore,
                through inattention,
                the sign of The Kingdom placed before their presence;
        who four times turn away from the sign placed before their presence;
        who murmur in dissent among their ilk and do not avail themselves of
                            Grace offered before their presence.

Man exhibits wisdom in accepting Grace prior to the establishment of a seat of Justice
                            from which he will not turn away.

Man will long regret his call before a seat of Justice that could have been avoided,
        remember the consequences of his actions both before and after his
                          appearance at a seat of Justice.

Repent!
Repent!
Repent!
And obviate appearance before a seat of Justice!

Turn!
Turn!
Turn!

From ways established without consideration to the longevity of man,
> established and recorded within the heart of man,
>> that wrote the records not erased and so accessed at a seat of Justice to the
>>> detriment of man.

Erase the records!
Erase the records!
Erase the records,
> while the time of Grace remains accessible to man through The Name Above
>> All Names,
>>> Jesus The Messiah,
>>> The Lamb of God!"

My Content Study Aid

Justice in Judgement

"In the sight of The Lord a seat of Justice and a seat of Judgement are indistinguishable and fully interchangeable.

Only in the surroundings of the flesh of man do justice and judgement offer the possibility of a conflict of intent."

My Content Study Aid

The Intent of The Lord

"The power of fellowship amongst The Saints is the strength of the Church across the
                                                                              races of man,
                   The Saints is the security of the orphans and
                                           the widows,
                   The Saints is the feeding of the body,
                                   the souls and the spirits,
                                        each according to the need.

The fellowship of The Saints is eternal,
            is the quest for relationships that will endure.

The fellowship of The Saints extends the spirit and the soul beyond the reach of time
                                                         and space:
                the restrictions imposed by the mortality of man.

The mortality of man is the time of the sifting of the spirit,
                of the harnessing of the soul.

The mortality of man is the springboard to—
                        all that has been promised,
                        all yet to be made known,
                        all prepared to be so accessed by the immortality
                                                       of man.

The immortality of man may lead to exaltation,
                leads to fulfilment of aspiration,
                may lead to judgement previously unrealized.

The immortality of man may lead to appreciation previously unacknowledged,
                may lead to awe previously unforeseen,
                may lead to wonders previously uncontemplated.

The immortality of man may lead to majesty previously undisclosed,
                may lead to Glory previously withheld,
                leads to all previously shielded by the curtain of eternity as
                                    positioned by The Spirit.

The Spirit speaks in comfort,
        speaks in counsel,
        speaks in tongues,
        speaks in knowledge,
        speaks in wisdom,
        speaks in Faith,
        speaks in truth.

The Spirit speaks all these,

        when invited,
        into the spirit of man.

The Spirit will speak in fire,
        speak in boldness,
        speak in needs,
        speak in desires,
        speak in blessings,
        speak in favour,
        speak in The Word.

The Spirit will speak in—
        as directed,
        as permitted,
        as received—
            the intent of The Lord.

The intent of The Lord is not capricious,
        stands in holiness before The Father,
        is in compliance with The Father's Will."

My Content Study Aid

The Servants of The Lord

"I,
   The Lord,
      speak to all My servants this day.

         As they live their lives so will I be blessed.
               so will their testimony stand.
               so will their reward be.

The servants of The Lord should be beyond reproach,
           should reflect The Word,
           should uplift The Kingdom.

To greet with joy,
to present with Grace,
to speak with dignity—
     so are My servants known among the gatherings of man:
             not to err from The Truth,
             not to reproach in anger,
             neither to amplify nor distort the events of life as they
                           are encountered.

The events of life are interpreted by man.

The spoken words of man should agree with the record of the events of life.

   A disparity between the records should be to man's concern.

   A disparity results in the re-interpretation of the record so harmony is achieved
                           between the two.

   A child of man erases the record upon becoming a child of God.

   All who seek the key will find the door.

The door is always opened to those who hold the key;
           all pass through the door who use the key;
           all those who enter through the door enter as a child of God.

My servants serve,
      hold the key,
      encourage the accepting of the key,
      direct the willing to the door,
      assist the passing through the door:
             to pass through and hence become a newborn child of God."

The Return of The Shepherd

"I love My sheep.

   My sheep are ready for the sheepfold.

      I protect all those within the sheepfold;
               who know My voice,
               who answer to their names,
               who seek the sanctuary of The Lord,
               who call My Name;
               known to The Father,
               known to My Spirit.

      I protect all those who would become a lamb,
                     a sheep,
                     a member of My flock.

         Those who answer to their names are blessed,
                     stay within the flock,
                     will hear The Call of God.

All those within the flock will know the sign of God.

The sign of God is for the sheep,
               is spread across the skies,
               heralds the Shepherd of the Sheep,
               calls the flock to gather and prepare.

The sign of God is the trumpet blast of God,
               the trumpet blast that wakens all the sheep,
               the trumpet blast that brings fear only to the lost.

All will hear the trumpet blast of God.

The trumpet blast of God heralds a new era into the life of man.

Listen for,
   hearken to,
   arise for,
   the trumpet blast of God that calls the sheep:
               the sheep within the sheepfold,
               the sheep with spotless coats,
               the sheep with fleeces that testify,
               the sheep whose hearts are pure,
               the sheep that do await the return of the shepherd to the fold."

The Hurdles of Man

"The fear of man precedes The Fear of God,
        stultifies The Fear of God,
        proscribes The Fear of God.

The fear of man lies within the soul,
        commands inertia towards God,
        is driven by the obsequiousness of man,
        is relegated to from whence it came,
        is vanquished from each soul by the boldness so attained as My Spirit
                speaks it into each spirit that requests.

  Each emboldened spirit can acquire The Fear of God.
  Each emboldened spirit can learn The Fear of God.
  Each emboldened spirit,
        walking in The Fear of God,
        can then acquire,
        if sought,
        The Wisdom of God.

The wisdom of God does not countenance the wisdom of man.

The wisdom of God leads to greater vision,
        supplants the acquisitiveness of the soul,
        is displayed throughout the heavens,
        interacts with the tongue of man,
        sets man on his course free of encumbrance.

  Man is encumbered by his acts of will not in alignment with his spirit.

  Man is encumbered by lifestyles he embraces,
        by the baggage that he carries,
        by the records that he keeps,
        by counsel that should be discarded,
        by lack of vision for his future,
        by the idols that he follows,
        by the debt he has assumed.

The encumbrances of man blind the eyes of man to God,
        are gathered on broad paths easily traversed,
        are not to be admired,
        are not worthy of emulation,
        are not the things of God.

  The cost of encumbrances in the freight yard of the soul are rendered due for
                payment after the filling of the grave.

The debts of the soul may quench the flickering of the spirit.

The debts of the soul are tear drops on the heart,
        have been already paid,
        may surely be erased.

The debts of the soul of man need not be judged,
        need not be retold,
        need not be regurgitated:
     for the debts of the soul have been paid,
            cancelled and erased:
     for all who have an entry in The Lamb's Book of Life."

My Content Study Aid

The Book of Life

"The Book of Life is the record of The Bride of The Lamb,
        is eternal,
              records the new names against the old.

The Book of Life records each spirit with each soul to be renewed,
                in each new body so designed,
           records each garland awarded for each race,
           records the allocation of each site of life within the new Jerusalem,
           records the wedding gown of each Bride,
           records each testimony of the linkages that adorn each gown.

  The linkages that adorn are traceable and true,
                bear testimonies of joy and celebration,
                are the fruit of the spirit of the gown.

The spirit of the gown has been found spotless as a sheep,
                as a lamb,
                    as a child of God.

The network of the gowns,
        each with its linkages,
                establishes a complexity of enduring relationships beyond the
                              comprehension of the present mind of man.

The network of the gowns foretells of visitations beyond the realms of space and time.

The network of the gowns foresees travel within the realms of universes not even
                            postulated by either the dreams
                            or the imaginings of man.

The networks of the gowns are each linked to The Bridegroom.

Each spirit of a gown has visitation rights to every other engowned spirit.

Every engowned spirit is aware of the individuality of preparation of each site of life.

The basis of allocation is the adornment of the gown,
                      the white linen:
              the deeds performed in love,
                  through callings,
                  in service to The Lord.

  The blood of the Martyrs is recorded on a special gown.

  As it is recorded,
     so it shall be treated—
     let those with wisdom understand.

The importance of adornment on a gown should not be under-estimated by the mind
of man.

Those who escape as through the fire have gowns without adornment.

Man is encouraged,
> while in the time of Grace,
> to ensure:
>> an entry in The Lamb's Book of Life;
>> the colour of his linen;
>> the adornments thereon.

The Book of Life is the record of the records—
> the books that will be opened.

The Book of Life stands supreme.

The Book of Life contains The Truth wherein justice is established for all involved to witness in the presence of The Lamb."

My Content Study Aid

The Battlements of The Mind

"The battlements of the mind protect or expose the spirit and the soul,
                  stand or fall according to the wisdom available within.

The battlements of the mind must withstand the storming of the mind,
                  must repel the onslaught of invaders,
                  must be prepared to fight.

The battlements of the mind can conquer with The Word,
                  can conquer by decree,
                  can conquer in The Name above all names.

The battlements of the mind can deflect missiles with the shield of Faith.

The battlements of the mind can surmount intrusions,
                  can surmount attacks,
                  can surmount the probings of the soul.

    The probings of the soul can undermine the battlements,
                    can collapse the battlements.

    The probings of the soul,
                when unchecked,
                  can bring down the defences of the mind.

    The probings of the soul lay bare the weaknesses of the soul.

Man should not permit a full assault on or by the weaknesses of the soul.

    For a full assault extends the battle plan of the foe to include the spirit.

    The capture of the soul concerns the spirit.

    The capture of the soul cannot occur without the concurrence of the agency of man,
                  brings prevarication to the knowledge of the spirit,
                  leads to the appellate call of the spirit,
                  brings tribulation to the fore within the life of man.

    The seeking of redemption is oft delayed for those with captured souls.

    Redemption is freely offered within The Age of Grace.

    Redemption is the Gift of God that brings salvation to the spirit and renewal to the
                  body and the soul.

Man should not delay the attainment of his salvation.
Man does not know when the grave will call.

    Salvation must be attained by man prior to the filling of his grave.

The foe of man invites delay to every captured soul that the attainment of salvation may
                                        be then curtailed by the filling of the grave.

Fortify the battlements of the mind with wisdom!
Strengthen the battlements of the mind with intent that will not falter!
Renew the battlements of the mind:
                remove the weaknesses of the soul!

Protect the battlements of the mind with a shield placed firmly before the soul.
Enlarge the battlements of the mind with the counsel of The Spirit.
Inspect the battlements of the mind that all may be in order.

Defend the battlements of the mind,
        with all the weapons made available,
                that the soul is not misled,
                does not succumb:
                but rather stands in honour with the spirit in thwarting all
                              activities of the foe of man.

The foe of man comes in many guises,
        comes one step at a time,
        comes to capture the soul,
        comes to corrupt the body and the soul,
        comes to subvert the plan of God.

    The capture of the soul is marked within a book.
    The capture of the soul results in the seduction of the body and the soul.

    The seduction of the soul impacts on the lifestyle of the body,
                on the testimony of the spirit,
                on the defences of the mind.

    The seduction of the soul impacts on the attitude:
                      to life;
                      to relationships;
                      to the marriage covenant;
                      to the truthfulness;
                      and so the destiny,
                          of man.

    The seduction of the soul impacts on the dignity,
                the honour,
                The Freewill of man.

Man should not invite the foe into the soul of man,
        suffer the foe of man within the soul,
        condone the weaknesses of the soul,
        permit man's destiny to be determined by the weaknesses of man's soul!

Man should prohibit and abjure the probings of the soul!

For the probings of the soul can be determined through the discernment of the spirit.

Man should be attentive to the voice of his spirit that speaks within his conscience.

Man should listen,
>> hear and act upon the guidance of his conscience as it is developed by the speaking of his spirit.

Man should act within his agency in denying validity and existence to the machinations arising from the probings of his soul."

My Content Study Aid

The Mystery of Life

"The mystery of life should not be sought by man,
    is a secret of God,
    is not open to discovery by man.
The discovery of man is counselled by The Spirit upon a new name being written in The
                              Book of Life.

The inquisitiveness of man's spirit;
  his quest for knowledge by his effort;
  man's effort of discovery via precept upon precept:
  all bespeak of a design far grander than any so attributed to the mind of man.

The grandness of the design of man,
    by wisdom,
      should preclude the meddling of man.
Man should not meddle in designs of grandeur he does not fully comprehend.

  For designs of grandeur,
        that innately secure the secrets of God from discovery by man,
        will never yield such secrets to the probings of man's soul.

The meddling of man into chains with cuts and splices will bring disaster in its wake:
    whether of man,
    or of those that also walk and jump and creep and crawl and swim and fly,
    even of all living things that procreate and have their generations counted.

  For man cannot foresee the admixture of degrees of stability and change required to
             preserve the functioning of each species
             through all the generations so ordained.

  For man does not know when to stop:
         man cannot prevent rebellion within his ranks,
         man cannot enforce cessation into the soul of man.

It is before the perversity of man's soul that the charge is laid:
      of man's lack of reverence for the mystery of life.

The slaughter of The Innocent cannot abound,
      should not be tolerated,
      could not exist:
         in the presence of due reverence for the mystery of life.

The lack of due reverence for the mystery of life supports the indictment of man,
      in his application of his agency,
      the exertion of his freewill:
        the diadem of his creation bequeathed by God to man."

The Turning Points in Life

"I,
   The Lord,
      speak to all those who read,
         all those who hear,
           all those who would take notice of the saying of The Lord.

Life is to be highly valued by the lifestyles of man.

The opportunities of life bring either growth or stunting to the life of man,
         bring decisions at the turning points within the life events
                         of man.

Man should consider thoroughly the portent of the decisions made at the turning points
            encountered within the life events of man.

   For turning point decisions cannot be erased,
         cannot be denied,
         cannot be ignored by man.

Turning point decisions should be recognized and subjected to wise counselling.

Man should not access man's knowledge for wisdom is required.

The wisdom of counsellors is appropriate to assess,
            prior to a decision at a turning point—
                the life events of man.

They who rush headlong past each turning point do threaten the future happiness and
              destinations of those lives.

Wise indeed are they who approach a turning point with caution and trepidation,
            to examine from all perspectives:
       a signpost placed so carefully at a crossroad that can change the life
                        events of man.

   For the future life events of man are modified,
         are changed,
      depending on the choice established at each turning point encountered.

Safe are they who so decide with moral principles fixed firmly in their minds:
          for the morality of man issues from The Wisdom of God.

The morality of man is absolute,
      stands as given throughout the mortality of man,
      stands as received without addition or revision.

   Unwise are they who follow man's school of ethics:
      that are both relative and established by perception.

For the ethics of man will always fail in the hour of need:
    will always be found at variance and needing adaptation,
    are not universal in extent,
    are dependent on the culture of each nation,
        each race,
        each isolated people.

The ethics of man are changed:
    by the speech of the eloquent,
    on the decrees of those empowered,
    by the tumult of the voices expressing opinions from the
        gatherings of man.

Man,
  in wisdom,
    should establish his chain of life events resulting from decisions in alignment with what is already written:

'Finally, brethren, whatever things are true, whatever things [are] noble, whatever things [are] just, whatever things [are] pure, whatever things [are] lovely, whatever things [are] of good report, if [there is] any virtue and if [there is] anything praiseworthy— meditate on these things.' *

For in acceptance of this counsel,
  in living by this counsel,
  in practising this counsel—
    will man's soul be nurtured and corrected,
    will man's spirit call in Faith,
    will man's development be not stunted,
    will man's potential be attained,
    will man receive acknowledgment of his spirit's call:
    will man therein achieve his life of immortality in the presence of his God."

Scribal Note:
  *The Bible, Philippians 4:8
    Scripture taken from the New King James Version®. Copyright © 1982 by Thomas Nelson. Used by permission. All rights reserved.

My Content Study Aid

_____

_____

_____

_____

_____

The Fickleness of Man

"The fickleness of man is to be deplored,
     invites derision of his mind,
     points to lack of zeal,
       lack of objective,
         the absence of a goal within the life of man.

The absence of a goal leads to the wanderings of man.

The wanderings of man may lead to his entrapment,
       to his captivity,
         to his entrenchment within the jungles of The Earth.

 For entrenchment within a jungle denotes the surrender of the soul,
  captivity within a jungle calls for a clarion call of the spirit,
  entrapment within a jungle requires the freeing of the soul.

 The freeing of the soul necessitates an act of Faith.

Free the soul before the spirit has to call,
     before the soul has been surrendered,
     while it is yet still possible!

 For man with a surrendered soul has depravity of the mind,
    has a subjugated spirit that can no longer call,
     that can no longer sound the clarion that would call the host of Heaven to deal
      with the calamity that entrapped the soul,
         captured the spirit and now enslaves the soul.

The fickleness of man should be abhorred.

The fickleness of man is as:
     the blowing of the winds of change upon his agency;
     the arbitrary direction of a whim;
     the erratic footsteps of freewill,
        unmustered,
        unaligned,
      recording for their posterity the random footstep placements that
          exhaust the mortal walk of man.

The fickleness of man should not be endured,
    should be overcome,
    will bring adversity to the soul.

The waverings of the mind of man should be made subject to his spirit:
   that man may be transformed by the renewing of his mind—
    that he may prove what is that good and acceptable and perfect will of God.*"

Scribal Note: *The Bible, Romans 12:2

'And do not be conformed to this world, but be transformed by the renewing of your mind, that you may prove what *is* that good and acceptable and perfect will of God.'

Scripture taken from the New King James Version®. Copyright © 1982 by Thomas Nelson. Used by permission. All rights reserved.

My Content Study Aid

The Message of Compassion

"I,
   The Lord,
      speak to the peoples of The Earth with a message of compassion in times of the troubling of man:
         where man now witnesses the diminishing of his wealth,
         encounters difficulties beyond his experience,
         can no longer be certain of the purchases of life,
         suffers anxiety within his soul,
         recognizes a trembling in his spirit,
         calls out for help and assistance,
            that is only answered randomly,
               from those in whom he put his hope for the comfort of his life.

I say I change not.

I remain true to The Word.

My time of dwelling within the lives of man was to bring reconciliation between man and God—
         to bring the pathway to eternal life and light the way for man—
         to bring assurance to man of his salvation from the sin within his soul.

   The sin within his soul is a stumbling block to man that I have overcome.

The message that I have proclaimed,
         and do,
         and will proclaim,
   is that The Kingdom of God is now touching the boundaries of man—
         of those who dwell in the kingdoms,
            in the nations,
               in the distant places,
         of the peoples over all The Earth.

I call the sheep who hear My voice to gather with the flock:
         the flock that I protect—
            the flock that awaits the coming of the shepherd and the provisioning of The Lord.

   Hope and expectation are the seeds of Faith embedded within the flock,
            built within the flock,
            evident within the flock.

For I will apportion Faith to each according to each need:
              sufficient for the day of each redemption;
              sufficient for the day of each salvation;
              sufficient for each day."

The Journey of Man

"The outcasts of Heaven are no longer before The Throne.

The outcasts of Heaven no longer curry favour,
        lied before The Throne,
        sought what was not to be,
        took power unto themselves,
        fell from grace and favour,
        are a pain in the neck to all who they accost.

The outcasts of Heaven meddle in the affairs of man,
        antagonize the entity of man,
        circumvent the defences of man.

The outcasts of Heaven are vengeful in nature and deceitful in character,
        are eternal,
        are very numerous,
        seek nothing less than the destruction of man.

The outcasts of Heaven can curb man's mortality,
        would deny man his salvation,
                his redemption,
                his destiny as designed.

The outcasts of Heaven are envious of man,
        culture the diseases of man,
        disseminate the diseases of man,
        collapse man's defences to disease.

The outcasts of Heaven jeer at the portals of man and swing on his gates at will.

The outcasts of Heaven have a commonality of purpose that unifies their intent,
        are present on The Earth,
        are the epitome of evil.

The outcasts of Heaven are entertained at man's peril,
        do not bow to man,
        have a determined destiny decreed within the heavens,
        will become the outcasts of Earth.

    Man is extremely foolish if he thinks he can befriend,
            can play with,
            can have as company,
                  any of the outcasts of Heaven.

    Man plays with fire that will consume him as the second death when he adopts any
                of the outcasts of Heaven as his figureheads.

The outcasts of Heaven,
        the gargoyles of this world,
                must,
                by man,
        be kept in abeyance whilst man is in his mortality.

Man can require the abeyance of all the outcasts of Heaven when he relies on
                the trumpet blast of God,
                the breath of God,
                the coercive power of God,
        that is both summoned and directed in the Name above all names.

The journey of man in the presence of his God has complete fulfilment for his life,
                is a travelogue of wonder,
                is a compendium of stars,
                is a record of the feasting of the eyes.

The journey of man in the presence of his God is the supreme achievement,
                the accolade of eternity,
            the ultimate expression of God's love for man unhindered by time,
                      by concept or by space.

God calls man,
        in love,
        to commence the journey."

My Content Study Aid

The Butterflies of Heaven

"Heaven is.

Heaven is beyond the curtain of eternity,
        is within the scope of man,
        is the home of agapé love,
        is the translator of man,
        is the upholder of dimensions,
        is the guardian of creation,
        is the architect of the mind of man.

Heaven is the dwelling-place of the butterflies.

The butterflies of Heaven have their counterpart on Earth,
            flit both to and fro,
            carry sweetness on command.

The butterflies of Heaven can pierce dimensions of time.

The butterflies of Heaven are not seen by man,
            are builders of goodwill,
            are now assigned to Earth,
            are present at a birth,
            are messengers with blessings.

The butterflies of Heaven are an agent of The Spirit.

The agents of The Spirit are both many and varied.

The agents of The Spirit ply both day and night,
            are not welcomed by an unconverted soul,
            are never rejected by a spirit that is assigned,
            know the thoughts of man,
            bring benefits to man,
            tender their condolences to man,
            sift the requests of man.

The agents of The Spirit recommend according to the need.

I,
    The Lord,
        declare the heavens are at rest after a time of preparation.

I,
    The Lord,
        declare the time of the examination of The Bride is nigh.

I,
    The Lord,
        declare the time of the sifting of The Bride—
            the sifting of the flock—
                    will follow examination;
                    will follow shortly thereafter;
                    will cause some anguish and some pain;
                    will bring both joy and jubilation.

The sifting of the flock is watched by all concerned.

The attention of the heavens will be riveted—
                upon the commencing of the sifting of the flock.

The outcasts of Heaven await with eager ears the results of their perturbations on
                the flock.

The sifting of the flock has been revealed.

The sifting of the flock should come as no surprise,
        is essential for the welfare of The Bride,
        reserves holiness and Glory and honour to The Lord.

The sifting of the flock is upon the request of The Father and the supervision of
                The Spirit.

The butterflies of Heaven are present with The Bride,
        are fluttering around The Bride,
        are focusing on The Bride,
        are showing care for The Bride until a season,
        are imparting blessings and goodwill to the spirits of The Bride.

The butterflies of Heaven are not churlish,
        do not chide,
        do not frown.

The butterflies of Heaven are like sprites that come and go,
        skip and dance along the way.

The butterflies of Heaven are welcomed with great glee—
            exceeding joy,
            by the spirits of The Bride.

The butterflies of Heaven are attentive to each guest,
        have little need of rest,
        always frequent the best,
        glory in their colours,
        select a scent for every guest,
        arrest lightly without weight,
        are the envoys of God.

The butterflies of Heaven do not stop to gossip as they pass,
                carry tears among their blessings,
                carry farewells and greetings at the crossing point of man,
                succour and caress,
                fondle and admire,
                giggle with delight,
                frequent the thrones of God.

The butterflies of Heaven announce their briefing to the spirit so assigned,
                bring forth each commission with much fervour.

The butterflies of Heaven assess the welcome,
                and report.

The butterflies of Heaven are the welcome-mat of Heaven,
                seek shelter from a storm,
                hearken to The Spirit.

The butterflies of Heaven beautify their landscape,
                embellish their surroundings,
                dress and magnify the residence of God."

My Content Study Aid

The Lion of Judah in Readiness

"The tail of the Lion twitches as he prowls.
The claws of the Lion are prepared for battle.
The spoor of the Lion indicates willingness to fight.

The posture of the Lion is one of might and majesty.
The mouth of the Lion opens to emit a roar.
The eyes of the Lion roam both to and fro.

The ears of the Lion are pricked and alert.

The stance of the Lion is of readiness to pounce.
The coat of the Lion has the sheen of oil.
The scent of the Lion both attracts and dispels.

The visage of the Lion invokes awe in confrontation.

The readiness of the Lion is evident to the oiled.

Behold!
    The Lion of Judah!
    About to leave the lair!"

My Content Study Aid

_____
_____
_____
_____
_____
_____
_____
_____
_____
_____
_____
_____
_____

The Lion of Judah

"The Lion of Judah prowls the night,
        puts to flight,
        is clothed in light.

The Lion of Judah awaits the sounding of a horn,
        knows of a new dawn,
        has a garment never before worn.

The Lion of Judah carries himself erect,
        appears to be at ease,
        has a sense of destiny.

The Lion of Judah mounts the rock to roar,
        roars within the folds of time,
        brings an awe of silence.

The Lion of Judah descends down to a feast."

My Content Study Aid

The Glory of The Kingdom

"The trees of the field and the lilies of the valley are dressed in the adornment of Heaven
that is presently masked from the eyes of man.

The trees of the field and the lilies of the valley display their verdancy to the eyes
of man.

The trees of the field and the lilies of the valley presently have their many varied hues
withheld from the eyes of man.

For man is in his infancy,
in his womb of development,
in his child-hood of understanding—
of discernment—
of all that now surrounds him.

When the eyes of man are opened to the full extent of Heaven then the eyes of man will
no longer be subject to the blindness of the fall.

The eyes of man will open wide in wonder and in awe as he sees the handiwork of God
everywhere abounding—
The Glory of The Kingdom:
then to be revealed.

The Glory of The Kingdom exhibits The Power of God,
The Authority of God,
The Majesty of God.

The Glory of The Kingdom contains sights and sounds beyond the present spectrums
available to man,
holds fragrances and textures yet not present in the
vocabularies of man,
is of relationships of families established by the
marriage covenant.

The genealogies of The Kingdom,
the linking of the families,
the love that will not perish;
is the remembrance,
the development,
the stories of The Saints in their journey home.

The Glory of The Kingdom is the completeness of man in the loving presence of
his God."

The New Day

"I,
    The Lord,
        speak to the people of this nation.

I,
    The Lord,
        speak to the government of this nation.

I,
    The Lord,
        speak to the councillors of this nation.

I,
    The Lord,
        speak to the stewards of this nation:
                all those in positions of accountability to the people of this nation;
                all those who oversee and apportion the resources of this nation;
                all those in tiers of command that affect the lives of their fellow citizens.

I,
    The Lord,
        speak to all the leaders across this land,
                across this island nation,
                where the new day of man begins with each rising of the sun.

I state for all to hear,
    'A new day approaches that will usher in a new era never seen before by man.

    The new day sets new boundaries for man,
            sets new goals for man,
            brings fulfilment of hope and the rewards of disbelief.

    The new day that breaks across the heavens will greet men who take a forward step,
                            will dismay men who take a backward step,
                            will greet children as they stand.

    Women are not bound to follow men who take a backward step—
                who turn their backs and run.

    The new day brings change and dissolution.

    The new day brings forth new allegiances,
        will establish fresh laws of governance,
        will bring forth the standards and the qualities of the day.

    The new day will bring safety to the family,
        will bring honour to each marriage,

will bring the voice of God as a restraint upon the bearers of the power of man.

The new day will bring the death-throes of laws that are unjust,
> will bring the sanctifying of The Spirit to this nation,
> will bring a turning of the minds of man,
> will bring an opening of heart to this nation,
> will bring the young to seek and serve,
> will bring forth wisdom from those who are mature.

The new day will bring forth purpose and intent,
> guidance and direction,
> exuberance and passion.

The new day will bring forth the blessings of The Lord upon this nation:
> at a crossroads in time and of opportunity.' "

My Content Study Aid

The Edifice of God

"The edifice of man is constructed according to his will.

The edifice of man is built upon the sand,
        stands but for a moment,
        topples on command,
        seeks but rejects the answer.

The edifice of man combines effort with lack of wisdom,
        wealth without assurance.

The edifice of man supplies appeasement without reward,
        marks but does not honour,
        denotes care without attention,
        is garrulous without restraint,
        has the ways of the blind,
        composes falsehoods within the soul.

The edifice of man attends at deafened ears,
        sacrifices without intent,
        adopts without consent,
        completes without approval,
        complies without restriction,
        goads without conviction.

When the edifice of man falls,
        man becomes distraught,
        man despairs of hope,
        man seeks solace in silence,
        man finds comfort in solitude.

The fall of the edifice of man brings despondency of the soul,
        the grieving of the heart,
        the recovery of the spirit.

The fall of the edifice of man speaks of a new beginning,
        of a restoration.

The fall of the edifice of man confuses the erectors of walls,
        upholds the written word as sanctified,
        precedes and heralds the foretold intent of God.

The intent of God has established The Edifice of God.

The edifice of God is built upon the rock,
        is constructed from The Truth,
        is for the benefit of man.

The edifice of God sustains The Family of God,
        boldly declares a welcome,
        quietly whispers a rebuke,
        comprehends each message from a heart,
        supports The Will of God,
        calls to man to enter.

The edifice of God consumes the boundaries of man,
        breaks down walls,
        retakes the land,
        takes captive the foe of man.

The edifice of God becomes the domicile of man,
        the residence of the graceful,
        confirms certainty of purpose.

The edifice of God seeks out man,
        calls out man,
        singles out man.

The edifice of God greets man,
        comforts man,
        enfolds man,
        instructs man,
        loves man,
        welcomes man.

The edifice of God is sensitive to the approach of man,
        the awe of man,
        the humbling of man,
        the return of man,
        the forgiveness of man,
        the redemption of man,
        that man may be at home within The Edifice of God."

My Content Study Aid

_____

_____

_____

_____

_____

_____

_____

The Spectacles of Heaven

"The veil of eternity is moved by The Spirit in the presence of The Father.

The veil of eternity is slightly withdrawn,
        opens vistas,
        is before the eyes of man.

The spectacles of Heaven reside behind the veil of eternity.

The spectacles of Heaven are known to those who dwell therein,
        are known to those who were cast out.

The spectacles of Heaven exist for eternity,
        are known to those who visit,
        surpass the grandeurs of The Earth.

The spectacles of Heaven inspire,
        exalt,
        confirm man in his newness of experience.

The spectacles of Heaven adjust themselves according to design,
        will not bore the mind of man,
        satisfy the quest for knowledge.

The spectacles of Heaven can be approached,
        can be tended,
        can be examined.

The spectacles of Heaven can be sought,
        can be admired,
        can be appreciated.

The spectacles of Heaven fulfil obligations,
        fulfil expectations.

The spectacles of Heaven sing to music of delight,
        orchestrate the music of the heavens,
        proscribe the anthems of the heavens,
        initiate the psalms of Heaven.

The spectacles of Heaven have structure and displays,
        will amaze The Kings,
        will silence The Lords,
        will be before The Saints,
        celebrate each victory,
        may be called as witnesses,
        fulfil The Will of God."

The Transgressors of The Soul

"The transgressors of the soul know not what they do.

The transgressors of the soul kindle conflagrations,
                lead others to the fire,
                are too foolish to fear the fire.

The transgressors of the soul forsake responsibility,
                have no recrimination,
                muddle on their way.

The transgressors of the soul treat the spirit with contempt.

The transgressors of the soul know no faith,
                share no faith,
                live no faith.

The transgressors of the soul mark time with a dead heart.

The transgressors of the soul carry time within their wallet,
                treat revenge as the plaything of tomorrow,
                carouse without a conscience.

The transgressors of the soul are covered in the dust of The Earth.

The transgressors of the soul have names and thoughts and deeds written in the dust.

The winds of change revel in and erase all that is written in the dust.

The winds of change reveal what underlies the dust,
                lay bare the rock of the foundation,
                cannot change the rock of the foundation,
                recognize the rock of the foundation,
                bypass in swirls the rock of the foundation.

The winds of change do not mingle with the winds of Heaven.

The winds of Heaven can superimpose their will on the winds of the heavens.

The winds of the heavens are known to the transgressors of the soul.

The winds of the heavens can interrupt the transgressors of the soul,
                can interfere with the transgressors of the soul,
                can call to account the transgressors of the soul."

The Healing of Man

"The life of man within his mortality is beset with damage to his flesh,
                                      with damage to his bones,
                                      with damage to his body.

The body of man is of interest to The Lord,
        has perfection of function,
        heals upon necessity.

The body of man suffers extraneous force,
                extraneous force that pre-empts the timeline set for healing.

The timeline set for healing may be hastened or extended according to the knowledge
                                                                                             of man,
                may be indefinitely extended by the foe of man.

The body of man suffers pain as a warning of the foe's attack upon the timeline set
                                                                                                          for healing.
                        Pain is the signal for when the body of man calls for help.

The signal can be cancelled when help is offered and accepted by the body of man,
                upon re-establishment of the timeline set for healing when
                                  voided of the foe,
        according to the knowledge of man.

Man has applied knowledge without wisdom when the signal is cancelled without
                                                        quenching the foe's attack.

Man has applied knowledge without wisdom when his arsenal of medicine is applied
                                                          throughout the body without
                                                          the power of directed prayer.

Man has applied knowledge without wisdom when he answers an evidenced call for help
                                  that ignores the quest of the spirit for freedom from
                                  the foe's attack upon the timeline set for healing.

Directed prayer from a called servant who seeks,
                        declares,
                        looses,
                        binds,
                        commands,
                        sets free:
                in the Name above all names,
        resets the timeline set for healing according to the need of the body,
                                                  the call of the spirit,
                                                  and the state of the soul.

Pain is not of Me.

Malfunction is not of Me.

Suffering from within the body of man upon his mind,
                                        his spirit,
                                        and his soul is not of Me.

For in perfection was man created,
                  was man given dominion,
                  will man again yet be.

Man may be healed within the counselling of My Spirit,
                  the prayers of My servants,
                  the confines of his medicines,
                  the skills of his surgeons.

Man may be healed within his body,
                  mind,
                  soul and spirit through deliverance that goes
                                                               to completion.

Man has applied knowledge without wisdom when deliverance fails the test
                                                                             of completion.

    Failure of completion is the failure of authority,
                      the failure of command,
                      the failure of preparation for the battle of the fall,
                                      the battle with the foe of man.

Man has applied knowledge without wisdom when committing to a battle unprepared.

Man has applied knowledge without wisdom when joining a battle unprotected by
                                                                                   his armour.

Man has applied knowledge without wisdom when believing Faith alone is sufficient in
                                                                            the battle with the foe.

Man with wisdom and My Spirit will always defeat the foe.

Man with knowledge,
    with wisdom,
    and with My Spirit will have deliverance liberate,
                                according to the utterance that signifies completion.

The joy of liberation is on the visage of those previously oppressed,
                          is the temporal reward of My servants,
                          is recorded in the soul as a turning point of man,
                          speaks to a diminishing of A Kingdom and the enhancement of
                                                                   A Kingdom,
                          has eternal consequences when protected and retained,

speaks to man of the reality of two kingdoms in their struggle for
the soul of man.

Man has insufficient knowledge,
is without wisdom,
if he does not forsake,
renounce,
reject,
the kingdom of darkness,
the kingdom of the foe,
the kingdom of the outcast prince.

Instead,
man is called to embrace The Kingdom of God that grants citizenship
through Grace,
that sets a light before his feet,
that welcomes those who so confess the way of The Lord.

The healing of man is The Will of The Father,
The Call of The Son,
The Delight of The Spirit.

The divine healing of man does not proceed by the pleading of man,
does not proceed by the promises of man,
does not proceed by the status of man.

The divine healing of man does not proceed by the abilities of man,
does not proceed by the wealth of man,
does not proceed by the begging of man.

The divine healing of man proceeds in The Love of God,
proceeds in the justice of God,
proceeds in the mercy of God,
proceeds in the sovereignty of God.

The divine healing of man testifies of answers,
is circumscribed by prayer,
is verified through results.

The divine healing of man is not limited by the reasoning of man,
sheds light and health and truth,
upholds The Word,
upholds the Rhema of My Spirit,
upholds My servants in their callings,
will increase,
will call through testimony.

The divine healing of man verifies the validity of a Faith in God,
of the existence of God,

> of the intent of God,
> of the nature of God.

The divine healing of man speaks I AM to man."

My Content Study Aid

The Death of Man

"The death of man is but a stepping-stone for man.

The death of man need not be a cause of anguish,
        need not commence a mourning,
        need not bring tears to the eye.

The death of man should not be planned by man,
        should not be caused by man,
        should not be hurried by man.

The death of man terminates the time of choice.

The death of man is the crossing point of man,
        is welcomed by those ready to receive,
        is feared by those not willing to receive.

The death of man brings tenure to the unrepentant soul,
        brings release to the mortal suffering of man.

The death of man changes the status of the spouse,
        the status of the children,
        the status of the family.

The death of man speaks of memorials and inscriptions.

The death of man causes man to question the prospect of eternity.

The death of man seals with a finality the opportunities,
        as offered,
        that are withdrawn without acceptance.

The death of man causes the appraisal of a life.

    The appraisal of a life is the judgement of man,
        is made in ignorance of the facts,
        is very rarely truthful,
        is not easily assessed by man.

The death of man initiates the examination of a life.

    The examination of a life is the judgement of God.

    The examination of a life is made in full knowledge of the facts,
        always reveals The Truth,
        is easily determined by God.

The death of man is the rendezvous of man,
        may be the exhilaration of man,
        may be the despair of man.

The death of man seals man as he is,
    seals his record—
        the record of his soul,
            of his spirit,
            of his mind,
            of his body,
            of his mouth,
            of his tongue;
        the record of his tongues,
            of his eyes,
            of his ears;
        the record of his recreation,
            of his procreation,
            of his desecration;
        the record of his character,
            of his actions,
            of his travels;
        the record of his hands,
            of his fingers,
            of his feet,
            of his toes;
        the record of his word,
            of his utterances;
        the record of his wealth,
            of his possessions;
        the record of his relatives,
            of his friends,
            of his encounters,
            of his assemblies;
        the record of his fruits,
            of his service,
            of his gifts,
            of his visits,
            of his labours;
        the record of his dealings,
            of his generosity,
            of his humanity,
            of his deeds,
            of his heart;
        the record of his life.

   The records are cross-referenced.

The records may be accessed by The Lamb's Book of Life.

The death of man causes prayers to be referred,
>> calls to account debts incurred in his mortality,
>> brings division within the family.

The death of man brings the inspection of estates,
>> the gathering of inheritances,
>> the devolution of the effort.

The death of man brings promotion to generations,
>> brings transfer of responsibility,
>> calls for care and attention of and to a spouse,
>>> a family when in need.

The death of man is measured within the dimensions of time,
>> is measured by the teaching of a child,
>> is measured by the honour rendered due.

The death of man is measured by the mantle that was carried,
>> the mantle that was worn,
>> the mantle that tipped the scales."

My Content Study Aid

The Birth of Man

"The birth of man is a new beginning,
>is a threefold event,
>>completes after the life event of death.

The birth of man extends past the measurement of time,
>brings man to fruition,
>>sees man full-grown in perfection.

The birth of man sees man assume his rightful place,
>sees man as he is intended.

The birth of man is modified according to his birth pangs:
>>the birth pangs of the womb,
>>the birth pangs of the water,
>>the birth pangs of the grave.

The birth of man results in a renewal as has been promised.

The birth of man culminates in an eternal union,
>culminates in an ecstatic reunion,
>culminates in the voyage of discovery.

>The voyage of discovery familiarizes man in his surroundings,
>>may have complexity or simplicity,
>>may be welcoming or foreboding.

>The voyage of discovery ends in justice,
>>prepares man for eternity,
>>cannot be retraced.

>The voyage of discovery completes the birth of man.

The birth of man expands his senses,
>expands his perceptions,
>increases his abilities.

The birth of man changes his modes of travel.

The birth of man increases his powers of recollection,
>his powers of memory,
>his powers of transportation.

The birth of man imparts knowledge,
>dispels misconceptions,
>installs truth.

The birth of man enables man to fulfil his destiny,
>removes the doubts of man,
>reflects the posturing of man in his period of Grace."

The Pathways of The Rain

"The commencement of the rain marks a time of refreshing,
                a time of replenishment,
                a time of extended growth.

The rain varies with the season,
        varies with the clouds,
        varies with locality.

The rain falls in differing forms depending on the height,
                depending on the winds,
                depending on its journey.

The rain falls as a blessing upon The Earth,
            upon its crops,
            upon the life of man.

The rain when deemed not to be a blessing has been subject to interference,
                        has been channelled upon landing,
                        has been made to flow in concentrated paths
                                    across the land.

  Man's lack of wisdom seen in building,
                seen in redirection,
                seen in usage,
                seen in treatment of the landing needs of rain—
                          speaks to the pathways of the rain.

The pathways of the rain were established in the heavens,
                were established on the land,
                were established within the seas.

    The network of creation depends upon the pathways of the rain.

The pathways of the rain should be reliable,
                      according to the season,
                      according to the record.

The pathways of the rain should be known,
                      according to location upon The Earth.

The pathways of the rain are not committed to fail in the environment of man.

The pathways of the rain were designed to be,
                were designed to bring water to the land,
                were designed to return a surplus to the seas,
                were designed to lie within the winds,
                were designed to be driven by the sun.

The pathways of the rain are necessary to life,
                are in trust for all,
                are of supreme importance,
                enable life on Earth,
                encircle The Earth.

The pathways of the rain should be studied by man within The Wisdom of God."

My Content Study Aid

The Tenants of The Mind

"The pygmies of the mind develop slowly.

The pygmies of the mind have to be stopped in their tracks,
        stay according to their acceptance,
        are sent to distract man.

The pygmies of the mind are a source of sin,
        the root of temptation,
        the seed of evil intent.

The pygmies of the mind are installed by the foe of man,
        can grow and fester as a wound,
        can call for support from others.

The pygmies of the mind can unleash attacks.

The pygmies of the mind can be forced to retreat,
        can be vanquished from the battlefield,
        can be despatched upon appearance.

The pygmies of the mind should not be made to feel at home,
        should not be welcomed,
        should not be encouraged to linger.

The pygmies of the mind frequent the cesspools of humanity,
        contaminate the mind,
        can grow to giants within the mind.

Giants within the mind can exercise control.

Giants within the mind endanger the spirit and the soul,
        can exercise the body,
        will bring shame to the body.

Giants within the mind are difficult to dislodge,
        can be transferred at a touch,
        jeopardise the prospects of man.

Giants within the mind should be slain with a slingshot,
        will stand awaiting the hit,
        are always felled by the hit.

    The hit that fells the giants is the immersion of the body.

The giants within the mind cannot again grow to maturity in a mind that has consented to
                                      the immersion of its body.

The giants within the mind then remain stunted and easily evicted.

The giants within the mind cannot then take control,
>   cannot usurp authority,
>   cannot subdue freewill.

The waters of immersion always clean the mind,
>   wash the mind,
>   purify the mind.

The waters of immersion always drown the giants.

The waters of immersion wash away the giants when supervised by My Spirit.

The waters of immersion—
>   the waters of baptism,
>   the waters of the covering,
>   the waters of rebirth,
>>   quell the presence of the giants."

My Content Study Aid

The Message of Healing

"The pinpricks of man are of little consequence.

The pinpricks of man are a nuisance in themselves,
        niggle at the surface,
        do not compare with the pinpricks of Heaven.

The pinpricks of Heaven have a message to make known,
        carefully select a site,
        are accurate and precise,
        study well the consequences of their strike,
        mark the strike-place of their pin,
        deliver their message to the depths of the mark,
        declare a message of healing to the surroundings at the mark.

The message of healing has an immediate effect,
        sets to work with a will,
        overcomes the venom of the foe,
        repairs the damage of the foe.

The message of healing stays around as needed,
        calls for reinforcements,
        rejoices at success.

The message of healing is vital to the longevity of the body,
        the health of the blood,
        the strength of the muscles.

The message of healing dresses the surface of the bones.

The message of healing heals the heart of man of the pinpricks of man,
        injustices of imagination,
        offences stored within the soul,
        denigrations that retract the spirit.

The message of healing cares for the emotions of man,
        the feelings of man,
        the depressions of man,
        the elixirs of man.

The message of healing attends the stability of man,
        the predictability of response,
        the socialising of behaviour.

The message of healing reaches out to comfort,
        stretches out to soothe;
        pacifies the restless spirit,

calms the troubled soul.

The message of healing is a blessing in disguise.

The message of healing is easily conveyed.,
    is not always understood,
    can lack appreciation,
    may not be well received,
    always achieves its purpose,
    has certainty of access,
    brings realization to the mind.

The message of healing originates from God."

My Content Study Aid

The Effects of The Fall on Man

"Man fell according to his will.

Man fell through misplaced belief,
        lack of questioning,
        lack of awareness,
        lack of leadership,
        the quest for wrongful dominion,
        seeking what was not his to have,
        not applying wisdom.
        grasping a deception.

Man has yet to learn the error of his ways,
        the importance of a new beginning,
        the message of the cross:
                of The Love of God.

For man continues in the lifestyle of the fall,
        in the forsaking of his God,
        in his belief of self-fulfilment;
continues to accept,
        to promote,
        to enjoy the causes of the fall.

The causes of the fall are not rejected by man,
        are still practised by man,
        are still holding man in bondage:
                with the foot of the foe upon his neck.

Man is comfortable with the foot of the foe upon his neck.

Man does not struggle to remove the foot of the foe upon his neck.

Man is extremely vulnerable with the foot of the foe upon his neck.

Man does not call for help even with the foot of the foe upon his neck.

Man no longer notices the foot of the foe upon his neck.

Man has come to accept the foot of the foe upon his neck.

The foot of the foe is about to increase pressure on the neck of man.

The foot of the foe is not there for the benefit of man.

The foot of the foe is capable of great pressure,
        is capable of crushing,
        is capable of destruction.

The foot of the foe damages the neck of man.

The foot of the foe makes it difficult to breathe,

>to think,
>to gather strength,
>to recollect a time of freedom,
>to resolve to attain it once again.

The foot of the foe makes it difficult to pursue,
>to reclaim,
>>the right to his freewill:
>>and thereby initiate the procedure to break free.

The neck of man must not be the chopping-block of the foe,
>at the beck and call of the foe,
>pressured by the foe.

The neck of man is protected by the breastplate,
>is protected by the shield,
>is protected by the sword.

The neck of man is protected by the wise,
>left vulnerable by the foolish.

The neck of man transmits commands,
>transmits reports.

The neck of man,
>when damaged,
>when constricted,
>>cannot conduct the fight,
>>cannot supervise the battle.

Man must turn from acquiescing with the fall of man.
must turn from a lifestyle that is in harmony with the fall.
must turn from acquiring,
>from accepting,
>from receiving the fruits of the fall.

Man must turn from the suffering of the foe.

Man should be in harmony with the purposes of God,
>the teachings of God,
>the instructions of God.

Man should acquire without delay the presence of God,
>The Fear of God,
>The Wisdom of God.

Man should ensure he is aligned with,
>does satisfy,
>>can meet the requirements for the entry to the destiny of man that
>>>is accompanied by God."

The Wrath of God

"The wrath of God is not easily incurred.

The wrath of God does not fall without a warning.

The wrath of God falls on goats and not on sheep,
        falls on kids and not on lambs,
        falls on tares and not on wheat,
        falls on the false and not on the true.

The wrath of God falls upon those who cuddle up to the foe,
        those who deny the existence of God,
        those who choose to worship items of creation—
        then bow before them as serving idols of their false beliefs.

The wrath of God will fall upon those who deny the sacrifice of The Son.

The wrath of God does not fall on those who cry out for forgiveness,
        who cry out for redemption,
        who cry out in Faith to God for mercy on their souls,
        who cry out to The Name above all names.

The wrath of God will fall in justice after judgement has been entered.

The wrath of God will destroy all hope and expectation,
        decrees destruction of all sin,
        falls on those who would carry sin into His Presence.

   Foolish are they who would attempt to carry sin.

The wrath of God melts in the refiner's fire.

The wrath of God will purify the heavens,
        will purify The Earth,
        will remove contamination."

My Content Study Aid

_____

_____

_____

_____

_____

_____

The Frustrations of God

"The frustrations of God echo within the heavens.

The frustrations of God return to the sender,
                return with blessings not received,
                return without progression.

The frustrations of God do not see development.

The frustrations of God see stagnation at its worst,
                see procrastinations without achievement,
                see callings remaining vacant,
                see callings partially fulfilled,
                see callings resigned,
                see servants uncommitted,
                see serving without excellence.

The frustrations of God see sheep that refuse discipleship:
                prophets that do not speak;
                evangelists that do not go;
                teachers that do not teach,
                      do not prepare,
                      do not impart;
                shepherds that do not dip the sheep,
                      that do not dag the sheep,
                      that only count the sheep.

  Much is expected from those who are called by God.

  Much will be required from those who accept a calling with crossed fingers and
                                          thereby block it for another.

  Much will not be given to those who bring reluctance with their call.

The frustrations of God do not carry mercy to the unrepentant.

The frustrations of God exercise His patience,
                tire out His other servants,
                delay the audition of The Kingdom of God.

The frustrations of God lead to repeated dress-rehearsals.

The frustrations of God will come to an end,
                will be excised from the flock,
                will not be seen within His Bride.

The frustrations of God are counted as sin.

The frustrations of God—

    the attitude of The Saints,
    the commitment of The Saints,
    the development of The Saints,
    the service of The Saints,
    the timeliness of The Saints,
    the utterances of The Saints,
    The Saints without their references:
        will live outside the flock.

Wise are they who retain a foot-hold within the flock.

Wise are they who protect their references—
    do not have them shredded,
    do not have them stolen,
    neither drop nor lose them on the journey.

Wise are they who can tender references in a golden scroll."

My Content Study Aid

_____
_____
_____
_____
_____
_____
_____
_____
_____
_____
_____
_____
_____
_____
_____
_____
_____
_____
_____
_____
_____
_____

The Entrance to Heaven

"I,
   The Lord,
      speak to My people and say,
         'The day of My coming approaches,
                        is nigh,
                        is at hand,
                        is about to burst forth,
                        is about to be fulfilled,
                        is about to cross the threshold of man.

The threshold of man is defended by the foe.

The threshold of man stands by a gate that is partly open,
                        is a site of a battle,
                        summons loyalties that are divided,
                        gives access to his dominion,
                        is a portal to mortality,
                        will be fully breached.

The threshold of man will be vanquished of the foe.

   The foe will not be seated at the threshold gate of man.

The threshold gate of man will be taken off its hinges,
                will be forever thrown away,
                will no longer mark a boundary between Heaven and
                                                          The Earth.

The threshold gate of man is to be pulled down to make way for a highway.

The guardians of the highway are angelic hosts,
                stand on either side,
                protect the thoroughfare to Heaven,
                never rest nor sleep,
                allow none to pass without permission,
                are instructed by My Spirit.

The guardians of the highway have a sacred duty,
                assist those with permission who find it difficult
                                                      to traverse,
                give protection from the foe.

The guardians of the highway celebrate their call of duty,
                stand very tall and straight,
                hold effective weapons,
                can use them with great skill,

     serve both God and man,
     will be seen by man.

The thoroughfare to Heaven levies no toll,
     is traversed in both directions,
     does not cause a stumble,
     is open and well lit,
     does not need a signpost.

The thoroughfare to Heaven can be travelled very quickly,
     can be travelled very slowly,
     can be travelled with inspections at discretion.

The thoroughfare to Heaven has only tears of joy,
     is constructed for great usage,
     has music along its length,
     opens the eyes of man,
     is a travel agent's dream.

The thoroughfare to Heaven leads man to and from his God.' "

My Content Study Aid

_____
_____
_____
_____
_____
_____
_____
_____
_____
_____
_____
_____
_____
_____
_____
_____
_____
_____

The Temple of The Body

"I,
   The Lord,
      speak to the people and say,
   'None can travel the thoroughfare to Heaven without repentance.

   None can travel the thoroughfare to Heaven without an entry in The Lamb's Book of Life.

   None can travel the thoroughfare to Heaven without understanding,
                                 without acceptance,
                                 without acknowledgement.

   Listen to the prompting of the spirit,
        the prompting of the conscience—
                      that incubates the sprouting of the seed of Faith.

   For Faith will lead to the presence of The Spirit and the learning of the Wisdom of God.

   The wisdom of God,
   the counsel of The Spirit,
       will lead man home to dwell in the presence of God.

   Man is led along a narrow way beset by temptation on every side during his mortality.

   But after the crossing point is reached,
       man sets foot on the thoroughfare to Heaven or the pathway to Hell.

   Man is not intended to take the pathway to Hell.

   Avoid temptations of the soul,
      indulgences of the soul,
      entertainment of the soul—
          avoid the feeding paths and roadways that lead man to travel the pathway to Hell.

   Read My Word and testimony that builds a hedge of protection around the soul.

   Procure and attain the knowledge that is necessary.

   Listen and enquire from those able to instruct.

   Implement the changes that have an eternal reward.

   Turn from the ways of man.

   Greet the ways of God.

   Repent of all that shames the spirit.

Receive a new beginning—
> erasing all the records by immersion—
> welcome the presence of God within The Temple of the body.

The temple of the body reacts to the presence of My Spirit,
> has a new direction,
> sets foot on a different route,
> is guided by My Spirit.

The temple of the body has company that upholds,
> that supports,
> that sustains.

The temple of the body denies the flesh.

The temple of the body reaches out for truth,
> for light,
> for a destiny that is complete in every way.

The temple of the body is preserved,
> will be renewed,
> will be exalted in a different form.

The temple of the body should not be sacrificed to man,
> should not be sacrificed to the foe,
> should not be sacrificed to idols.

The temple of the body should be preserved by man for a higher use.

The temple of the body has yet to attain full Glory,
> yet to reach its pinnacle,
> yet to be furnished in The Kingdom of God.'"

My Content Study Aid

_____
_____
_____
_____
_____
_____
_____
_____
_____
_____

The Guidance of God

"The authority of man is limited within the heavens,
            is limited by his position,
            is limited by his relationship.

The authority of man is limited by belief,
            is limited by Grace,
            is limited by status;
            is limited by wealth,
            is limited by health,
            is limited by his standing before God.

The authority of man is encouraged by the foe,
            is encouraged by his soul,
            is encouraged by his ambition.

The authority of man can command respect,
            can command obedience,
            can command servility.

The authority of man can command assistance,
            can command relief,
            can command the hand of healing;
            can command by proxy,
            can command under duress,
            can command with stress.

The authority of man can be upheld upon appeal,
            can be dismissed upon appeal,
            can be punished upon appeal;
            can be ignored,
            can be overridden,
            can be underpinned.

The authority of man can bind and loose,
            can imprison and set free,
            can punish and reward;
            can be unjust,
            can be foolishly applied,
            can usurp the power of others.

The wielding of authority calls for much restraint,
            improves with age,
            should be limited to the wise;
            should not be exercised in haste,
            causes the weak to yield,

may cause a house of cards to fall.

The wielding of authority can bring nations to their knees.

The wielding of authority can cause the fall of kingdoms.

The wielding of authority can expose corruption,
        can bring darkness into light,
        can instigate a reign of new beginnings.

The wielding of authority can install and usher in,
        can capture and dismiss,
        can be just and done in love,
        can be carried out in wisdom.

The wielding of authority can support the hopes of man,
        the dreams of man,
        the aspirations of man in a new beginning.

A new beginning does not always discard the old.

A new beginning can modify,
    can repair,
    can superimpose,
    can renew,
    can add,
    can destroy.

A new beginning can bring change.

A new beginning can bring a new direction.

A new beginning can usher in an era of belief,
        an era that promotes the welfare of man,
        an era that speaks of the guidance of God."

My Content Study Aid

_____

_____

_____

_____

_____

_____

_____

_____

The Handshake of Creation

"The gift of God is eternal life.
The gift of God transforms man after his mortality.
The gift of God can be refused in its fullness.

The gift of God,
       without its fullness,
         respects The Freewill of man.

The gift of God,
       with its fullness,
         honours The Freewill of man.

The gift of God is intended as the handshake of creation.

The handshake of creation is the wellspring of a welcome,
       seals a friendship that continues,
       has no need of an agreement,
       is founded on love and trust,
       will never be withdrawn.

The handshake of creation partners man and God,
       brings man into his Glory,
       is the clasp that is not broken,
       brings man into His Presence,
       honours The Freewill of man.

The gift of God is not intended for the brewing chamber of despair.

The brewing chamber of despair does not comfort man,
       has no door that man can open,
       is not visited by God,
       continues,
       has many rooms,
       permits no visitors to those assigned,
       has rooms to serve the needs.

The brewing chamber of despair is not a pleasant place,
       has rooms of lakes of fire,
       has rooms of darkness,
       has rooms of silence,
       has rooms of denial,
       has rooms decreed by justice,
       respects The Freewill of man.

The freewill of man determines the destiny of man,

is not intended to lead man to the brewing chamber of despair,
is intended to be confirmed by the handshake of creation.

The freewill of man will either demand respect or deserve honour.

God upholds The Freewill,
    the agency,
    of man:
    and so confirms man's destiny of choice."

My Content Study Aid

The Silence of God

"The silence of God is at The Will of God.

The silence of God can be an answer to a prayer,
        can be thunderous in effect,
        can teach wisdom,
        can cause an echo in the spirit,
        can signify the absence of consent.

The silence of God brings holiness to the silent.

The silence of God does not ask a question,
        does not require repetition,
        does not demand a response.

The silence of God varies in its purpose.

The silence of God may be heard without acceptance,
        may be blamed for rebellion,
        may indicate agreement with The Word.

The silence of God may only slowly dawn.

The silence of God can be broken,
        can come as a rebuke,
        can indicate restraint,
        can be a time of reflection,
        can be a blessing to man."

My Content Study Aid

_____
_____
_____
_____
_____
_____
_____
_____
_____

The Pathway of The Son

"The Son was born.
He lived.
He Died.
He rose.

So will it be with man.

The agony of The Son is not transferred to man.
The radiance of The Son is not transferred to man.
The inheritance of The Son is not transferred to man.

Man cannot walk,
        in its fullness,
           the pathway of The Son.

The pathway of The Son is the pathway of God,
              is exemplary,
              does not seek,
              is walked without sin,
              complements the pathway of The Father,
              is aligned with the pathway of The Father,
              has the blessing of The Father.

The pathway of The Son is witnessed,
        in part,
        by man.

The pathway of The Son testifies,
        in part,
        to man.

The pathway of The Son brings,
        in part,
        salvation for man.

The pathway of The Son justifies,
        in part,
        the hope in man.

The pathway of The Son trammels the foe,
        the enemy of man.

The pathway of The Son has widespread jurisdiction.

The pathway of The Son invites the company of the soul of man,
        encircles The Earth,

> reaches throughout the heavens,
> is not bound by time,
> continues on for ever.

The pathway of The Son stops and waits for man.

The pathway of The Son widens to accommodate the guests.

The pathway of The Son is neither constrained nor hurried,
> is no longer harried,
> is worthy of the journey,
> has guests that do not straggle,
> has guests that tend to flock.

The pathway of The Son knows who is about to wed.

The pathway of The Son carries those who will rejoice.

The pathway of The Son is not onerous to tread,
> leads to reconciliation,
> bestows security of tenure,
> leads to the presence of The Father,
> passes acclamation.

The pathway of The Son passes the scenes of battles,
> climbs steadily to the light,
> stands in the victory of The Son,
> bows in honour to The Son,
> shows the love of The Son.

The pathway of The Son confirms the miracle of Heaven:
> the love of The Father,
> the love of The Son,
> the love of The Spirit—
> the redemption through Grace of the fallen state of man."

My Content Study Aid

_____
_____
_____
_____
_____
_____
_____

The Fall of a House of Hell

"The fellowship of Hell turns man on his head.

The fellowship of Hell is a fellowship of Hell.

The fellowship of Hell is the fellowships of the iniquities of man,
        the fellowships of the foe,
        the fellowships of the cartels of man,
        the fellowships of business cronies,
        the fellowships of defensive encirclings that still extort.

The fellowship of Hell scavenges the wealth of man,
        the labour of man,
        the time of man.

The fellowship of Hell has no redeeming feature,
        ignores all cries of distress.

The fellowship of Hell pays lip service,
        addresses by way of token,
        always seeks publicity:
            for the dregs of assistance offered.

The fellowship of Hell excessively extorts,
        minimally returns.

    The wisdom of man should not commend the fellowship of Hell,
        should be at variance with the fellowship of Hell,
        should not condone the fellowship of Hell.

The fellowship of Hell satisfies the greed of man,
        grows in nests of corruption.

    The knowledge of man will eventually bring destruction upon the fellowship of Hell,
            the kidnapping of Hell,
            the blackmail of Hell.

The knowledge of man will eventually attack the nests of corruption.

The nests of corruption will be unseated from where they are built.
The nests of corruption will be located wherein they shelter.

The locations of the sheltering are in great peril from man,
        are open to attack,
        are rotten to the core;
        will fall with a gentle push,
        will fall like a wall that once divided.

The fall of the locations will cause a scramble to re-locate.

The knowledge of man can prevent a re-location.

The knowledge of man can cause a house of Hell to fall—
                        the house that houses a fellowship of Hell.

A house of Hell will fall when the wealth of man is dried up for a season,
        when the wealth of man is redirected,
        when the wealth of man is selectively with-held.

The power of man is yet to be achieved within the wealth of man,
        currently sleeps,
        can be marshalled via a network.

The network power of man is yet to be fully realized.

The network power of man can bring nations to their knees,
        can place them in the hands of their enemies,
        can operate at the speed of light,
        can cause assets to be released from the clutches of a
                house of Hell,
        can bring to no avail the funds held in reserve,
        can repeatedly attack a house of Hell that is dependent on
                the marketplace of man.

A house of Hell stands defenceless before the attack of the network power of man upon
                the marketplace of the house of Hell."

My Content Study Aid

_____
_____
_____
_____
_____
_____
_____
_____
_____
_____
_____
_____
_____
_____

The Miracle of Christmas

"The Miracle of Christmas was born in the need for reconciliation.

The Miracle of Christmas waited for A Kingdom,
                lived within A Kingdom,
                died before A Kingdom,
                was born with A Kingdom,
                inherits many kingdoms,
                reigns as The King of kings.

The Miracle of Christmas offers citizenship of His kingdoms,
                is seated on a throne,
                is attended by the courtiers.

The Miracle of Christmas understands the mind of man,
                brought a message heard by man,
                brought a message seen by man,
                brought a message lived by man;
                commends the message to man,
                spreads a message of goodwill.

The Miracle of Christmas calls on choirs of angels.

The Miracle of Christmas calls on angelic symphonies,
                calls on angelic trumpeters,
                calls on angelic harpists that play the harps of light.

The Miracle of Christmas presents choirs singing beyond the pitch of man,
                far beyond the octaves of the voice of man,
                sustaining notes until curtailed that blend in colour with the
                                      music masters' patterns.

The Miracle of Christmas hears,
        sees,
        scents,
        the music of the senses being played on instruments of light.

The Miracle of Christmas watches the endeavours of man,
                encourages and frowns on the endeavours of man,
                is not surprised by the endeavours of man.

The Miracle of Christmas reaches for the children,
                puts one on each knee,
                listens with both ears to two mouths that speak at once.

The Miracle of Christmas takes note of the whispers of each mouth,
                      the smile upon each face,

>   the love within each heart.

The Miracle of Christmas revisits when requested.

The Miracle of Christmas sends a counsellor when invited.

The Miracle of Christmas smiles upon,
>   heeds,
>   these signs of love.

The Miracle of Christmas gathers children round about for stories of A Kingdom.

The Miracle of Christmas oversees their growth,
>   oversees their life,
>   oversees their decisions and their choices as they wend their way back home."

My Content Study Aid

The Body of Man 1— Designed

"The body of man is a masterpiece of construction.

The body of man has built in talent,
        has attributes of speciality,
        has uniqueness of abilities,
        has expansion capabilities.

The body of man has the power of self-repair,
        has the power of self-determination,
        has the power of self-belief,
        has the power of self-assessment,
        has the power of self.

The body of man has the authority to wander,
        has the authority to stray,
        has the authority to meander all his days.

The body of man has the gift that orders his steps,
        that aligns his steps,
        that brings structure to his steps.

The body of man has the right to be preserved,
        the right to be renewed,
        the right to be eternal.

The body of man has a destiny with the soul,
        a destiny with the spirit,
        a destiny with the mind.

The body of man has an existence that has been planned,
        an existence that develops,
        an existence that has a forward extension.

The body of man has potential not yet realized,
        has potential for a time hidden behind the future time of man.

The body of man should be treated with all honour,
        should be consecrated to God,
        should be baptized by man,
        should be baptized by The Spirit,

The body of man needs to receive The Promises of God that arise from a second birth.

The body of man has need to be prepared for the third birth:
                the passing through the grave,
                the life event of death.

The body of man is conveyed on the voyage of discovery by The Promises of God.

The body of man is in the image of God.

The body of man did neither evolve by error,
                             nor by trial.

The body of man was created by the spoken word of God.

God does not rely on chance to carry out His will.

God has no need for cause,
     has no need for effect,
          in validating the spoken word of God.

The scholarship of man has failed in apportioning The Glory of creation to the assumed
                                                                                sequencing of time.

Time is not random;
 time is not consistent;
 time is not continuous;
 time is multi-dimensioned:
               within the scholarship of God."

My Content Study Aid

_____
_____
_____
_____
_____
_____
_____
_____
_____
_____
_____
_____
_____
_____
_____
_____
_____

The Gathering of The Bride

"The day of The Kingdom is coming.

The day of The Kingdom approaches as an express train nearing its destination.

The express train has not stopped between stations,
        is about to sound its whistle of impending arrival,
        is slowing as it prepares to stop.

Crowds are gathering at the station waving flags,
    can hear the whistle of the train coming nearer.

The crowds are showing much excitement at the station.

Those on the carriages are preparing to alight,
        have been planning this journey for a while.

There is eager anticipation on the faces peering out the windows,
        shuffling in the corridors as positions are sought.

Those on the seven carriages are ready to detrain.

Those on the six carriages become silent now in honour,
        are to form the guard of honour:
            the choristers,
            the music masters,
            those in attendance upon the visitor.

The crowds at the station are no longer waving flags,
        are now orderly and quiet,
        are now dressed in white,
        are all dressed in gowns,
            in gowns that sparkle and are embellished.

The crowds at the station gently curtsy with a bowed knee—
        their bands of gold glisten in the sunlight,
        their hands are all joined together,
        their faces reveal smiles of awe and expectation.

The crowds at the station move to form a seven-fold semicircle.

The last is first as the seventh carriage stops in its position so appointed.

The seventh carriage unfolds and opens upwards.

The station and the crowds are enveloped by the light that is released.

The crowds do not push forward,
    do not jostle,
    do not encroach on the footway of the visitor.

The footway of the visitor is now bordered by those transparent,
                        bordered by those alighting from the carriages numbering six.

The visitor alights but does not touch the ground.

The visitor is enrobed,
        with a stature of regality.

The visitor moves,
        without walking,
        along the footway so defined.

The visitor approaches and processes along the ranks.

The visitor lifts each hand presented,
                bent at the knuckles,
                to his lips.

The visitor greets each enthusiastically by the given name.

The visitor moves backwards in reversal and beckons the greeting crowd to follow—
                                entrained aboard the seventh carriage.

    Those transparent re-locate within the carriages numbering six.

The express train is about to sound the whistle of departure,
        is bound for the next assigned station along the way,
        displays The Standard marking the presence of the visitor.

The express train travels extremely fast.

The express train can expand the seventh carriage as needed:
        will fulfil its purpose,
        will achieve its goal,
        will not be impeded,
        will not leave anyone at a station;
        is the fulfilment of a promise,
        has an appointment with a wedding."

My Content Study Aid

_____
_____
_____
_____
_____
_____

The Sequencing of Time

"The sequencing of time is not easily understood by man.

The sequencing of time is not experienced by man,
        does not permit experiments,
        makes judgements based on time unreliable to man,
        permits occurrences that would be strange to man.

The sequencing of time allows for time to trough and peak.

The sequencing of time is at The Will of God.

    Time can stop and start,
        be accelerated and slowed,
        run forwards and backwards,
        be cut and spliced.

    Time can be inserted and deleted,
        be repeated and omitted,
        be interrupted and confirmed,
        be condensed and expanded.

    Time is but a variable within the existence of man.

    Time can be dimensioned and be multifaceted.

    Multiple time dimensions can transfer matter to and fro without the loss of energy
        when position is maintained.

    Time can be extrapolated only with great caution.

    The knowledge of man fails when accepting,
        without due thought,
        the time extrapolations of man.

The passage of time depends upon equations that may not be known to man.

The measurement of time is uncertain for man.
The continuity of time should not be assumed by man.
The management of time is beyond the ability of man.

Time can change and vary as the eddying in a stream,
        wander far from a straight line,
        follow complex curves and paths,
        control jurisdictions and paths across the sky.

The time sphere of man can be impacted by events,
        can be modified by collisions,
        can be penetrated and left,

can be viewed internally and externally.

Change occurs within the time sphere of man.

Change cannot be seen outside the time sphere of man.

The time sphere of man is quite extensive.

Man cannot escape,
during his mortality,
the time sphere of man.

The time sphere of man has external controls.

The control of time enables travel to very distant places.

The control of time,
the application of time,
the persistency of time,
is reserved to The Will of God."

My Content Study Aid

The Body of Man 2— A House

"The body of man is prepared as if a temple,
        is intended to be a temple,
        is a temple when in-dwelt by My Spirit.

The body of man stands in honour as The Temple of The Spirit,
        stands in shame at the abuse of the enemy of man,
        should not be required to suffer shame.

The body of man cannot withstand the onslaught of the enemy of man,
        withstand onslaughts with permission,
            onslaughts of connivance,
            onslaughts of premeditation,
            onslaughts bred through compliance.

The body of man cannot combat repeated abuses of the halls of access,
        handle the duress of contamination within the halls of access,
        cannot prevent the transference of control that opens the halls
                of access.

    The halls of access open to rooms that are all occupied,
           to rooms that function according to the plumbing,
           to rooms that recognize the handshakes offered by
                the rooms.

    The halls of access are emptied and cleaned,
        lead to all the rooms.

  A room that refuses a handshake causes trouble in the halls,
            trouble for the room refused,
            trouble for the housekeeper.

The housekeeper quarantines the occupant of the offending room,
        sends a team of friends to attend the occupant,
        is most distraught when encountering an occupant who still refuses to
                shake hands,
            who shakes hands weakly,
            who lets his grasp slip to the floor.

The housekeeper partly closes the door to such a room.

An occupant who is recalcitrant vexes the resources of the housekeeper,
    who is sleeping does not vie for the attention of the housekeeper,
    who is sick can cause a life event of contamination.

An occupant of uniqueness cannot have the room's door closed,
        cannot have the plumbing blocked,

cannot prevent the attention of the housekeeper.

The occupants of the rooms are at home throughout the house,
                chatter constantly,
                discuss their levels of activity,
                talk of workloads that come and go.

The occupants of the rooms can each call for attention,
                can pretend to go to sleep,
                can exercise in a frenzy.

The occupants of the rooms grow and develop,
                are strong and virile,
                age and weaken.

The occupants of the rooms become tired and ask for little sustenance,
                            offer little sustenance,
                            produce little sustenance.

The housekeeper watches very carefully the sustenance available,
                      the sustenance accepted,
                      the sustenance rejected.

  The halls of access have defences along their corridors.

  The halls of access have defences that are continually surveyed,
                that are continually inspected,
                that are continually maintained.

The housekeeper is responsible for the level of security,
                the maintenance of security,
                the breaches of security.

  The breaches of security are serious and real,
                may be minor or massive,
                may be physical or spiritual.

  The breaches of security ring alarms,
                are reported,
                call support.

  The breaches of security scares the housekeeper,
                prepares for attack,
                brings support to the fore.

  The breaches of security may be of short or long duration,
                may lead to the establishment of a foreign colony of a
                                        single warlord.

  The breaches of security grow worse when not repaired,
                when not foiled,

       when not rebutted,
       on the first alarm.

The author of the house does not attack the house,
    has a different agenda,
      desires to convert houses into temples.

The enemy of man failed to become a co-author.

The enemy of man inflicts his enmity on the house of man,
       the shell of man,
       the glove of man,
       the habitation of man,
       the body of man,
       The Temple of man.

The enemy of man has forces that can breach the security of the house,
       that can rampage down the halls of access,
       that can lay waste the rooms of residence.

The enemy of man must be kept outside the house,
    must be promptly evicted when found at home,
    must not be tolerated while in the process of destruction.

The enemy of man is too dangerous to invite in as a guest,
       to concur with in agreement,
       to ignore when in the guise of innocence.

The enemy of man desires to destroy The Temple prior to rebirth,
      to destroy the house before conversion,
      to capture the soul while still vulnerable.

The enemy of man is correctly so called,
    is serious and determined,
    attacks with ferocity and vengeance,
    never rests nor sleeps.

The enemy of man selects the weakest point,
    delays attention,
    uses stealth.

The enemy of man is the master of procrastination,
    is Satan in his guises,
    is the prince of darkness,
    is Beelzebub,
    is the fallen angel,
    is the inquisitor of the heavens,
    is the current ruler of The Earth.

Foolish,
    indeed,
        are those who are likely to condone;
            who deny his existence;
            who believe the lies of centuries;
            who don't defend themselves;
            who fail to take up the weapons of defence;
            who don't cry out for assistance:
                      to the allies of man,
                      to the friends of man,
                      to the readers of the Book,
                      to the author of the house,
                      to the author of The Temple,
                      to the author of the Book:
                          the book that has as author The Name
                                  above all names."

My Content Study Aid

The Body of Man 3— A Temple

"The enemy of man would stalk the halls of entry of the body of man.
The enemy of man is no respecter of man.
The enemy of man records each success.

The enemy of man is not easily repelled,
        is not easily evicted,
        is not easily overcome.

Overcoming the enemy of man restores function to the body,
        enables full recuperation,
        confirms the restoration as a gift of God.

  Pain is the signature of the enemy of man.

  Infection running wild is the signature of the enemy of man.

  Failure of the function of a room is the signature of the enemy of man.

  The signature of the enemy of man can be erased from that on which it is written.

Man should not carry the signature of the enemy of man.
Man should crave for freedom from the signature that convicts.

Man can regain freedom with care and understanding,
        obedience and defiance,
        Faith and repentance.

  Success does not come through the shortcuts of man,
        from the anguish of the soul,
        from partial movements of the lips.

  Success comes from the desire of the heart,
        the contriteness of the spirit,
        the warmth of the welcome,
        the mastery of the soul.

  The house with all its rooms or The Temple with its chambers,
        can both be cleansed and purified from the virus of the foe.

The virus of the foe comes in many different clothes,
        should not be placed in wardrobes,
        should be seen for what it is,
        should not be let to incubate;
        has a deadliness of purpose,
        does not accept responsibility.

  The house should be repainted,

        should be refurnished,
        should be trimmed to size,
        should be re-piled,
        should be maintained so function is retained,
        should be made inviting for a guest that may come and stay.

The temple has a guest that is at home.

The temple should be maintained so function is retained.

The temple may need to be renewed,
        may need a coat of paint,
        may need water-blasting first.

The temple has foundations that need to be reinforced,
        has walls that may need straightening.

The temple has a roof that may sometimes leak,
        that may result in the catching of a cold,
        that may give reason for reflection.

The temple should not lean,
        should be erect,
        should not cast a shadow.

The temple should not harbour a rubbish bin within,
        should not have a signature hidden in a wardrobe.

The temple should be full of light,
        should be fitted with loudspeakers that broadcast to the world,
        should be a lighthouse to the ships at sea,
        should point to a safe haven in a foggy world.

The temple is protective.

The temple carries honour.

The temple is worthy of admiration,
        worthy of a future,
        worthy of great care.

The signatures of the foe can be erased through a fourfold pronged attack
                                        that repents,
                                        confesses,
                                        evicts,
                                        renews or repairs:
                by repentance for the lack of maintenance,
                          the lack of care,
                          the lack of appreciation of the home.

    Repentance is a change of heart,

        commitment to repair,
        urgency to clean,
            to prevent contamination,
            to keep the defences of the halls of access in pristine condition.

Confession of repentance is announced by the lips,
        gauged by the actions,
        confirmed by the heart,
        rejoiced over by the spirit,
        modifies the soul.

Confession of Faith is the adjunct to repentance.

The eviction of the foe is by the commanding prayer of Faith,
        the commanding prayer accepted,
        the commanding prayer of completion issued with
            authority in The Name above all names.

The evictor does not need to converse with an evictee.

The renewal or repair of the house and of The Temple is The Will of God manifested
            in the life of man.

Renewal or repair is accomplished by the prayer of earnestness,
        of sincerity,
        of righteousness.

The prayer that is as incense in a golden bowl.

A prayer that is in agreement reaches past the heavens.

A prayer that requires,
    that seeks,
    that deserves,
        a miracle in the life of man is carefully considered by The Word."

My Content Study Aid

The Body of Man 4— Protected

"The body of man is not endowed to flee,
        is not endowed to scent the wind,
        is not endowed with a skin of camouflage.

The body of man is endowed to think,
        is endowed to wield,
        is endowed to take dominion.

The body of man is not endowed to crawl,
        is not endowed to slither,
        is not endowed to swim.

The body of man is not endowed to fly,
        is not endowed to lie in wait,
        is not endowed for stealth.

The body of man is endowed to talk,
        is endowed to sing,
        is endowed to play.

The body of man is endowed to stand,
        is endowed with self,
        is endowed with the awareness of God.

The body of man is for a wondrous journey.

The body of man can change form and appearance,
        is for supervision and command,
        has been prepared by God.

    The soul knows the potential of the body of man.
    The spirit regards as precious the body of man.
    The mind must learn the value of the body of man.

The foe has the body of man targeted for destruction prior to its transition to a
                                                  higher state.

    The target for destruction is again to separate man from God,
                to nullify the sacrifice of God,
                to make forever permanent the loneliness of man.

The enemy of man has no mercy,
        is constant in harassment,
        has successes when he shouldn't,
        has a future that is foretold.

Foolish are they who befriend,
> accommodate,
>> do not evict the entity of spirit whose future has been
>>> so declared.

The entity of spirit,
> the immortal entity of spirit,
> the enemy of man,
> has a place prepared for him that is not to his satisfaction.

Foolish are they who choose to follow the vicious entity of rebellion
>> to that place preserved,
>> to that place reserved,
>> to that place that imposes,
>>> that inflicts,
>>> that exacts,
> just tribulation for decisions made.

Foolish are they who do not recover while they can,
> who do not listen when they hear,
> who do not decide to act without procrastination.

The foolish will regret—
> the stupidity exhibited in their mortality,
> the misspending of their youth,
> the loss of opportunity,
> as they stand before a judgement throne that is unlikely to reprieve.

The foolish are in denial of their God,
> have chosen other Gods,
> have accepted the fate of Satan.

The foolish are called to repent,
> to walk a higher path,
> to build on their potential within the framework of creation that
>> leads home to an existence in the
>> presence of the Three-in-One.

The foolish are in mortal danger of allowing the stealth of procrastination to remove their opportunity of Grace."

My Content Study Aid

_____

_____

_____

The Variety of Choice

"The variety of the choice of man is to be exercised with wisdom.

The variety of the choice of man is tempting to his taste,
                is tempting to his sight,
                is tempting to his hands.

The variety of the choice of man lightens the pocket of man,
                lightens the chores of man,
                lightens the workload of the hands.

The variety of the choice of man is produced by experimentation,
                is produced by lines of tools,
                is produced at the request of man,
                      through the quest of man,
                      at the behest of man.

The variety of the choice of man is marketed to empty out the pocket,
                      to appeal to slothfulness,
                      to emphasize the fears of man.

The variety of the choice of man is enhanced by the folding coinage of the realm of man,
                is enhanced by transport,
                is enhanced by distance—
                            the freight ways of the far-off lands.

The variety of the choice of man is dependent on imagination,
                      on a source of energy,
                      on the hands of man that cuddle bags
                                  of wealth.

The variety of the choice of man brings payment to the poor that keeps them poor,
                      brings payment to those who cannot read,
                            those who cannot write—
                            which is insufficient to buy chalk.

The variety of the choice of man transfers labour to those who must,
                            just to survive.

The variety of the choice of man is priced without concern for the need of chalk,
                                the need of a teacher,
                                the need of human dignity,
                                the need for hope.

The variety of the choice of man does not dwell on those who must grovel for
                                            their bread,
                                            cry out for assistance;

> have eyes that size the saucers* of the soul.

Those who feed on the variety of the choice of man would do well to reconsider their
> lack of wisdom that maintains,
> that encourages the grovelling,
> > the deafened ears;
> > the enlarging of the
> > saucers of the soul.

Those who feed on the variety of the choice of man,
> who surround themselves in plenty,
> who know no lack,
> who see no lack,
> who feel no lack,
> who experience an abundance:

those are they who have a responsibility before God to exercise their wisdom of
> selection that justice may encroach upon the poor;
> > that they may not gobble at a table and see no
> > crumbs fall to the floor;
> > that they may insist on justice and see the winds
> > of change blow through an opened door."

Scribal Note: *saucers of the soul* "storage and handling capacity of and for the content resulting from the greed of the soul."

My Content Study Aid

_____
_____
_____
_____
_____
_____
_____
_____
_____
_____
_____
_____
_____
_____
_____
_____

The Chains of Choice

"The chains of choice affect the disempowered.

The chains of choice are used unwittingly by some,
        provide a service to the wealthy,
        do not service the needy.

The chains of choice have links that form the marketplace of man.

The chains of choice do not purchase the labour of the poor,
        the produce of the poor,
        without an eye upon excessive gain.

Excessive gain does not denote fairness of approach,
    incriminates the wealthy,
    speaks volumes of the heart,
    is a reason for arraignment,
    is the ploy of the cartels sheltering within the marketplace.

Excessive gain is watched by God,
    is frowned on by God,
    carries a warning of God.

A warning of God is for the benefit of man,
    should be heeded promptly,
    will be followed up.

Unheeded warnings of God can be counted as infringements of intent.

Infringements of intent have repercussions on anticipated rewards,
        on gifts that were reserved,
        on the spectre of despair.

Infringements of intent need immediate repentance and offers of reparation.

Offers of reparation should be easily accepted.

Offers of reparation not easily accepted fail as insincere.

Offers of reparation,
    reparation made,
    excessive gain removed,
        amend the records previously as written in the library of man.

An amended record in the library of man counts as repentance before God.

An amended record is evidence that cannot be discerned,
        cannot be accessed,
        acts as a reprieve.

The chains of choice do not bind the wealthy.

The chains of choice bind the struggling with lost opportunities of advancement,
> cannot justify their stance by selective examples that are few
>> in number,
> will thrive when they can stand and deliver with a conscience that
>> is clear,
> can move within the confines of God when they so choose.

The chains of choice can bring hope to those who struggle in their daily needs,
> those who would advance their lives through the
>> hope that is within,
> those who cry out for assistance that is
>> currently withheld."

My Content Study Aid

The Abilities of Man

"The abilities of man are always to the fore,
            always on their guard,
            always striving for expansion.

The abilities of man are lightly regarded,
            are taken for granted,
            are often forgotten.

The abilities of man are at his beck and call,
            are sometimes overestimated,
            are sometimes insufficient for the task at hand.

The abilities of man seek alliances that augment,
            grow with experience,
            evaporate with consciousness.

The abilities of man can recognize a presence,
            can operate at distance,
            can aspire to greatness.

The abilities of man canon into conflict,
            canon into injury,
            canon into realms of the unknown.

The abilities of man collide with others,
            collide with achievements,
            collide with ambition.

The abilities of man do not retreat from collision,
            are not deterred by collision,
            are not fearful of collision.

The abilities of man retreat from embarrassment,
            retreat from superiority,
            retreat from a lack of knowledge.

The abilities of man are allowed to fail,
            are allowed to succeed,
            are allowed to capture.

The abilities of man are for the purposes of man,
            come with the nature of man,
            are integrated in application.

The abilities of man are limited by power,
            are limited by authority,
            are limited by freewill.

The abilities of man are approved of God,
      are overseen by God,
      are defended by God."

My Content Study Aid

The Fiefdom of The Lord

"The day of The Lord arises with the sun.

The day of The Lord,
    the return of The Lord,
    the second coming of The Lord,
            has long been awaited,
            has long been expected,
            has long been a recurring disappointment—
                          by and to the mind of man.

The mind of man has often called for rescue,
        has often called for solace,
        has often called in chagrin.

The mind of man has often pleaded,
        has often given voice,
        has often committed to a song.

The mind of man has often ignored the call to proclaim,
        has often regarded silence as completion,
        has often sought to sever the lost's call from the found.

The mind of man has sometimes been extremely diligent,
        has sometimes set off in obedience,
        has sometimes reported far off success.

The mind of man has sometimes been committed unto death,
        has sometimes embarked without the cost,
        has sometimes been supported by Faith and promises.

The mind of man has accepted a commission,
        has travelled extended distances,
        has passed a lifetime in the lands of the lost.

    All has been recorded—
            both action and reaction.

    All has been appraised—
            the level of attainment.

    All has been rewarded—
            according to disclosure.

All was,
    all is,
    all will be,
    commemorated—

        as the teacher taught—
        as the disciple lived.

The day that is awaited,
        now is.

The day that is awaited now rolls to the forefront of the stage,
        awaits the curtain call,
        awaits the fanfare of immediacy.

The day that is awaited will culminate an age,
        will unroll upon command,
        will change the lives of man.

The day that is awaited will dispense with Grace,
        will dispense with Faith,
        will dispense a new beginning—
              of love,
              of justice,
              of provisioning.

The day that is awaited has need of the sanctuaries of The Lord.

The sanctuaries of The Lord are a part of The Edifice of God.

The sanctuaries of The Lord are open to all who know the key—
        the key of access to a sanctuary of The Lord.

The key of access cannot be lost,
        cannot be transferred,
        cannot be stolen,
        cannot be acquired through force of arms.

Possession of the key of access is confirmed by The Spirit as access is sought.

The key of access provides shelter within a sanctuary,
        knowledge when distressed,
        protection when threatened.

The sanctuaries of The Lord defy marauding bands,
        defy kings that do not honour,
        defy armies that wreck destruction.

The sanctuaries of The Lord will not fall,
        will withstand,
        will overcome.

The sanctuaries of The Lord will uphold The Kingdom of The Lord,
        will grow,
        will expand.

The sanctuaries of The Lord will not suffer duress at the hands of any man,
>> will survive dissent,
>> will welcome the homeless.

The sanctuaries of The Lord are respites,
>> are for the benefit of the sheltered,
>> will confirm the safety of the soul.

The sanctuaries of The Lord are precursors of the coming Kingdom,
>> model the coming Kingdom,
>> typify the coming Kingdom.

The sanctuaries of The Lord herald the coming Kingdom:
>> The Kingdom of The Lord,
>> The Kingdom of God,
>> The Kingdom that will honour heads that bow to,
>>>> tongues that worship,
>>>> Earth that acknowledges,
>>> Jesus as The Lord of His creation—
>>>> the King seated on His throne of majesty,
>>>> the Master of all that He surveys.

The Name above all names has come unto His own,
>> has come into His own,
>> has come onto His own—
>>> The Earth whereon He reigns."

My Content Study Aid

The Plunder of The Soul

"The bounty of man is garnered where he will.

The bounty of man is supervised by man,
        has claim laid to it by man,
        contains items of abuse,
        contains results of theft,
        contains items acquired without good title.

The bounty of man is laid up by pirates who procure at any cost,
        who treat frontiers as thresholds,
        who travel to accumulate,
        who treat a frontier of a nation as a threshold of
                a home,
        who ransack and carry off the plunder of the soul,
        who will not return their plunder regardless
                of entreaty.

The plunder of the soul should not be counted as gain,
        is not recognized by The Spirit,
        is hidden with great care,
        is owned by he who counts,
        does not bring wealth of honour,
        speaks of the presence of a pirate.

The plunder of the soul speaks of greed in action,
        speaks of roving eyes,
        speaks of the covetousness of the soul of man.

The plunder of the soul speaks of scruples long forsworn,
        speaks of conspiracies of success,
        speaks of rampant disregard.

The plunder of the soul is very rarely viewed,
        is hidden in rooms that have a lock,
        is counted only in times of solitude.

The plunder of the soul possesses he who holds it,
        destroys he who acquires it,
        has no value in the future world of man.

The soul of man often seeks to plunder,
        often seeks to hoard,
        often seeks to treasure the plunder of the soul.

The soul of man can be taught a lesson,
        can be taken under reins,

can be checked and then reformed.

The pirate of the plunder can become the gentle man of God,
 can become the committed man of God,
 can become the sacrificial temple of his God."

My Content Study Aid

Christmas Day

"Christmas day has nearly again come to completion in this land,
                              is yet to come in others.

Christmas day is loved by The Lord for its intent of holiness,
            is for the pause of man,
            is for the reflection of man.

Christmas day is for the call of man based on remembrance of things past,
                        based on the pleasure of the day,
                        based on the forward hope of what will surely come.

Christmas day calls for righteousness before God.

Righteousness is the herald of peace.

Peace is victory over the soul.

Victory over the soul is applauded by God.

The applause of God is a welcome sign to man.

Welcome signs to man point to the way home.

The way home is sign posted for man—
            at the turning points in the life of man—
            at the turning points where sign posts are most welcome.

Christmas day was,
      is,
      shall forever be,
            a turning point in the life of man.

Christmas day gave birth to a promise of great Glory,
            to a sacrifice of great gain,
            to a resurrection of great significance.

All for the life of man.

The life of man has been ransomed,
        has been plucked to safety,
        has been secured for his freewill.

The freeing of Man's freewill from imprisonment was born on Christmas Day."

My Content Study Aid

_____

_____

The Banner Prepared

"The Banner of The Kingdom is now to go into the marketplace of man,
    is now to be unfurled,
    is now to confront the beliefs of man.

The Banner of The Kingdom is prepared for the heralds,
    will witness as declared,
    will enter the mind of man.

The Banner of The Kingdom will murmur to the soul,
    will shout to the spirit,
    will bring recognition to the eye.

The Banner of The Kingdom is to have its history disclosed.

The Banner of The Kingdom has origin divine,
    has counsel divine,
    has guardianship divine.

The Banner of The Kingdom has authority divine,
    has seals divine,
    has approvals divine.

The Banner of The Kingdom has ownership divine.

The Banner of The Kingdom reaches out,
    confirms,
    stipulates a presence.

The Banner of The Kingdom enervates a people,
    summons those to whom it speaks,
    enthuses young and old to continue with a journey.

The Banner of The Kingdom stands on The Earth pointing to the heavens,
    dances in the wind pointing to The Spirit,
    revels in the radiance pointing to The Son.

The Banner of The Kingdom speaks of the presence of great purity,
    speaks of the presence of the meeting of great boundaries,
    speaks of the presence of the great coming of eternity.

The Banner of The Kingdom of God on Earth speaks of Jesus—
    The Lord of His creation—
    the returning King of kings.

    Maran atha!"

The Wings of Heaven

"The wings of Heaven float upon a breeze,
        very rarely sneeze,
        give a loving squeeze,
        never seem to wheeze,
        like the scent of cheese,
        are remembered in a frieze.

The wings of Heaven are masters of their flight.

The wings of Heaven can dive,
        can hover,
        can twirl,
        can twist,
        can soar,
        can glide,
        can loop.

The wings of Heaven can fly with wings that touch,
        that flex,
        that curve.

The wings of Heaven surpass the wings of Earth.

The wings of Heaven do not compare with the wings of man.

The wings of Heaven are alive,
        are coloured according to their role,
        are gentle in their touch,
        are fearsome in their approach,
        are awesome in their bands.

The wings of Heaven gather for their pleasure,
        have widespread scope to operate,
        can draw near in silence,
        can whip up a storm of dust.

The wings of Heaven can be made visible to man,
        can cloak their wings when needed,
        can match their age upon appearance.

The wings of Heaven protect,
        defend,
        uplift.

The wings of Heaven are agents of The Spirit.

The wings of Heaven love to change their colours,

    love to change their wing shape,
    love to change their roles.

The wings of Heaven can escalate their speed,
    can escalate their vibrations,
    can escalate the life-beats of their wings,
    have mastery of the mediums in which they fly.

The wings of Heaven do not need air to fly,
    do not tire,
    can look like fire,
    sound as a lyre.

The wings of Heaven are great in number,
    attend the thrones,
    disseminate as instructed.

The wings of Heaven bring Glory when folded,
    bring honour when in part extended,
    bring unity when quivering.

The wings of Heaven are submissive when trailed,
    are attentive when drooped,
    are loving when enfolding.

The wings of Heaven worship with full extension upwards,
    praise with full extension outwards,
    rest in white.

The wings of Heaven are the masterstrokes of God,
    are the master-strikes of God,
    are the masterminds of peace.

The wings of Heaven can be damaged upon landing,
    always land with great caution,
    are repaired with great care.

The damagers of the wings of Heaven never regret their action,
     crow at their success,
     keep the score with smirks.

The keepers of the score lie about their failures,
    do not count their damage,
    never speak of territory that is lost.

Only the keepers of the score with the damagers of the wings of Heaven,
     believe what they have recorded,
     what has been spread abroad,
     what part-victories won.

The wings of Heaven know the scent of victory,
        know the battle plan,
        know the surety of the final victory.

The wings of Heaven are prepared to concede territory that is not reinforced,
        that is not critical,
        that has no lingering support,
        will cause no lasting damage.

The keepers of the score with the damagers of the wings of Heaven,
        can themselves be damaged by The Word,
        can be bruised by the shield,
        shy from the belt,
        try to dent the helmet,
        try to trip the shod feet,
        flinch from the spoken rhema,
        flee from a strong attack.

The keepers of the score with the damagers of the wings of Heaven,
        take a long time to recover,
        dread a fresh encounter,
        find it difficult to retain unity in the face
                of such defiance.

The keepers of the score with the damagers of the wings of Heaven,
        would rather launch a probe elsewhere and not count the loss,
        would rather launch attacks and lie about the outcome,
        would rather not finish what they have started,
        would rather not believe the outcome of the war."

My Content Study Aid

_____
_____
_____
_____
_____
_____
_____
_____
_____
_____

The Bones of The Earth

"The bones of the fields and the bones of the valleys,
  the bones of the mountain tops and the bones of the plains,
  the bones of the seas and the bones of the lakes,
  the bones of the streams and the bones of the rivers,
  the bones of the glaciers and the bones of the forests,
  the bones of the cities and the bones of the hamlets:
        the bones of The Earth;
        the remnants of man;
        all will be uplifted from their resting places—
            from their graves within the dust,
            from their graves within the water.

        All will be uplifted at the time of the upheaval of man.

The remnants of man will no longer rest within The Earth,
    will no longer rest beneath the surface of the waters of The Earth,
    will reach out and link together,
    will be recovered in the resurrection of man.

The resurrection of man will split asunder beliefs of error,
    opens all the graves still sealed,
    overcomes the enemy of man.

The resurrection of man marks the end of Grace,
    marks a new beginning,
    marks the end of time.

The resurrection of man enables judgement to occur and justice to prevail,
    enables sentences to commence,
    introduces understanding of eternity to the soul of man.

The resurrection of man declares The Power of God,
    confirms The Love of God."

My Content Study Aid

_____
_____
_____
_____
_____

The Waters of Life

"The waters of life dwell within the soul,
                are shared by the spirit.

The waters of life,
 the streams of living water,
                have eternal properties,
                hold an eternal promise,
                quench the thirst of those who sup.

The waters of life are as an oasis in the desert,
                an oasis to a soul,
                an oasis that does not run dry.

The waters of life are as an oasis that is not encroached by sand,
                are as an oasis that supplies needs in abundance,
                are as an oasis where all may freely drink,
                offer hope to those who have no hope.

The waters of life are not a secret in a desert.

The waters of life can be seen from afar,
                can be tasted and rejected,
                can be tasted and accepted.

The waters of life exist in many pools,
                flow in many streams,
                have signs pointing to their presence,
                should be imbibed by all.

The waters of life wash,
        cleanse,
        immerse,
        cover,
        teach,
        lead,
        point to a life that only they provide.

The waters of life are known by those they whet,
                are known by those they save from drought,
                are known by those on whom The Spirit rains."

My Content Study Aid

_____

_____

The Earth of God

"The Trinity of God pervades the heavens,
        has yet to pervade The Earth of man,
        stretches The Faith of man.

The Earth of man has yet to be The Earth of God.

The Earth of God will not know The Earth of man,
        will not be built upon The Earth of man.

The Earth of God will arise from a rebirth,
        a renewal,
        a change of ownership,
        a change of authority,
        a change of purpose of existence.

The Earth of God will comprehend the Trinity of God,
        will be a colony of Heaven with its King in residence,
        will know its God—
            The God of Heaven.

The Earth of God will bring an entourage from Heaven,
        constructions of majesty,
        constructions of praise,
        constructions of worship.

The Earth of God will inaugurate an edifice of God:
        an edifice in which God is at home,
        an edifice which distributes power,
        an edifice that shares authority,
        an edifice that ensures justice,
        an edifice of love.

The Trinity of God speaks both of function and of form,
        speaks both of presence and description,
        speaks both of separation and derivation,
        speaks both of graduation and immersion,
        speaks both of purpose and pursuit,
        speaks both of being and existence,
        speaks both of holiness and humanity.

The Trinity of God is as a plaited rope,
        can be splayed as per each strand,
        can be separated when needed.

The Trinity of God can be as gentle as a finger-tip,
        as enveloping as a cloud,

      as united as a brook upon a fall of rain.

The Trinity of God can be as unyielding as a lake of ice,
      as impenetrable as a moving avalanche,
      as loving as the warmth in water when heated by the sun.

The Trinity of God created the natural laws of man within the experience of man.

The Trinity of God determined the natural laws of man to control his rite of passage.

The Trinity of God has natural lines of force in place to encourage man to choose his
        lifelines with great care while on The Earth of man.

The death-lines of man are offered in temptation,
    are offered in a lie,
    are offered to subvert—
  are coarse and not transparent,
    ensnare and do not free,
    suffocate without release,
    infect and do not cure,
    still and do not resuscitate,
    decry without redemption.

The death-lines of man are held taut by the enemy of man,
    are played in earnestness with skill by the enemy of man,
      attempt to become a stranglehold upon the life of man through the
          twitches of the foe."

My Content Study Aid

_____
_____
_____
_____
_____
_____
_____
_____
_____
_____
_____
_____
_____
_____

The Messages of Life

"I,
   The Lord,
      speak to My people this day of the difficulties of life.

         The difficulties of life are so-named by man:
            the messages of life are known to God.

The messages of life do not speak of evolving over time.
The messages of life speak of the witness of the cell of life.

The witness of the cell of life is of those parts that save,
                read,
                transmit,
                copy,
                construct life within the cell.

The witness of the cell of life is now perceived by man.

The witness of the cell of life does not offer confirmation to the hypotheses of man that
        he has myriads of extended cousins in the chains of life on Earth.

The witness of the cell of life has patterns that are recognizable to man that speak of
                information carried:
           minimized complexity that cannot further be resolved,
           the presence of activities now understood by man.

The witness of the cell of life demolishes the theories of the vain,
          bounces off the ears of the proud,
          are not seen for what they are by the eyes of the blind.

The messages of life speak to those who would know The Truth,
            to those who are not bound to suppositions that are false,
            to those who revel in knowledge built on a rock foundation.

The messages of life speak of strings that go to completion,
          speak of the origins of the molecules of creation,
          speak of the mastery of their control.

Man should not meddle in the grand designs of life.
Man can only watch the working of the grand designs of life.
Man has no concept of how to originate a grand design of life.

The grand designs of life are not for man to emulate,
          are not for man to copy,
          are not for man to simulate in the process of trial and error.

Man cannot allow for the generations that are counted to fluctuate for
>the safety of the counted,
>the longevity of the counted,
>the future of the counted.

The future generations of the counted are not safely preserved when in the hands of man. The future life events of the counted are not safely determined when in the hands of man. The future viability of the counted is not safely constructed when left in the hands of man."

My Content Study Aid

The Banner of Effects

"The Banner of The Kingdom stands before man,
        raises the awareness of God,
        speaks of the future of man;
        causes eyes to be averted,
        causes excuses to be brought forth,
        causes tongues to become silent.

The Banner of The Kingdom gives cause for contemplation to the thoughtful,
        gives cause for action to the wise,
        gives cause for rejoicing to the repentant.

The Banner of The Kingdom foretells an act of significance,
        foretells a sea change on The Earth,
        foretells of water that overflows a cup.

The Banner of The Kingdom initiates events upon The Earth,
        initiates events within the heavens,
        initiates events in Heaven.

The Banner of The Kingdom awaits the day of the sun,
        awaits the day of The Earth,
        awaits the day of The Son.

    The day of the sun is a day of heat.

    The day of The Earth is a day of scarcity.

    The day of The Son is a day of living water bringing life.

    The day of The Son approaches,
        unlocks the waters of Zion,
        brings streams of living water,
        waters a thirsty Earth.

    The day of The Son sees The Earth reclaimed,
        sees The Earth re-seeded,
        sees The Earth prepared."

My Content Study Aid

_____
_____
_____
_____

I, The Lord

"I,
    The Lord,
        would speak to My people that they may know I AM.

I,
    The Lord,
        would speak to My people that they may sense the urgency for preparation.

I,
    The Lord,
        would speak to My people that they may be reassured that My love for them will
                                                              not fade away.

I,
    The Lord,
        would speak to My people that they may realize how much I love My Disciples,
              how much I love those who follow in My footsteps,
              how much I will testify for those who testify of Me.

I,
    The Lord,
        would speak to My people that they may have Faith I will return.

For a day comes,
        that shall not be long delayed,
              when The Earth will resound to the trumpet call of God,
              when The Earth will arise in anticipation,
              when The Earth will tremble at The Word,
              when The Earth will shake with trepidation,
              when The Earth will swarm together for protection,
              when The Earth will writhe in agony,
              when The Earth will struggle for rebirth.

For a day comes that will herald a new beginning,
        that will herald the capture of the foe,
        that will herald a reign of peace on Earth,
        that will herald the end of the organisations of man,
        that will herald the inauguration of The Edifice of God,
        that will herald a change in lifestyle for man,
        that will herald the coming Kingdom of The King of kings—
                visible to all creation.

For a day comes when righteousness prevails,
        when peace prevails,
        when justice prevails,

> when plenty prevails,
> when freedom prevails,
> when fairness prevails throughout The Earth.

For a day comes when happiness abounds,
> when laughter fills the throats of throngs,
> when life is equitable to all.

For a day comes when those who carry weapons will be excluded,
> when those who would use weapons will be excluded,
> when those who would make weapons will be excluded.

For a day comes when weapons of destruction,
> weapons of the stockpiles,
> weapons of wealth extortion,
> weapons of illness,
> weapons of coercion,
> weapons of greed,
> will be no more.

The weapons of the air,
> of The Earth,
> of the sea,
> of man,
>> shall no longer bear man a reward.

A day comes,
> that none can miss,
> of which all will be aware,
> that will leave an imprint on the soul of man for ever."

My Content Study Aid

_____
_____
_____
_____
_____
_____
_____
_____
_____
_____

The Banner of Destiny

"The Banner of The Kingdom falls upon The Earth and is not uplifted.

The Banner of The Kingdom is there to be beheld,
                is there for a time of preparation.

The Banner of The Kingdom speaks of God in action,
                speaks of A Kingdom with a vacant throne,
                speaks of coming events,
                speaks of the coronation of the King.

The Banner of The Kingdom has a purpose and a destiny,
                focuses the mind of man,
                calls for a decision.

The Banner of The Kingdom is not without authority,
                brings expectation to the forefront,
                shouts to all mankind.

The Banner of The Kingdom is not to fall upon The Earth.

The Banner of The Kingdom is there to be lifted high,
                to point the way,
                to invite the lost to seek.

The Banner of The Kingdom deserves the notice of man,
                offers respect to all,
                is the reaching out of God.

The Banner of The Kingdom is being carried by the angels,
                now decorates The Earth,
                lines the passage of The King.

The Banner of The Kingdom is visible in the retinue of The King,
                waves as Standards where trumpets play,
                flies as Flags with anthems present,
                is as Standards beside The Throne on which The King
                                is crowned.

The Banner of The Kingdom is the Colours of the King.

The Banner of The Kingdom is asserted at the crowning of The Kings.

The Banner of The Kingdom speaks of the end of times,
                speaks of new beginnings,
                speaks of a hope long awaited.

The Banner of The Kingdom will have substitutes of deception,
                will have proximities of design,

will have proclamations made in error,
will reflect the efforts of man,
will reflect the foe of man,
will reflect efforts at deflection of The Kingdom's call."

My Content Study Aid

The Fire and The Tribulation

"A day of fire and tribulation befalls The Earth.

A day of fire and tribulation encompasses The Earth,
                sequesters The Earth,
                overlays The Earth,
                circumscribes The Earth,
                purifies The Earth.

The fire is The Word of God aflame,
            The Word of God in Glory,
            The Word of God enthroned.

The tribulation is the wrath of God in action,
            the wrath of God displayed,
            the wrath of God that falls on the unrighteous.

Fire and tribulation follow the coming of The Kingdom,
            follow a journey of mortality,
            follow the sheep and the goats,
            follow the time of Grace,
            follow the call of angels,
            follow the seating of the elders,
            follow the gestures of The Lord.

Fire and tribulation bestow and withdraw reward,
            are the face of Faith and of ignominy,
            result from seeking and dismissing,
            are rewarded and inflicted,
            endure for eternity,
            are neither quenched nor pleaded,
            are deserved.

Fire and tribulation do not come in silence,
            do not come in ignorance,
            do not come in agreement,
            do not come together,
            do not come in unity,
            do not come in secret,
            do not come in contact.

The Word of God aflame ignites the flame of The Spirit,
            ignites the bowls of incense,
            ignites the dragon's lair.

The Word of God in Glory is the mantle of The Kingdom,

      is the stature of the regal,
      is enrobing by The Father.

The Word of God enthroned accepts an audience,
      addresses affairs of state,
      is attended by The Bride of The Lamb.

The wrath of God in action is terrible to behold,
      rolls as a thunderstorm across the heavens,
      surges as a wave across the lands.

The wrath of God displayed causes the loss of courage,
      causes all before to flee,
      causes monuments to fall.

The wrath of God that falls on the unrighteous has long been withheld,
      occurs with disappointment,
      speaks of enslaved souls and spirits that
            are bound.

The coming of The Kingdom is about to be,
      determines the destiny of man,
      seals the fate of the confession-less.

A journey of mortality ends in the spirit,
      has purpose and design,
      progresses the being of man,
      maintains the link with eternity for man,
      creates the character of man,
      tests the soul of man.

The sheep and the goats are not inseparable,
      will no longer inter-mingle,
      have differing destinies that do not cross,
      appear similar from a distance,
      sound similar from a distance,
      seek different pastures.

The Time of Grace draws to an end,
      cannot be refuted,
      verifies The Love of God.

The call of angels inaugurates the convocation of a court,
      announces readiness to proceed,
      ensures silence prevails.

The seating of the elders brings all to attention,
      causes records to be opened,
      causes throats to be cleared.

The gestures of The Lord are watched with great intensity,
        promote and despatch,
        are made with great solemnity.

Bestowal and withdrawal of reward accords with the records,
        does not come as a surprise;
        brings fluttering of hearts,
        brings dismissal by the elders,
        brings transfer to a location,
        brings amazement or rejection.

The face of Faith and the face of ignominy are diametrically opposed,
        can be recognized at a glance,
        highlight their expectations,
        are not present in one place,
        are no longer changeable,
        had the same beginnings.

Seeking and dismissing are not comfortable companions,
        are for the wise and for the foolish,
        testify to the failure and success of the enemy of man,
        are as white and black,
        honour and dishonour,
        elevate and subjugate.

Rewarding and inflicting accesses the records of man,
        recognizes the agency of man,
        is occasioned by the soul of man,
        does not surprise the spirit of man,
        does not give cause for complaint,
        is always seen as just.

Enduring for eternity is not lived one day at a time,
        speaks of the absence of time,
        speaks of sameness of experience.

Quenching and pleading are no longer possible,
        were reserved for mortality,
        have no recourse to The Throne-rooms.

The deserving receive in line with their deeds,
        their thoughts,
        their approach to wealth,
        their stance towards the needs of brothers,
        their authority,
        their ear for mercy.

Silence flees before the voice of man,

> before the ears of man,
> before the memory of man.
>
> Ignorance does not exist in these presences,
> > in these environments,
> > in these courses of action.
>
> Agreement is implicit when in a course of action,
> > when not combined together,
> > when resolved in isolation.
>
> Coming together is not practical,
> > implies lack of understanding,
> > negates one with the other.
>
> Unity does not speak of opposites,
> > can speak of selection,
> > can indicate The Will of God.
>
> In secret are the works of God not done,
> > are the edicts of God not made known,
> > do the trials of God not eventuate.
>
> Contact is not made by those with opposing destinies,
> > with opposing agency of freewill,
> > with opposing masters whom they follow.
>
> The mortality of man,
> > that seeks in the time of Grace with fervency,
> > finds the Fire:
> > The Word of God,
> > and the triumphant soul of man.
>
> The mortality of man,
> > that dismisses the time of Grace as of little consequence,
> > leads to tribulation:
> > the wrath of God unleashed,
> > and the downfallen soul of man."

My Content Study Aid

_____
_____
_____
_____
_____

The Banner Brings Response

"The Banner of The Kingdom now becomes a witness,
  now invites enquiry,
  is positioned for acceptance.

The Banner of The Kingdom is supported by all involved,
  is not an orphan left alone,
  appeals to the inner man.

The Banner of The Kingdom arouses an excited response,
  arouses thoughtless disdain,
  polarises man for all to see.

The Banner of The Kingdom causes attitudes to be updated,
  positions to be declared,
  the mouth of man to show the colour of his soul.

The Banner of The Kingdom instigates The Fear of The Lord,
  intensifies The Fear of The Lord,
  welcomes The Fear of The Lord,
  acknowledges The Fear of The Lord,
  completes The Fear of The Lord,
  dwells in The Fear of The Lord,
  dwells in the presence of The Lord.

The Emblem of The Spirit on The Temple of The Spirit states truth to those encountered,
  invites discussion of a sign,
  brings recognition to the wise.

The Emblem of The Spirit on The Temple of The Spirit approaches as a laughing friend,
  is gracious in a greeting,
  has a testimony on lips.

The Emblem of The Spirit on The Temple of The Spirit ensures a divine appointment,
  causes listening with interest,
  invites queries without rancour.

The Emblem of The Spirit on The Temple of The Spirit always offers prayer,
  always offers a way of progress,
  always offers an address of meeting.

The Emblem of The Spirit on The Temple of The Spirit moves and intermingles,
  hears lips without reproof,
  brings honour to The Temple of The Spirit.

The Emblem of The Spirit on The Temple of The Spirit encourages a turning point,
  encourages the joy of life,

encourages the winning of lost souls.

The Emblem of The Spirit on The Temple of The Spirit speaks of devotion to A King, speaks of the redemption of A King, speaks of the sign of The King of kings."

My Content Study Aid

The Banner in The Role

"The Banner of The Kingdom of God shall arise,
      shall shine forth,
      shall proclaim possession.

The Banner of The Kingdom of God augurs well for the future,
      augurs well for a future of enlightenment,
      augurs well for the onset of a new way of life.

The Banner of The Kingdom of God forestalls attacks of the foe of man,
      forestalls attacks of ill health for man,
      forestalls the indignity of the spirit of man.

The Banner of The Kingdom of God overlooks The Kingdom,
      the citizens of The Kingdom,
      the welfare of its citizens.

The Banner of The Kingdom of God is protective of its citizens,
      is protected for its purpose,
      protects those who shelter.

The Banner of The Kingdom of God will not wear away,
      will always be renewed,
      will always state a claim.

The Banner of The Kingdom of God denotes excellence of belief,
      excellence of attitude,
      excellence of favour.

The Banner of The Kingdom of God speaks of a plenitude of love,
      a plenitude of life,
      a plenitude of knowledge,
      a plenitude of wisdom,
      a plenitude of relationships,
      a plenitude of activity.

The Banner of The Kingdom of God is never boring,
      is never false,
      is never misunderstood.

The Banner of The Kingdom of God has been a long time in coming,
      is now here for ever,
      is as originally planned.

The Banner of The Kingdom of God should be acquired by the wise,
      will speak to the seekers,
      will service the servants,

>
> will govern the lost,
> will curtail the unjust,
> will set a standard of behaviour,
> will precede the seating of a throne.
>
> The Banner of The Kingdom acclaims the reign of the coming King,
> acclaims the reign of justice,
> acclaims the reign of love,
> acclaims the reign of righteousness,
> acclaims the reign of light,
> acclaims the reign of Heaven,
> acclaims the reign of the Will of God made known."

My Content Study Aid

The Banner as A Signpost

"The Banner of The Kingdom speaks of the Triumvirate of God,
                speaks of the Triumvirate of Spirit,
                speaks of the Triumvirate of Light.

The Banner of The Kingdom rolls forth upon The Earth under the guidance of the
                                            Triumvirate of God,
                has confirmation as the Will of God,
                has the eye of God firmly fixed thereon.

The Banner of The Kingdom will overcome impediments.

The Banner of The Kingdom will not be trammelled,
                will not stumble at a roadblock,
                will not be slowed in an advance.

The Banner of The Kingdom will achieve the objectives of God,
                will achieve the designs of God.

The Banner of The Kingdom flies in the face of evil,
                flies in the face of hatred,
                flies in the face of greed,
                flies in the face of pride,
                flies in the face of envy,
                flies in the face of deceit.
The Banner of The Kingdom circumvents corruption,
                circumvents pockets of resistance,
                circumvents chains of command.

The Banner of The Kingdom circumvents strongholds of lies,
                circumvents temples of idolatry,
                circumvents dens of thieves.

The Banner of The Kingdom is stationed on land recaptured,
                on land reclaimed,
                on land with authority re-established.

The Banner of The Kingdom is a new signpost to man.

The Emblem of The Spirit on The Temple of The Spirit is a new signpost to man.

The Emblem of The Spirit on The Temple of The Spirit signposts
                                an acclamation of Faith,
                                a proclamation of Truth,
                                a declamation of Redemption:
                                the application of Salvation.

The Emblem of The Spirit on The Temple of The Spirit speaks of a witness bearing arms,

speaks of a witness with a testimony,
speaks of a guiding light in this time of Grace."

My Content Study Aid

The Banner of The Battle

"The Banner of The Kingdom speaks of the battle for humanity,
                          the battle for each soul,
                          the battle that recoups what has been lost.

The Banner of The Kingdom speaks of the battle fought in the time of Grace,
                                    was fought in the time of temptation,
                                    was fought in the time of redemption.

The Banner of The Kingdom speaks of the battle fought in the time of salvation.

The Banner of The Kingdom culminates the battles for the soul of man.

The Banner of The Kingdom culminates the battles of Redemption,
                          the battles of Grace,
                          the battles of Salvation.

The Banner of The Kingdom culminates in battles for all that man has at risk:
                                    the ownership of his soul and,
                                    therein,
                                    his agency.

The Banner of The Kingdom is trooped as the Colours of The Kingdom.

The Banner of The Kingdom is guarded for the benefit of souls that may yet be lost.

The guardians of The Banner of The Kingdom frown on those who would fight battles
                                                    under law,
                       know no souls were saved in the time of
                                law when reliant on the law,
                       know no souls are saved in the time of
                                Grace when solely reliant on the
                                mind of reason and of intellect.

The guardians of The Banner of The Kingdom know that Grace requires a seed of Faith,
                                          an act of freewill,
                                          an act that terminates in a leap of Faith.

The guardians of The Banner of The Kingdom witness the first step of Faith
                                         that can be very tentative,
                                         that can grow with confidence,
                                         that can grow in certainty of commitment.

The guardians of The Banner of The Kingdom witness the reins put on each soul,
                                            the circumspect nature of control,
                                            the seeking of wisdom that befits
                                                      a destiny.

The mind of reason and of intellect can be robbed of possession of its soul when
                                      entwined in the tendrils of evolution.

    The tendrils of evolution capture the mind,
                entangle the mind,
                constrict the paths of thought in the mind of man.

    The tendrils of evolution overturn the mind when struggling to handle the
                                  implications of a single tendril.

    The tendrils of evolution are not of consequence in the cell of life.

    The tendrils of evolution isolate the mind of man,
                imprison the mind of man,
                restrict alternatives to the mind of man.

    The tendrils of evolution can caress,
                can appeal to,
                can snuggle up to,
                the mind of man.

The mind of man dwells within the soul of man.

The mind of man when beset by tendrils loses control of the direction of his walk,
                      loses control of his agency of choice,
                      loses control through the muffling of his soul.

The Banner of The Kingdom presents queries to the mind of man,
                      is confirmed by the free spirit of man,
                      is defensive or offensive depending on the need.

The Banner of The Kingdom has a multitude of tasks,
                      reveals when justified,
                      conceals in the absence of demand."

My Content Study Aid

The Keys of The Kingdom

"The Kingdom of God is as The Kingdom of Heaven,
        images The Kingdom of Heaven,
        and The Kingdom of Heaven have keys that cross fit.

The Kingdom of God has keys that are not unique,
        that turn the locks,
        that open doors.

Keys that are turned on Earth are turned in Heaven,
        that are immobile on Earth are immobile in Heaven,
        that enable access on Earth enable access in Heaven.

Keys that are held by the righteous are honoured in Heaven,
        that are operated by the righteous are upheld in Heaven,
        that are used with authority have predictable results.

The Keys to The Kingdom of God are there for man to seek,
        are there for man to find,
        are there for man to use with wisdom.

The Keys to The Kingdom of God recognize authority,
        recognize the settings of the locks,
        recognize the actions presently requested.

The Keys of The Kingdom of God were buried in The Cross,
        were slotted in The Cross,
        were withdrawn from The Cross.

The Keys of The Kingdom of God are operated with imparted wisdom,
        are known by those who would,
        are a blessing to those who hold them securely in
                their spirit.

The Keys of The Kingdom of God have been presented to man,
        have been made available for use,
        have been located in The Word.

The Keys of The Kingdom of God can be disclosed by The Spirit,
        can be encouraged by The Spirit,
        can be enfranchised by The Spirit.

The Keys of The Kingdom of God are of significance to The Saints,
        are of significance in their lives,
        of significance in their walk with God,
        are a secret of God made known to man.

The Keys of The Kingdom of God offer access to many things,
> are offered to each soul.

The Keys of The Kingdom of God sometimes rust through a soul's disuse,
> should show the marks of constant use,
> slot in easily when polished.

The Kingdom's keys play many tunes,
> tinkle as they turn,
> delight in scales unheard by man.

The Kingdom's keys operate as if for a music box,
> are heard by those attuned,
> contribute to the music of the soul."

My Content Study Aid

The Banner Setting Forth

"The Banner of The Kingdom is for acceptance by The Saints,
        is for understanding by The Saints,
        is for the blessing of The Saints.

The Banner of The Kingdom is there to bless The Saints within the marketplace,
        to direct footsteps to their doors,
        to encourage an exchange of blessings.

The Emblem of The Spirit is there to proclaim belonging,
        to make known the liked with like,
        to comfort those who travel.

The Emblem of The Spirit speaks of covenants established,
        speaks of covenants upheld,
        speaks of hopes that can be herewith shared.

The Emblem of The Spirit frees the spirit of man in recognition,
        frees the soul of man to share a testimony,
        frees the mind of man from the fear of man.

The Emblem of The Spirit uplifts the eyes of The Saints,
        uplifts the hearts of The Saints,
        uplifts the walk of a lonely saint.

The Emblem of The Spirit invites communication,
        invites the breaking of a barrier,
        invites a long and lasting friendship.

The Emblem of The Spirit seeks to share an understanding,
        seeks to start a new beginning,
        seeks to save the wounded with a desolated soul.

The Banner of The Kingdom has started on a journey of succession,
        has started on a journey with no end,
        has started on a journey of exaltation.

The Banner of The Kingdom has started on a road that it will conquer,
        has started on a road with many offshoots,
        has started on a voyage of discovery in a ship that will
                not sink.

The Banner of The Kingdom has started on the back of revelation,
        on the back of the white horse,
        as an arrow in a quiver on the back of one with
                eyes of fire."

The Banner on The Way

"The Banner of The Kingdom has a journey in the making.
The Banner of The Kingdom has a journey worth following.
The Banner of The Kingdom has a journey of accompaniment.

The Banner of The Kingdom has a journey of participation,
      a journey of declaration,
      a journey of restoration.

The Banner of The Kingdom has a journey of the record,
      a journey of assistance,
      a journey of service.

The Banner of The Kingdom has a journey of great distance,
      has a journey of great heights,
      has a journey of great depths—
            into the soul of man.

The Banner of The Kingdom seeks company that sings,
      seeks company that is joyous,
      seeks company that prays.

The Banner of The Kingdom is at home within the vanguards,
      is at home within the residents,
      is at home within the travellers.

The Banner of The Kingdom is at home within The Saints.

The Banner of The Kingdom has a time-frame for succession,
      is as the trumpet call of God,
      is at the crossroads of time.

The Banner of The Kingdom sees the changing of an age.

The Banner of The Kingdom has been blessed by The Father,
      has been unfurled by The Lion,
      accompanies The Lamb.

The Banner of The Kingdom has edges hedged with fire that does not scorch.

The Banner of The Kingdom confirms the future of man,
      confirms the life expectancy of man,
      confirms the importance of the placement of The Faith
                of man,
       the importance of The Faith of man,
       the importance of the being of man.

The Banner of The Kingdom confirms the lifelong need of the soul of man."

The Rising of The Son

"The Son rises to meet the new dawn,
      rises in The Will of The Father,
      rises with The Spirit,
      rises in His Glory,
      rises entrained,
      rises enrobed,
      rises acclaimed.

The Son rises to the sound of Heaven,
      rises to the sound of Earth,
      rises to a chorus,
      rises to ovations,
      rises to an inheritance,
      rises to His wedding,
      rises as The Groom.

The Son rises for a purpose,
      rises for bestowal,
      rises to receive,
      rises to speak,
      rises to declare,
      rises to accept,
      rises to acknowledge.

The rising of The Son is an event of grandeur,
      is an event of majesty,
      is an event of first magnitude in lives,
      brings shadows to the pastures of The Earth,
      brings areas not lit by light,
      shows where darkness still resides.

The rising of The Son is greeted with great glee,
      is greeted with some ignorance,
      is greeted by much dissent,
      is a promise long foretold,
      is a change to the life of man.

The rising of The Son is of benefit to the jubilant,
      of concern to the lawful,
      of disaster to the rebellious.

The rising of The Son brings gratitude to the wise.

The rising of The Son leads into a new realization of surroundings,
    into a new standard of behaviour,
    into a new appreciation of what is meant by justice.

The rising of The Son leads into a new expression of love,
    into a new storehouse of provisioning,
    into a new Kingdom of The Kingdom."

My Content Study Aid

The Banner of Assails

"The Banner of The Kingdom assails corruption on The Earth,
        assails the hands of greed,
        assails the feet that trample.

The Banner of The Kingdom assails the narrowing of eyes,
        assails the deafened ear,
        assails the closed mind.

The Banner of The Kingdom assails The Truth-denying soul.

The Banner of The Kingdom assails the might of conquest,
        assails the force of intimidation,
        assails the power of injustice.

The Banner of The Kingdom assails the flames of desolation,
        assails the caves of obscenity,
        assails the walls of captivity.

The Banner of The Kingdom assails the iniquity of man.

The Banner of The Kingdom assails the broadcasting of lies,
        assails the broadcasting of enmity,
        assails the broadcasting of deception.

The Banner of The Kingdom assails the assault of ignorance,
        assails the assault of poverty,
        assails the assault of hunger.

The Banner of The Kingdom assails all that precludes man's attaining of his destiny of
        walking in the garden of The Kingdom.

The Banner of The Kingdom asserts the right to love,
        asserts the right to peace,
        asserts the right to a life of victory.

The Banner of The Kingdom asserts the right to be,
        asserts the right to live,
        asserts the right to exercise freewill.

The Banner of The Kingdom asserts the authority of light,
        asserts the positioning of The Kingdom,
        asserts the coming of The Kingdom.

The Banner of The Kingdom builds on the victories of the past,
        builds on the martyrdom of saints,
        builds on the willingness of the righteous.

The Banner of The Kingdom builds on testimonies made known,
>builds on Faith declared,
>builds on the counsel of The Spirit.

The Banner of The Kingdom builds on the groundswell of commitment,
>builds on the groundswell of the church,
>builds on the groundswell of the body of The Bride.

The Banner of The Kingdom is building on what has gone before,
>is building on the sacrifices made,
>is building on the ordination of The Word."

My Content Study Aid

The Banner in its Presence

"The Banner of The Kingdom of God is not a matter with which to trifle,
        is to be taken seriously,
           exists before the eyes of man.

The Banner of The Kingdom of God is accompanied by the revealed word of God,
        is accompanied by The Spirit of God,
          is accompanied by signs.

The Banner of The Kingdom of God is not to be forsaken after a cursory glance,
        is not to be dismissed without understanding,
          is not to be ignored with the revealed word of God put aside.

  The revealed word of God is for these end-times of belief.

  The revealed word of God values the passage of time in the life of man.

The Banner of The Kingdom with the revealed word of God will segregate the level of
                            belief in man.

  Ponder diligently on the revealed word of God.

  A lack of understanding speaks of diligence not pursued,
        of seeking not sought,
          of wisdom not exercised.

  A lack of understanding is the defence of the fool.

  A lack of understanding convicts the tongue as it so speaks.

  A lack of understanding profanes the revealed word of God,
        profanes The Holy Spirit,
          profanes the seal of God.

The Banner of The Kingdom of God is as a golden umbrella,
        is as a refuge in the mountains,
          is as an extended wing of a dove.

The Banner of The Kingdom of God has descended from Heaven to The Earth.

The Banner of The Kingdom of God will bring delayed regret when declined,
        will bring delayed searching when needed,
          will bring delayed peace when close at hand.

The Banner of The Kingdom of God is a tool of The Kingdom.

The Kingdom of God has tools that are useful,
        has tools in frequent use,
          has tools that defy description.

The Kingdom of God has tools to be carried,
>> tools to be sent for,
>>> tools that have no weight.

The Kingdom of God has tools that can be seen,
>> has tools for the unforeseen,
>> has tools that can be sworn.

The Kingdom of God has tools for every purpose.

The Kingdom of God has tools that act like keys,
>> that are used as keys,
>> that are known as keys.

> The Keys of The Kingdom are offered to the hands of the righteous:
>> to the hands of the wise,
>> to the hands of each servant of The Lord."

My Content Study Aid

_____
_____
_____
_____
_____
_____
_____
_____
_____
_____
_____
_____
_____
_____
_____
_____
_____
_____
_____
_____
_____
_____
_____
_____
_____

The Banner at Home (& Pottage of Stew)

"The Banner of The Kingdom is at home in the garden of The Earth,
        is at home in the oases of wonder,
        is at home in the waterfalls of the veils.

The Banner of The Kingdom is at home in the adornment of the flowers,
        is at home in the delight of webs within the mists,
        is at home in the beauty of the decoration of the skies.

The Banner of The Kingdom is at home in the majesty of mountains near the seas,
        is at home in the expanses of the shorelines with
                seaborne scents,
        is at home in the nesting of mankind in the locations for
                their souls.

The Banner of The Kingdom loves the variety of life,
        the decoration of each nest,
        the hope expressed with each new birth.

The Banner of The Kingdom loves the relationships of man,
        the laughter of man,
        the dancing of man.

The Banner of The Kingdom loves the myriads of aspirations,
        the myriads of opinions,
        the myriads of expressions:
                that compose the face of man.

The face of man has many aspects worth reflection,
        many aspects worth noting,
        many aspects worth remembering.

The face of man:
        the presence of man,
        the integrity of man,
        the who of man,
        the what of man,
        the why of man—
            are not the occurrences of microbes in a mess.

The pottage of man's stew does not exist,
        has never been,
        will not be.

The pottage of man's stew is only there for the basis of dissent,
        never gave man birth.

The pottage of man's stew is a concept bred in minds that are berserk,
>   that have stopped thinking,
>   that would only justify.

The pottage of a mess decries a grand design,
>   denies man's common sense.

The pottage of a mess destroys the concept of a soul,
>   the concept of a spirit,
>   the concept of a destiny beyond the time of man.

The pottage of a mess has been proposed by Satan,
>   is supported by the enemy of man,
>   installs the proposition of the foe.

The pottage of a mess of stew as the birthplace of man beggars the imagination of man,
>   beggars the hopes of man,
>   beggars the future of man,
>   beggars the history of man,
>   beggars the presence of man,
>   beggars the activities of man.

The beggaring of man is done in the laboratories of Hell,
>   in the halls of hate,
>   in the caverns of the dead.

The beggaring of man is done by man himself.

The beggaring of man is under the guidance of the foe with a ring firmly set in the noses
>   of those who do not stop to think.

The beggaring of man results from the learned lacking wisdom,
>   the learned following their noses,
>   the learned behaving as lemmings in the race for
>   high esteem.

The Banner of The Kingdom will be seen at a judgement seat of justice when those who
>   led the beggaring of man,
>   who accepted,
>   by default,
>   the master of iniquity as their figurehead,
>   who did not join the battle of the just:
>   will be forever in the company of
>   those with the smell of sulphur in
>   the nostrils that were pierced.

The Banner of The Kingdom is never led by,
>   does not follow,
>   will not recognize:
>   noses that are pierced.

The Banner of The Kingdom leads to a destiny of Glory,
>	where The Son never sets,
>	where The Son has already risen."

My Content Study Aid

A Land of Plenty

"Far from The Kingdom of God lies a land of plenty.

A land of plenty that sacrifices to unknown gods,
        breeds a cult of worship of gods not known to the Risen King,
        believes it has no need for The God of its scriptures.

A land of plenty that has accepted gods of materialism,
        gods of humanism,
        gods of idolatries.

A land of plenty full of recriminations,
        full of anxieties within its soul,
        full of the cravings of its eyes.

A land of plenty that does not value life yet are hypocrites over deaths from the hands
        of others,
        that does not value the marriage bed but approves beds of defilement,
        that does not reverence the scriptures in the raising of a child.

A land of plenty that supplies poisons to its youth,
        poisoning its soul,
        poisoning its future.

A land of plenty that is governed by,
        exists within,
        slowly dying through,
        the destitution of its own morality.

A land of plenty that does not honour any flag in its respect for nationhood,
        that staggers as a drunkard with no place to sleep,
        that is without direction—
        to arrive at only God knows where,
        that belches from its stomach the sins of yesterday,
        that gurgles down its throat the sins set for today,
        that feeds into its soul—
            its mind—
                the sins that feed tomorrow.

A land of plenty is admired from many shores,
        is mired in its own mess;
        that extends welcomes to its guests,
        often claimed to be God's own.

A land of plenty that harbours great delusions,
        no longer in the shelters of God,
        no longer embraces the sanctity of life,

        no longer confesses its heritage of Faith,
        no longer honours the gifts of children in its midst,
        no longer has integrity in those with sporting prowess,
        no longer gives voice in concert to prayers of thanksgiving.

A land of plenty is not a land of greatness,
    is not a land of wisdom.

A land of plenty is not the harbinger of The Spirit,
        is not the harbinger of example,
        is not the harbinger of enlightenment.

A land of plenty can yet be the epitome of nationhood,
            the epitome of righteousness,
            the epitome of Truth.

A land of plenty can yet turn from,
        can yet be the antithesis of,
            the past;
                in the fulfilment of a vision,
                as the adoptee of a new beginning,
                in this:
                the onset of the three fold seventh century by
                      which the wise do measure time.

A land of plenty that once had wisdom can attain it once again,
        that knew and shed its blood on a distant land of favour.

A land of plenty that is a friend of God,
        that grieves the heart of God,
        that walks in the sight of God.

A land of plenty should reset its standards,
        should fly high its flags of jubilation,
        should uplift its banners of proclamation,
        that all may know a purpose re-established:
            a renewed belief,
            a turning from the past,
            a celebration of the future,
            the new dawn of righteousness—
                    the new dawning of things to come."

My Content Study Aid

_____

_____

The Favour of The Lord

"The favour of The Lord signifies a blessing,
        signifies a delightful occurrence that is unexpected,
          signifies the awareness of God to the lives that He attends.

The favour of The Lord falls as a daily occurrence,
        falls on hearts of thanksgiving,
        falls as a daily response.

The favour of The Lord is in response to prayer,
        in response to gratitude,
          in response to the acceptance of a call.

The favour of The Lord is in response to the loving of a heart,
        is in response to a lifestyle revealed,
        is in response to obedience displayed.

The favour of The Lord can be appreciated by discernment,
        should never be allocated to luck,
        should not be discarded with contempt.

The favour of The Lord is for each day's recognition,
        is for each day's prompting of the spirit,
        is for each day's communing with The Lord.

The favour of The Lord is for acknowledgement by the spirit,
        is for recognition as to origin,
        is for accompanying a walk in friendship.

The favour of The Lord should not be greeted with a yawn,
        should not be tolerated as to dust,
        should not be treated with irreverence that defiles a sacred act.

The favour of The Lord follows the servants of The Lord,
        follows the friends of God,
        follows the upholding of The Standard of The Kingdom.

The favour of The Lord is not to be easily dismissed,
        is not lightly bestowed.

The favour of The Lord encourages the perceptive,
        uplifts the poor in spirit,
        confirms a walk in fellowship.

The Favour of The Lord keeps the angels busy.

The Favour of The Lord reminds of incompleteness.

The Favour of The Lord is a sign from the presence of The Light."

Scribal Note:
> *Refer: 'The Favour of The Lord (2)', Bk 2,* 'GOD Speaks to Man on The Internet'

My Content Study Aid

The Race of The Righteous

"The walk of the righteous is inspected by God,
    reflects a walk of Faith,
    is determined by the level of Faith,
    is often not a walk,
    can become the running of the righteous,
    can become the race of the righteous.

The race of the righteous is a joy to behold,
    has no losers in its midst.

The race of the righteous has an end in sight,
    has a goal of attainment at the mountain top,
    has constant communing with The Spirit throughout their
        journey into Glory.

The race of the righteous is known by the songs heard by the angels as they come and go.

The race of the righteous has no stragglers at the tail,
    gathers stragglers into their midst,
    has mighty power in its momentum,
    is very difficult to stop,
    is viewed with dismay by eyes of knowledge without wisdom,
    hurdles obstacles in its path.

The race of the righteous is run by those with batons,
    shares and places the batons,
    quickly recovers a baton that is dropped,
    intends to hand each baton on,
    has inscriptions on their batons,
    is refreshed at the way-stations of The Lord.

The race of the righteous has onlookers galore,
    collects signatures of sincerity,
    carries scrolls of supporters.

The race of the righteous encourages onlookers to join,
    encourages onlookers to sign,
    encourages onlookers to participate with the baton they
        are offered.

The race of the righteous passes on the scrolls within their batons when they reach the
    victors' stands.

The race of the righteous ends with celebrations,
    ends with congratulations,
    ends with the gift of promise.

The race of the righteous starts with a commitment,
ends with a transition."

My Content Study Aid

The Beauty of The Earth

"The beauty of Earth does not compare with the beauty of Heaven.

The beauty of Earth is there for all to behold,
        for all to tread its paths,
        for all to wonder at its being.

The beauty of Earth oscillates with seasons,
        oscillates with light and dark,
        oscillates with rise and fall.

The beauty of Earth oscillates with tempest and calm,
        oscillates with life and death,
        oscillates with discovery and loss.

The beauty of Earth oscillates at The Will of God.

The beauty of Earth is for the perception of man,
        is for the education of man,
        is for the appreciation of man.

The beauty of Earth enhances the life of man,
        opens the eyes of man,
        opens the ears of man.

The beauty of Earth is there for the senses of man,
        for the growth of his spirit,
        for the harbouring of his soul.

The beauty of The Earth,
    the beauty of the seas,
    the beauty of the air,
    the beauty of all life:
        all are there to testify of a guardian with authority,
                one with a vested interest,
                one with a grand design.

The beauty of The Earth shudders at an onslaught,
        struggles to repair,
        has her dresses ripped.

The ripping of a dress depletes the wardrobe of The Earth.

The ripping of a dress signifies a loss,
        does irreparable harm,
        leads to a dustbin without a lid.

    A ripped dress releases dust from within the dustbin.

Dust will spread widely once released.

Dust should be confined within the dustbin for the benefit of life,
>> the destiny of man,
>> the beauty of The Earth.

The ripping of a dress speaks of lack of care,
> speaks of lack of stewardship,
>> speaks of snubbing the designer of the dress.

The ripping of a dress speaks of an attitude of greed,
> an attitude of selfishness,
>> an attitude that is not amenable to the sustainability
>>> of life.

The ripping of a dress leads to the destruction of the mantle of The Earth.

The ripping of a dress leads to the need for a new wardrobe.

The ripping of a dress leads to the need for a change of government."

My Content Study Aid

_____
_____
_____
_____
_____
_____
_____
_____
_____
_____
_____
_____
_____
_____
_____
_____
_____
_____
_____
_____

The Troops of The Lord

"The troops of The Lord gather in preparation for the storm,
        gather in preparation for the battle,
        gather in the vanguard of the storm.

The troops of The Lord lead in the storm of the citadels of darkness.
    The citadels of darkness will not stand intact against the storm of the troops of
                                              The Lord.

The troops of The Lord have long been aware of their assignment.

The troops of The Lord are glad of an imminent command,
        are in serried ranks,
        are in close formation.

The troops of The Lord have their Standards at the ready,
        their weapons presented,
        their shields all to the fore.

The troops of The Lord arrayed in their battle armour are a sight to behold,
                are a sight that intimidates,
                are a sight that has the scent of victory.

The troops of The Lord have diverse modes of operation,
        are very difficult to wound,
        have their wounds dressed on the fields of battle,
        do not march to the beating of drums,
        scurry back and forth.

The troops of The Lord are listening for,
        are watching for,
        are moving with,
                the clarion call of God.

The clarion call of God is always heard above the din of battle,
        marshals and directs,
        commands the battles of The Spirit,

The troops of The Lord hearken to the clarion call of God.

The clarion call of God strikes fear into the foe,
            fear into the inhabitants of the citadels,
            fear into those commanding the high places,
            fear into those self-instated at the gates of entry.

The fear of God precedes a rout.

The fear of God precedes the emptying of the citadels,
> the deserting of the high places,
> the vacating of the gates.

The fear of God precedes the advancement of the troops of The Lord,
> precedes the proclamation of possession by The Standard of
>> The Kingdom,
>
> precedes the territory forsaken by the foe,
> The Freewill of man regained:
> the freedom for man to choose his destiny with wisdom not besmirched."

"Who can stand before the battle plan of The Lord?
Who can stand before the breath of The Lord?
Who can stand before The Hosts of Heaven to take the territories so declared?
> Only My servants."

My Content Study Aid

_____
_____
_____
_____
_____
_____
_____
_____
_____
_____
_____
_____
_____
_____
_____
_____
_____
_____
_____
_____

The Candles of The Lord

"The fireworks of The Earth fascinate the eyes of man,
                capture the imagination of man,
                keep man at abeyance.

The fireworks of The Earth speak of a grand design,
                speak of a great furnace,
                speak of a great outpouring.

The fireworks of The Earth intimidate with molten majesty,
                intimidate with plumes of spectacle,
                intimidate with tongues that utter from within the depths of
                                                          The Earth.

The fireworks of The Earth secrete the sweatings of The Earth,
                escalate then fade,
                display with prior warnings,
                can be measured and assessed,
                are uncontrollable by man,
                hold man in their thrall.

The fireworks of The Earth are spectacles of wonder,
                are testimonies of power,
                are monuments to the sculptor that releases them from
                                                            The Earth.

The fireworks of The Earth play and dance to a tune that they know well,
                      to an orchestrated cycle that ebbs and flows,
                              swelling by additions,
                              repelling all intrusions.

The fireworks of The Earth simmer to an oft repeated chorus that bids no life approach,
                            that bids no life infringe,
                            that bids no life to dwell
                            within allotted reservations.

The fireworks of The Earth shout in announcement as with a crash of thunder,
                      withdraw into departure as with an exhausted sigh.

The fireworks of The Earth mesmerize the wayward,
                give warning to the wise,
                provide warmth to the intrepid.

The fireworks of The Earth are the candles of The Lord.

    Man should not try to blow-out,
                to snuff,
                to stand before the candles of The Lord."

The Sanctity of Life

"The sanctity of life carries a crown of preservation.

The sanctity of life is an edict from The Lord,
        has overtures of eternity,
        has the highest of priorities.

The sanctity of life speaks of a commitment of love,
           a commitment of unselfishness,
           a commitment of humility.

The sanctity of life requires a commitment of protection,
           a commitment of sharing,
           a commitment of enlightenment.

The sanctity of life calls for a soul filled with respect,
        calls for a soul that wills no harm,
        calls for a soul that abhors violence.

The sanctity of life forbids the withdrawal of the needs of life,
        forbids the withdrawal of the seeds of life,
        forbids the withdrawal of the embryos of life.

The sanctity of life is at the forefront of creation,
        is at the forefront of humanity,
        is at the forefront of the wonder of new birth.

The sanctity of life is built on generations counted,
        on generations surviving,
        on generations not breeding monsters of destruction.

Monsters of destruction are not limited by gender,
        defile the integrity of the womb,
        breach the seal of protection,
        ignore the sovereignty of the crown,
        discount priorities as set,
        tear open the envelope that carries a letter to the world.

Monsters of destruction burrow into the sacrosanct,
        burrow past the walls that testify,
        burrow round the screens of conscience.

Monsters of destruction burrow where they should not,
        dismember tenants that they should not,
        care not when they should.

Monsters of destruction care not for past oaths,
        care not for such sanctity,

care only for the pay cheques that their bloodied hands have
usurped from the living that are dead.

Monsters of destruction,
the coterie of vultures,
all that hover round and wait to feed:
have themselves,
their lives,
in danger of destruction.

Monsters of destruction will soon stand before a robed bench where the edict of The Lord
will be laid before their feet,
the edict of The Lord that they scuffed into the dust,
the edict of The Lord that they swore to uphold:
the edict of The Lord that will call them to account."

My Content Study Aid

The Plank of A Nation

"A nation should rejoice in celebration of its birth,
        should know of the purpose for its creation,
        should be grateful for a history with A Lion.

A nation's plank of creation should be an object of thanksgiving,
            should uplift the peoples thereby committed,
            should give security of tenure.

A nation's plank of creation holds a vision for the future,
            has signatures bound in agreement,
            has brevity with wisdom,
            has hope laced with trust,
            has sharing of resources that neither favour nor deprive.

A nation's plank of creation is the start of a new beginning.

    The journey of a nation never follows a straight path.

    The rearward glance at a nation's footsteps is there for all to see.

    The rearward glance slows a forward journey,
            causes a conference of souls,
            spreads missions of dissent.

The creation planks of nations rarely have splinters at their birth.

The creation planks of nations are hacked at by the greedy,
            are whittled by the wily,
            are spliced for expansion,
            are bonded to abstraction,
            are later heard to utter what the tongues of the signatures
                      never spoke when signing.

The creation plank of a nation is not open to re-interpretation when the journey's
                      well begun.

The creation plank of a nation is to be honoured without equivocation.

The creation plank of a nation does not change according to discoveries,
            according to the self-aggrieved,
            according to the benefits that fall into the
                hands that labour.

The creation plank of a nation does not fluctuate in intent because of more recent values.

The creation plank of a nation is not to be splintered to rejection,
            is not to be splintered born through malice,

is not to be splintered born through murmuring from those
with their own agendas.

A nation cannot be of one voice if the plank of its creation is later filled with splinters
of injustice.

The journey of a nation is as according to the divisions of man.

The forward glance at a nation's future encourages a vision made known.

The forward glance shines as a light on a way of life with wonders,
speeds all to a common goal,
brings unity of purpose not easily distracted.

The creation plank of a nation is steeped in hallowed ground.

The creation plank of a nation speaks to the present of the past,
speaks to the present of the future,
makes possible a vision on a tablet for the herald with
which to run.

The creation plank of a nation speaks of The God that first invested in a plank,
that invested in the builder of the nations,
that was invested with due reverence within the lives of
those who knew.

The creation plank of a nation should not be readily overturned,
stood before the faces of men who swore that it was so.

The creation plank of a nation stands before The God who witnessed it and knows."

My Content Study Aid

The Galleons of Service

"The galleons of service move wares to and fro,
                move over the face of The Earth,
                move at the will of man,
                fade into the night,
                broach a new dawn.

The galleons of service have a myriad of pathways,
                have a myriad of commanders,
                have a myriad of owners.

The galleons of service satisfy the demands of the marketplace of man:
                satisfy the demands of elapsed time,
                satisfy the demands of the method of propulsion,
                satisfy the demands of each selected pathway.

The galleons of service satisfy the needs of man,
                satisfy the wants of man,
                satisfy the cravings of man.

The galleons of service operate without a soul,
                operate with names of fancy,
                operate with a moving rate set by the one who counts the gain.

The galleons of service are the new behemoths of The Earth,
                the unequal consumers of its fuel,
                the contributors to the winds of change.

The galleons of service care not where they go,
                care not for their frequency,
                care not for the depth of ill will that they carry.

The galleons of service are created by man with eyes set on the purse-strings of the gain.

The galleons of service do not yet use the wind,
                know how to use the sun in part,
                do not yet use the embrace of the moon on the woman who
                                    continues on her way,
                to separate the waters so they can recombine.

The galleons of service have cargoes fit for the hungry,
                have cargoes fit for construction,
                have cargoes fit for destruction.

The galleons of service have cargoes of enslavement,
                have cargoes of little use,
                have cargoes eagerly awaited.

The cargoes of The Earth have manifests that cheat,
>have manifests that defraud,
>have manifests that were written in the dark.

The galleons of service can be directed by those that serve in righteousness,
>those that serve with the honour of their house intact,
>those that maintain the integrity of A King,
>those that transport in justice for the benefit of all:
>those are they whose galleons will serve under The Flag of The Kingdom,
>those are they who will stand with The Standard of The King,
>those are they who know The Emblem of The Spirit and this move of God."

My Content Study Aid

The Vapours of The Earth

"The vapours of The Earth are of concern to man.
The vapours of The Earth are of concern to God.

The vapours of The Earth form the breath of man,
           form the breath of animals,
           form the breath of all that have the gift of life.

The vapours of The Earth rest upon The Earth.

The vapours of The Earth are stable within bounds.

The vapours of The Earth do not vie to escape,
           do not vie to compensate,
           do not vie to extend a zone.

The vapours of The Earth is a dress within a wardrobe,
           a dress that is daily worn,
           a dress that fits tightly,
                  that restricts freedom of movement,
                  that hinders full production.

The vapours of The Earth are added to by man,
           are not subtracted from by man.

The vapours of The Earth have their stability under threat.

The vapours of The Earth depend on the pathways of the seas,
           on the pathways of the rain,
           on the winds of change.

The vapours of The Earth depend on the candles of The Lord.

The vapours of The Earth depend on the canopies of The Earth,
                on the depletion of resources long buried beneath
                                            The Earth,
                on the labouring of the tools of man.

The vapours of The Earth no longer tend the purity of covering that falls upon The Earth.

The vapours of The Earth bring oscillations of variance.

The vapours of The Earth notice the shrinkage in the dress of covering that removes a
                                                        balance of a surplus.

The vapours of The Earth regard,
           respond to,
           withdraw from,
                the changes in the visage of The Earth,

> the dressage of The Earth,
> the wardrobe of The Earth.

The wardrobe of The Earth hangs dresses of differing sizes,
> hangs dresses that may be changed depending on The Son,
>> depending on the need,
>> depending on the day.

The wardrobe of The Earth has dresses of a size that should not be needed,
> of sizes that can only burst at the seams.

The wardrobe of The Earth pants and does not shiver,
> has its doors flapping open,
> has dresses for selection that hang in need of repair,
> dresses that are torn,
> dresses that are damaged,
> dresses that are crumpled:
> so their domes no longer fit the anchor points of Earth.

The wisdom of man is yet to be seen in concerted action.

The wisdom of man is evident as slash and burn,
> as hack and hoe,
> as net and plunder.

The wisdom of man is yet,
> in his dominion,
>> to return to the ancient shepherd's love that would sustain both
>>> the flock and the pasture whereon they need to graze.

The wisdom of God may yet be taught to the men of the north.

The men of the north have long ago descended on The Earth with intent to violate
> and pillage,
> to commandeer,
> to subjugate,
> to bring into,
> to keep within,
> the bounds of subservience in their quest for
>> expansion of their spheres of influence.

The men of the north are now over all The Earth in their pursuit of the wealth of man:
> continue on their ways,
> are devious in their ways,
> have caused distress to peoples of nobility,
> have sown seeds of destruction in peoples far and wide.

The men of the north did not bring happiness as their companion;
> brought enslavement to time and labour for a pittance;
> stand atop their mountains and frown on others as they climb,

>discourage with a kick,
>block the pathways as they climb;
>guard their wealth with a ruthlessness that beggars other men.

The men of the north are under the eye of The God of Nations,
>are under the imprint of The Spirit,
>are under The Call of God to their souls.

The God of their forbears,
The God who was there when they launched upon their journeys,
The God who remembers well the prayers that were uttered,
>by tongues at departure,
>by tongues upon arrival,
>holds the families of inheritance responsible for their actions:
>the actions that now oscillate the vapours of The Earth and cause
>>the wardrobe's doors to flap."

My Content Study Aid

The Coming of The Son

"The coming of The Son Lights a certain day.

The coming of The Son begs patience from a few,
               predicates belief upon the word,
               beseeches preparation by the sheep,
               astonishes the goats,
               confounds those in denial,
               is a day as no other in the memory of man.

The coming of The Son brings changes of governments,
               starts the endowing of the nations,
               confirms the settlement that precedes the coronation of a
                    monarch of royal descent.

A monarch of royal descent is decreed by Heaven.

The monarch of royal descent knows of an empty throne,
               is of the lineage of David,
               claims The Throne that is destined to be His,
               will never be deposed,
               is ordained to rule.

The Monarch of Royal Descent,
          The I AM of the Heavens,
          The Prince of Peace,
          The Lamb of God,
          The Son of God,
          The Bright and Morning Star,
          The Lord of All Creation,
          is about to be seated on The Throne of Homage.

  The Throne of Homage stands before the face of man,
               before the face of all creation that will admit "Jesus
                                      is Lord".

The coming of The Son has the seal of Heaven,
               has the seal of reconciliation,
               has the seal of a new covenant upheld.

The coming of The Son signifies a change of habitation,
               a change of residence,
               a change of presence.

The coming of The Son denotes A King about to take up residence,
               His Standard soon to so mark,

His Flag soon to so lay claim for the authority that will reside.

The coming of The Son is welcomed by The Banner of His Kingdom."

My Content Study Aid

The Commitments of Man

"The fall of Rome was based on a fall of confidence,
        occurred because of a lack of belief,
        was because of a commitment that was missing.

A commitment that is missing is of short duration,
        without strength does not arm the soul,
        made of straw has no weight behind it,
        with no heart will not see out the day.

A commitment born of greed will increase with the gain,
        will shrink with the loss.

A commitment of the spirit will support the uttered word,
        has no need of a signature,
        does not quibble at the consequences,
        teaches honour to the soul,
        validates belief,
        has Faith in an outcome.

A commitment of the spirit is extended without rancour,
        rewards the righteous walk,
        is not broken by the spirit,
        sees the end result,
        is transferred at a handclasp,
        is settled with a smile.

A commitment with a scrutiny brings anxiety to the soul,
        is settled out of favour,
        seeks ways of escape,
        carries ill-will behind a veil,
        oft calls for the presence of a judge,
        has signatures disowned.

A commitment with a scrutiny breeds an offence that lasts,
        speaks of scales that no longer balance,
        is a warning to the wise,
        is through eyes that water in advance,
        seeks an advantage that did not exist,
        attempts to share a loss.

A commitment always has important overtones,
        always has far reaching effects,
        should not be entered into lightly.

A commitment always imparts a lesson,

        always has an end result,
        always ends with honour or disgrace.

The commitment of the spirit outweighs the commitment of the soul.
The commitment of the conscience outweighs the commitment of the mind.
The commitment of the conscience lingers in the mind.

The commitment of the body is not held to account,
        is but a spasm of intent,
        has to be continually renewed,
        generates demands for relief,
        often wants to rest,
        is fragile in extension.

The commitment that is offered depends upon the security of the servant,
        depends upon the way it was imparted,
        depends upon the history of the soul,
            the history of the spirit,
            the history of the body,
        depends upon the means of acceptance.

The commitment that is in force depends upon:
        the longevity of temptations,
        the activities of a foe,
        the source of that commitment:
            whether of the soul,
                the spirit,
            or the body,
        the resolution of a scrutiny,
            and the purpose thereof.

A commitment is fulfilled by the wise,
        is breached by the transient,
        is forgotten by the foolish.

The commitments of The Lord stand,
        will be upheld and fulfilled,
        will be honoured and secure,
        as are the releases of The Cross with the promise of
            salvation in this time of Grace."

My Content Study Aid

_____
_____
_____

The Birthday of A Saint

"The birthday of a saint is to be remembered,
                was not achieved without an effort,
                exists because of time.

The birthday of a saint is a milestone in a career,
                signifies a commitment to the future,
                spreads relationships within a family,
                focuses the eyes of the parents,
                is marked with presents from afar,
                is a life event of man.

The birthday of a saint is shouted far and wide,
                should never be a secret,
                is a time of learning,
                is a time of salutation,
                bestows pleasure on the gathered,
                is cause for celebration.

The birthday of a saint brings smiles to many faces,
                initiates events that are eagerly awaited,
                is echoed in the heavens,
                commences a battle royal,
                commences the quest for a settled destiny,
                commences the journey home.

The birthday of a saint leads to the teaching of the signposts,
                marks the abilities of man,
                brings memories to the present,
                brings honour to the parents,
                is a blessing of grey hair,
                is a blessing at a wedding.

The birthday of a saint speaks of the birthday of a saint."

My Content Study Aid

_____
_____
_____
_____
_____

The Garden of The Lord

"The garden of The Lord is tended by expert hands,
        exhibits all of creation.

The garden of The Lord has reflections of vast proportions,
        has shadows of many colours,
        has aromas that question the senses of the mind.

The garden of The Lord has the vistas of The Spirit,
        has meanderings of magnitude,
        has scopes that fill the outlook of the eye that stares in wonder.

The garden of The Lord has plantings that follow footsteps of deliberation.

The garden of The Lord has moonbeams with the icicles,
        has sunbeams dancing with the birdsong,
        has flowers in minuet with the whispering of leaves.

The garden of The Lord is a celebration of design.

The garden of The Lord glories in reflection,
        glories in relaxation,
        glories in remembrance.

The garden of The Lord is a place to linger,
        is a place to learn,
        is a place to comprehend where a previous impossibility is not
                even an improbability.

The garden of The Lord has clashes with prior reasoning,
        has items that defy the logistics of supply,
        has nurture and nature in perfect harmony.

The garden of The Lord has content not previously seen,
        has content not previously available to assail the senses of man,
        has content long at home in the garden of grand design.

The garden of The Lord has flora and fauna that never went extinct.
        contains no fear of any occupants.

The garden of The Lord reflects the serenity of surroundings of each living thing,
              as planted in a masterpiece of perfection.

The garden of The Lord can be a walk through time,
        can be a walk on time,
        can be a walk outside time.

The garden of The Lord will never be forgotten,
        will never be contaminated,

will never evict its guests.

The garden of The Lord will always greet the righteous,
        will always greet the beloved,
        will always greet those who hold and operate The Keys of
                            The Kingdom.

The garden of The Lord is bypassed by those who shunned the sanctuaries of attendance,
        is closed to those who were foolish beyond belief,
        is non-existent for those who had no faith.

The garden of The Lord is for those with their gowns bejewelled,
                      that were not razed by fire."

My Content Study Aid

The Coming of The Spirit

"The coming of The Spirit is not on the timelines of man,
                varies with the season,
                is auspicious to man.

The coming of The Spirit is an encouragement to The Saints,
                is evident to the lost,
                confirms the actions of The Saints.

The coming of The Spirit brings a balcony of fire,
                attends those most in need,
                shepherds all before.

The coming of The Spirit is as a whirlwind of fire,
                neither harms nor hurts,
                heals and enlightens.

The coming of The Spirit justifies existence,
                hurtles to the fore,
                is directed by The Lord.

The coming of The Spirit is attended by many angels,
                breaks barriers of time,
                brings Glory with His freedom.

The coming of The Spirit is never not noticed,
                is the luxury of The Word,
                frightens and delights.

The coming of The Spirit eliminates all doubt,
                enhances Faith that captures,
                gives meaning to 'Disciples'.

The coming of The Spirit brings frequent falls of ecstasy,
                brings mentoring of the mind,
                farewells the flight of demons.

The coming of The Spirit brings momentum to the fight,
                fortifies the battlements of The Temples,
                girds with The Will to conquer.

The coming of The Spirit is only in the walk with Christ,
                does not exist with other gods,
                is The Herald of Preparation.

The coming of The Spirit is distinct from an indwelling.
The coming of The Spirit leaves man wide open-mouthed.
The coming of The Spirit seeks The Saints who worship."

The Coming of The Trumpet Call

"The Coming of the Trumpet Call has a place in the history of man,
        reverberates throughout The Earth,
        alerts the listening and the watchful.

The Coming of the Trumpet Call is sounded from the heavens,
        is as a burning fuse,
        approaches at a gallop.

The Coming of the Trumpet Call is not bound by walls,
        permeates the waters,
        emanates from angels.

The Coming of the Trumpet Call will not be a whistle in the dark,
        will not be mistaken,
        will arouse the servants of The Lord:
                penetrates the longing hearts,
                vibrates within the waiting souls,
                speaks volumes to the waiting,
                determines right from wrong,
                verifies belief.

The Coming of the Trumpet Call brings the thunder of many hooves,
        heralds the rider on the white horse.

The Coming of the Trumpet Call is The War-cry of The Lord."

My Content Study Aid

The Coming of The Turmoil

"The coming of the turmoil is closer than is thought,
                brings grief for the unprepared,
                frees the hands of the iniquitous,
                brings sanctity of purpose,
                carries tribulation on its wings,
                warns of upheavals across the lands.

The coming of the turmoil destroys the trust of neighbours,
                imposes trust in God,
                will be recognized by all,
                changes governments and thrones,
                invests the weak with Kingdom authority,
                vacates the ways of man.

The coming of the turmoil metes out the ways of God,
                is the rampage of the souls,
                is the cowering of the spirits,
                is the boldness of the foe,
                convicts man of the right to govern,
                satiates man's lust.

The coming of the turmoil vindicates the righteous,
                strengthens the woebegone,
                gives voice to the cry for peace,
                awaits in the calm before the storm,
                ushers in the flames of man,
                ushers in the assaults of man.

The coming of the turmoil ushers in the atrocities of man,
                encounters The Call of hope,
                encounters The Call of Faith,
                encounters the cry that cannot be ignored,
                will terminate with the new dawn,
                terminates upon a single command.

The coming of the turmoil terminates with the rider who is just,
                        the rider who is Faithful,
                        the rider who is mounted on a steed seen to
                                          be white."

Precept upon Precept

Scribal Note: *I am directed to Isaiah 28:5–29 and thereon inscribing boldness, as requested:*

(The Bible, New King James Version)

Isa 28:5   In that day The Lord of hosts will be For a crown of glory and a diadem of beauty To the remnant of His people,

Isa 28:6   For a spirit of justice to him who sits in judgement, And for strength to those who turn back the battle at the gate.

Isa 28:7   But they also have erred through wine, And through intoxicating drink are out of the way; The priest and the prophet have erred through intoxicating drink, They are swallowed up by wine, They are out of the way through intoxicating drink; They err in vision, they stumble [in] judgement.

Isa 28:8   For all tables are full of vomit [and] filth; No place [is clean].

Isa 28:9   "Whom will he teach knowledge? And whom will he make to understand the message? Those [just] weaned from milk? Those [just] drawn from the breasts?

Isa 28:10   For precept [must be] upon precept, precept upon precept, Line upon line, line upon line, Here a little, there a little."

Isa 28:11   For with stammering lips and another tongue He will speak to this people,

Isa 28:12   To whom He said, "This [is] the rest [with which] You may cause the weary to rest," And, "This [is] the refreshing"; Yet they would not hear.

Isa 28:13   But the word of The Lord was to them, "Precept upon precept, precept upon precept, Line upon line, line upon line, Here a little, there a little," That they might go and fall backward, and be broken And snared and caught.

Isa 28:14   **Therefore hear the word of The Lord, you scornful men**, Who rule this people who [are] in Jerusalem,

Isa 28:15   Because you have said, "We have made a covenant with death, And with Sheol we are in agreement. When the overflowing scourge passes through, It will not come to us, For we have made lies our refuge, And under falsehood we have hidden ourselves."

Isa 28:16   Therefore thus says The Lord GOD: "Behold, I lay in Zion a stone for a foundation, A tried stone, a precious cornerstone, a sure foundation; Whoever believes will not act hastily.

Isa 28:17   Also I will make justice the measuring line, And righteousness the plummet; The hail will sweep away the refuge of lies, And the waters will overflow the hiding place.

Isa 28:18   Your covenant with death will be annulled, And your agreement with Sheol will not stand; When the overflowing scourge passes through, Then you will be trampled down by it.

Isa 28:19   As often as it goes out it will take you; For morning by morning it will pass over, And by day and by night; It will be a terror just to understand the report."

Isa 28:20   For the bed is too short to stretch out [on], And the covering so narrow that one cannot wrap himself [in it].

Isa 28:21   For The Lord will rise up as [at] Mount Perazim, He will be angry as in the Valley of Gibeon— That He may do His work, His awesome work, And bring to pass His act, His unusual act.

Isa 28:22   Now therefore, do not be mockers, Lest your bonds be made strong; For I have heard from The Lord GOD of hosts, A destruction determined even upon the whole Earth.

Isa 28:23   Give ear and hear my voice, Listen and hear my speech.

Isa 28:24   Does the ploughman keep ploughing all day to sow? Does he keep turning his soil and breaking the clods?

Isa 28:25   When he has levelled its surface, Does he not sow the black cummin And scatter the cummin, Plant the wheat in rows, The barley in the appointed place, And the spelt in its place?

Isa 28:26   For He instructs him in right judgement, His God teaches him.

Isa 28:27   For the black cummin is not threshed with a threshing sledge, Nor is a cartwheel rolled over the cummin; But the black cummin is beaten out with a stick, And the cummin with a rod.

Isa 28:28   Bread [flour] must be ground; Therefore he does not thresh it forever, Break [it with] his cartwheel, Or crush it [with] his horsemen.

Isa 28:29   This also comes from The Lord of hosts, [Who] is wonderful in counsel [and] excellent in guidance.

My Content Study Aid

_____

_____

_____

_____

The Carriers of God's Wisdom

"The sails of the fortunate are set to catch the wind,
                trade before the wind,
                are not often caught by gusts,
                stay on an even keel,
                bend with a constant purpose,
                drive the galleons of commerce.

The sails of the fortunate are not found in the doldrums of the garage,
                in the doldrums of the harbour,
                in the doldrums of an airport.

The sails of the fortunate are not forced to linger in the dock,
                are blessed with fair winds for a journey,
                are not forsaken by its crew.

The sails of the fortunate are renowned for reliability,
                are renowned for trading that is fair,
                are renowned for their integrity.

The sails of the fortunate never seek to lure,
                never seek to bribe,
                never seek to dishonour The Standard they proclaim.

The sails of the fortunate drive the galleons worthy of their hire.

The wise seek out the galleons that are worthy,
        shun the galleons of the pirates,
        look past the jeopardising of the future for a benefit today.

The wise know full well the bargain of today is the robbery of tomorrow,
                the pleasure of the few is the discontent of the many,
                the scattering of largesse accompanies a meatless bone.

The wise do not break bread with the careless and the greedy,
            clasp hands with commitments written in the dirt,
            consider commitments with the stench of broken promises.

The wise are the carriers of The Wisdom of God,
        are made aware of the intent of a wayward heart,
        are repelled by promises of gain that appeal to avarice,
        are circumspect until they understand.

The wise do not commit in haste,
        do not have second thoughts.

The wise know The Fear of God,
        have been taught,

have sought.

The wise acknowledge The Truth revealed,
>> The Truth sustained,
>> The Truth proclaimed.

The wisdom of God imparts responsibility that the foolish will never know."

My Content Study Aid

The Footpaths of The Lord

"The footpaths of The Lord lead to the destination that is true,
> have no snares for the feet,
> are always in the light,
> are wide enough for wheels with seats,
> are curbed to mark the bounds,
> guide feet along their ways,
> stream with merry bands.

The footpaths of The Lord are neither walked in silence nor in solitude,
> are bereft of tollgates to despair,
> do not cause the feet to ache,
> are filled with arms that link.

The footpaths of The Lord share the sounds of laughter,
> share the music of the spirit,
> share the singing of the soul.

The footpaths of The Lord cross over all the paths of man,
> carry hurts until discarded,
> can be ridden as on a moving ramp,
> neither stall nor stop.

The footpaths of The Lord can be entered on,
> can be exited from.

The footpaths of The Lord are re-entered at the egress point that brought the journey to
> a halt.

The footpaths of The Lord will not carry those with second thoughts,
> those who choose to walk in directions that are contrary,
> those who mock or scorn along the way.

The footpaths of The Lord are trod in golden slippers,
> are lit for all the feet,
> carry the travellers past the grave,
> end in the garden of The Spirit.

The footpaths of The Lord lead through the gates of Heaven,
> pass by the gates of Hell,
> permit the boarding of those escaping through the flames.

The footpaths of The Lord are shepherded by angels,
> coalesce into a highway,
> gather far and wide,
> serve all who were once lost,
> have glimpses of a future,

> carry the counted of The Lord,
> carry those with entries in The Book of Life.

The footpaths of The Lord form the thoroughfare to Heaven,
> the route that does not waver,
> the way of all Disciples that leads all servants home."

My Content Study Aid

The Distractions of Man

"The distractions of man are many and varied,
    are not to be confused with the works of God,
    serve gods of double-mindedness.

The distractions of man draw man to himself,
    draw man away from God,
    steal the contents of his time.

The distractions of man bear resemblances to the placement of a child's toys upon
                     a floor,
    require a bended knee to repair the damage,
    cause lapses in concentration.

The distractions of man are instigated by the one who comes to plunder the time-span
                     of man,

The distractions of man give no surety of return,
    give no surety of reward,
    give no surety of love in an old age,
    give no surety that all is well within a family,
    do not care for man.

The distractions of man bring a holocaust of poverty,
    are designed to beggar,
    are intended to enslave with things of little worth attained at
                     great expense,
    occupy his life time,
    do not bring happiness upon reflection,
    enhance an image only in the imagination.

The distractions of man tear children from a throne,
    send spouses to a dungeon,
    are evidence of selfishness,
    accumulate and are stored,
    break and are discarded,
    do not decorate the gowns of life.

The distractions of man dwell with lips open with excuses,
    with ears immune to many pleas,
    with eyes that do not want to see.

The distractions of man should be seen for what they are,
    should be ignored without commitment,
    should not be picked-up and examined.

The distractions of man bring sorrow to a home,

        bring contentment for a moment,
        supersede the heart-cries for attention that would normally
                      be heard,
        change lifestyles for the worse,
        create no sense of gratitude,
        oversee the wayward passing of the time of man.

The distractions of man are of little or no benefit when seen on the landscape of a life.

The distractions of man will eventually be impounded,
        will eventually be deeply regretted,
        will eventually become spears of accusation that will wound
                      the soul,
        will eventually be burnt in flames of fire that cause no shadow on
                      The Earth,
        will eventually put in jeopardy a destiny considered safe."

My Content Study Aid

The Confines of The Spirit

"The confines of The Spirit are applied to man.

The confines of The Spirit keep man within his time,
        restrict man to his space,
        blind man beyond his scope.

The confines of The Spirit are for the benefit of man.,
        are for the benefit of other beings.

The confines of The Spirit are for the benefit of other spaces,
        the benefit of other locales,
        the benefit of other times.

The confines of The Spirit are essential for the management of time.

The confines of The Spirit do not have yearnings from restriction,
        have many vistas from which to choose,
        are not hesitant in application,
        have eternal considerations,
        vary with the imposition of man's variables to his state of being,
        determine the dwelling place of man.

The confines of The Spirit never cause tears of remorse,
        do not select a destiny,
        neither punish nor judge,
        neither reward nor exalt.

The confines of The Spirit match surroundings to a way-station of The Lord.
        may be temporary or permanent,
        are permanent outside the time sphere of man.

The confines of The Spirit are so great that they cannot be breached by a traveller from within,
        are solely set by God,
        measure attributes by different rods.

The confines of The Spirit contain the handiworks of God,
        showcase the creations of God,
        display their masterpieces to a traveller.

The confines of The Spirit have their being in a palm."

The Polishing of The Soul

"The polishing of the soul is in the care of man.

The polishing of the soul smoothes out the wrinkles and the bumps,
        enables its reflection to shine with all due brightness.

The polishing of the soul relinquishes control of the tongue,
        threads a crystal needle with a golden thread,
        adopts The Spirit as its guide,
        brings no argument to the fore,
        makes it a joy to be around,
        gives fortitude to surf the waves of life without a fall.

The polishing of the soul occurs after the dross has been removed,
        occurs after images have been replaced,
        occurs after jurisdiction is established,
        occurs after responsibility is accepted,
        occurs after a torch lights the reflection,
        is the process of refining the blurred image of the soul.

The polishing of the soul requires attention to detail,
        exerts pressure on the senses,
        strains the rashness of intent,
        follows the counsel of The Spirit,
        brings control of the expressions on a face,
        removes impulses that do not honour.

The polishing of the soul banishes flights of fancy,
        banishes the lies of friendship,
        checks the tongue from an utterance that invites a denial of
                        The Truth,
        comes from perseverance,
        comes through the desire for change,
        teaches after much practice.

The polishing of the soul is tarnished by disunity in a marriage,
        is tarnished by the giving and the taking of offence,
        revels with delight in the approval of The Spirit.

The polishing of the soul acquires a sheen through fasting,
        acquires a sheen through acquisition of The Word,
        acquires a sheen through discipleship with an active walk,
        an orientated walk with a goal fervently in mind,
        a walk that halts before a step that may be false,
        a walk that brings due honour in the precision with which the
                        feet are placed.

The soul is polished by placing guards upon the senses that pre-empt the tracing of a
    probing finger of the foe,
    that reject the probing of the soul,
    that do not countenance the probings
    that give rise to flights of fancy.

The soul is polished by placing guards upon the tongue,
    by placing guards upon the face,
    by placing guards upon the body.

The soul is polished when the guards are no longer needed,
    for the new nature is established that basks in the soul's reflection:
    upon the visage of presentation.

The polishing of the soul follows understanding of the process,
    has watchers who cheer each step,
    has reporters who record each degree of clarity attained.

The polishing of the soul spreads like fire across the heavens,
    spreads via word of mouth,
    spreads in shouts from the tops of temples.

The polishing of the soul is an event no-one wants to miss,
    is always encouraged,
    supplies jewels to the gown of life.

The polishing of the soul brings snarls from those defeated,
    curls the lips of the profane,
    turns the back of those who failed to capture.

The polishing of the soul is the joy-stick of a flight,
    is as an apple on a tree when fully ripe and free of rot,
    is waiting to ride the clouds of conquest in the presence of
    A Groom.

The polishing of the soul fits arrows to a bow.
The polishing of the soul enables the horse ride of a life.
The polishing of the soul puts a gowned figure on a horse."

My Content Study Aid

_____
_____
_____
_____
_____

The Stepping-Stones of The Lord

"The coming of The Son is a stepping-stone of The Lord.

The stepping-stones of The Lord are marked as milestones along the way,
        do not wet the feet,
        mark a pathway among the debris of distractions.

The stepping-stones of The Lord are not resting places,
        mark progress to a goal.

The stepping-stones of The Lord are there when sought,
        are there when needed,
        are there to light the path that all must follow.

The stepping-stones of The Lord are not slippery to shod feet,
        are not slimy to unshod feet.

The stepping-stones of The Lord can be trusted to carry weight.

The stepping-stones of The Lord carry the sole of the foot,
        carry the soul and the spirit,
        carry the hope and The Faith of each journeyman.

The stepping-stones of The Lord are discernible by man,
        are made known to man.

The stepping-stones of The Lord are encountered on the way to salvation,
        on the way to redemption,
        on the way to the presence of The Kingdom.

The stepping-stones of The Lord are there for all to use.

The stepping-stones of The Lord were placed by a toll that has been already paid,
        exact no further fee,
        exist in the time of Grace.

The stepping-stones of The Lord do not require a jump,
        are placed with great precision,
        will never cause a stumble.

The stepping-stones of The Lord are each inscribed with their function,
        are numbered seven.

The stepping-stones of The Lord,
    as laid for man,
        are the birth of the womb,
            the confession of Faith,
            the re-birth of the water,
            the tongue of fire,

        the sacraments of the supper,
        the walk of the disciple,
        the new-birth from the grave.

The stepping-stones of The Lord record each footprint on each note,
        can cope with many feet at once,
        have angels on assignment.

The stepping-stones of The Lord require commitment to traverse to the end,
        can be run across with safety,
        have the angels cheering as each step is taken.

The stepping-stones of The Lord can be navigated with the aid of a stick,
        with the aid of a chair,
        with the aid of a bed.

The stepping-stones of The Lord have notes of distinction that each footstep plays,
        play many merry tunes,
        accompany the songs the angels sing.

The stepping-stones of The Lord have each merry tune created by each passage for that saint to hear when the race is won."

My Content Study Aid

The Attendants of The Bride

"The seven angels of Heaven are coming to The Earth,
                are descending in unison.

The seven angels of Heaven,
                each with his own entourage,
                are the surveyors of The Earth.

The seven angels of Heaven carry lamp stands ready for a service,
                carry the vestments of The Lord,
                  the vestments of The Father,
                  the vestments of The Spirit.

The seven angels of Heaven have decrees ready to be spoken,
                have not been this way before,
                will not be this way again,
                verify and conform to the sequence of man's time.

The seven angels of Heaven chart a course of majesty:
                are in charge of celebrations,
                are in charge of all festivities,
                are in charge of the progress of a procession.

The seven angels of Heaven know the timing of events and apply it to The Earth,
                co-ordinate activities within the time frame of man,
                mix and mingle as required.

The seven angels of Heaven organise the feast,
                extend the invitations,
                check acceptances against a scroll.

The seven angels of Heaven prepare the venue for the host,
                have authority to declare what is to be,
                inspect progress with a smile,
                inspect progress with great care,
                inspect progress with the schedule.

The seven angels of Heaven know what is required,
                are not hindered in application,
                proceed with confidence and certainty.

The seven angels of Heaven will furnish the finished venue,
                  the venue as designed,
                  the venue in its Glory.

The seven angels of Heaven dress the table of the carpenter,
                lay the table with the keepsakes,

     decorate the room of fellowship.

The seven angels of Heaven have hands of holiness,
     have songs of worship,
     have music from Heaven and the ages.

The seven angels of Heaven view all with satisfaction,
     view all with great delight,
     view all in a state of readiness.

The seven angels of Heaven await the gathering of the invited,
     the presence of the honoured,
     the appearance of the host."

My Content Study Aid

_____
_____
_____
_____
_____
_____
_____
_____
_____
_____
_____
_____
_____
_____
_____
_____
_____
_____
_____
_____
_____
_____
_____
_____
_____
_____

The Tongue of Fire

"The tongue of fire is spoken by The Spirit.
The tongue of fire has the attention of the soul.
The tongue of fire dumbfounds the soul.

The tongue of fire settles doubts of direction.
The tongue of fire sets the record straight.
The tongue of fire calls the spirit to attention.

The tongue of fire speaks in a mode of freedom,
                    only when released,
                    for a witness of salvation.

The tongue of fire has full communication,
        can control the tongue,
        can escape from the lips.

The tongue of fire can by permission commune directly to The Spirit.

The tongue of fire knows what is required,
        recounts what has been suffered,
        whispers quietly in recline,
        proclaims boldly on a footstep,
                for comfort in distress.

The tongue of fire calls for healing at an injury.

The tongue of fire confirms reception of each gift,
        acceptance of each gift,
        the usage of each gift.

The tongue of fire is easily installed in a temple that confesses,
        is never discarded from a temple through non-use.

The tongue of fire speaks the language of the moment,
        speaks the language of His choice,
        speaks the language that suits the content.

The tongue of fire always remains in The Temple,
        always bursts forth when released,
        always re-iterates when requested.

The tongue of fire can carry on a conversation,
        can ask a query,
        can seek responses from afar.

The tongue of fire is modified by prayer,
        is fulfilled by modulation,

        is enhanced by changes in the topic.

The tongue of fire can speak languages galore,
        can switch an utterance in a moment,
        can call forth languages formerly familiar.

The tongue of fire re-stokes the fire of The Temple,
        causes the flaring of the soul,
        the flaming of the spirit.

The tongue of fire complements the life of man,
        insures the walk with God,
        blesses and transmits The Will of God.

The tongue of fire has a witness of its own,
        witnesses to the lost,
        confirms The Faith of The Saints.

The tongue of fire gives credence to The Saints from The God that says,
                'I AM'.

The tongue of fire is a wonder to observe,
        is a blessing to encounter,
        is a gift expressed upon The Temple at the miracle of new birth.

The tongue of fire imbues a character of righteousness,
        imbues one who knows the way,
        imbues the discovery of the impact of the fire.

The tongue of fire awaits the kindling of the spirit,
        awaits the glow of self-control,
        awaits the fury of the righteous.

The tongue of fire is wielded by the righteous,
        is wielded when in battle,
        is wielded by the bold.

The tongue of fire is fed by The Spirit,
        is encouraged by The Spirit,
        is developed through The Spirit.

The tongue of fire,
        when roaring,
                is an adjunct to the raising of the dead.

The tongue of fire,
        when roaring,
                banishes the foe.

The tongue of fire,
        when roaring,

clears the battlefield.

The tongue of fire awaits its time of maturity amongst The Saints,
>   awaits for the free fall of The Spirit,
>   awaits for tongues of fulsome worship.

The tongue of fire empowers,
>   defends,
>   restores the battlements of the mind.

The tongue of fire conquers the temerity of the soul,
>   the shrinking of the spirit.

The tongue of fire overcomes intent without commitment.

The tongue of fire verifies the opened door,
>   verifies the sought,
>   verifies The Word."

My Content Study Aid

The Mission of My People

"The mission of My people is to copy and proclaim,
        is to seek and reclaim,
        is to gather and to scatter.

The mission of My people is to spread The Word with The Power of God,
        is to enact The Word with the authority of God,
        is to live The Word with the blessing of God.

The mission of My people is to build linking chains of life,
        is to build networks of the marriage covenant,
        is to build repentance into Faith,
        is to build Faith into righteousness,
        is to build on righteousness so wisdom can reside.

The mission of My people is to lead others through the streets of darkness until they can see the light.

The mission of My people has been a mighty conquest,
        reaches out with open hands.

The mission of My people has a history of tears,
        has a history of smiles,
        has a history of sacrifice.

The mission of My people counts every single soul.

The mission of My people maintains Faith upon The Earth,
        circulates the hope of a new day,
        bears witness that I AM,
        occurs upon the overcoming of their fear,
        is fulfilled within The Fear of God,
        is overlain with the presence of My Spirit.

The mission of My people causes an upheaval of The Earth,
        a dislocation of the demons,
        a withdrawing of the tentacles of the prince of darkness.

The mission of My people amplifies A Kingdom,
        diminishes another,
        welcomes deserters in their tens of thousands.

The mission of My people rescues people with abrogated rights,
        welcomes the dissenters from a binding doctrine,
        welcomes the past persecutors of The Saints."

The Mark of The Beast

"I abjure the defilement of The Temple of man.

The temple of man is in the image of God.

The temple of man,
       of My Spirit,
       of the resurrection,
          should not willingly inflict mutilation at the hands of man.

The temple of man is prepared for the redemption of man.

The temple of man fills the eye of God with beauty,
         fills the senses of God with approval,
         fills The Earth with the summit of creation.

The temple of man is prepared for The Faith of man,
         is prepared for the righteousness of man,
         is prepared for the journey of man until the end of time.

The temple of man supports the mind of man,
         supports the endeavours of man,
         supports the presence of My Spirit.

The temple of man does not support the desolation of idolatry,
         does not support the wilderness of vanity,
         does not support the conquest of the soul.

The temple of man awaits for the repentance of man,
         awaits on the judgement of man,
         awaits in anticipation for the opening of the grave.

The temple of man hopes for an extended life,
         hopes for the welcome held in reserve,
         hopes for a time of wonder in the clouds of Glory.

The temple of man is converted by The Faith of his confession,
         is extended by an invited guest,
         is sealed by affirmation of The Word.

The temple of man is adorned by the gown of life,
         is furnished by discipleship,
         is supported by the three-fold washing:
                    of the water,
                    of The Spirit,
                    of the grave.

The temple of man cannot attain perfection when carrying the mark of the beast.

The mark of the beast is the threefold confirmation of the mark of man.

The defilement of The Temple of man is the threefold confirmation of the mark of man.

The mark of man appeals to the pride of man,
>> the vanity of man,
>> the idolatry of man.

The mark of man is evidenced through the flesh of man,
>> in the flesh of man,
>> on the flesh of man.

The mark of man bears witness of man's rejection of his temple,
>> of the desecration of his temple,
>> of the defilement of his temple.

The mark of man has the count increased at each session of intrusion.

The mark of man is established for the record by embedding,
>> by piercing,
>> by cutting,
>> all in the absence of a quest for healing.

The staining presence of the mark of man is not easily removed from the surface of
>> the soul.

The initial mark of man speaks to the folly of man,
>> the impetuousness of man,
>> the soulishness of man,
>> the lifestyle choice of man.

The initial mark of man is not recorded as to judgement,
>> is not recorded to man's detriment,
>> is not recorded with a declaration:
>>> as for a child in arms.

The secondary mark of man sears his conscience amidst the writhing of his spirit as the
>> entrapment poises to foreclose.

The secondary mark of man declares intention to proceed.

The secondary mark of man comes at a great cost to the spirit,
>> at a great cost to the seed of Faith,
>> at a great cost that darkens understanding.

The secondary mark of man signals attention being paid to the foe of man.

The tertiary mark of man confirms the intent to mutilate the handiwork of God,
>> has the soul in rebellion,
>> silences the spirit.

The tertiary mark of man speaks of foreign invasions that lay claim to permissive
                authority under the auspices of the enemy of man.

The tertiary mark of man speaks of ownership by the beast,*
        speaks of a sacrifice made in vain.

The mark of the beast can be deleted from the flesh,
        can be removed as if it never were,
        can re-adjust the record upon repentance.

The mark of the beast can be obliterated from the flesh,
        can be expurgated from the flesh,
        can be cleansed as if by fire.

The mark of the beast should not be left intact upon repentance,
        should not be allowed to bear false witness,
        must not insinuate a lie.

The fullness of the mark of the beast stands as an eternal witness of rebellion,
        stands in confirmation of a destiny made known by
                The Word,
        stands unless renounced threefold in confession.

The mark of the beast is not washed by the grave,
        occurs in the stock-take of the foe,
        prevents healing by My Spirit.

The mark of the beast will not be present within My Bride,
        will not be seen upon informed reflection,
        will be absent from the Disciples of The Lord."

Scribal Note: *of Tattoos and/or Cutting.*
        Refer: Leviticus 19:28, 1 Kings 18:28, Jeremiah 47:5,
                The Bible (New King James Version)

Leviticus 19:28
    'You shall not make any cuttings in your flesh for the dead, nor tattoo any marks on you: I *am* the LORD.

1 Kings 18:28
    So they cried aloud, and cut themselves, as was their custom, with knives and lances, until the blood gushed out on them.

Jeremiah 47:5
    Baldness has come upon Gaza, Ashkelon is cut off *With* the remnant of their valley. How long will you cut yourself?

The Way Home

"The power of the mind does not exist within itself,
        arises from the confusion of identity.

The confusion of identity arises from the teachings of man,
        should be correctly attributed to the master of confusion.

Confused thinking within the body of man emanates from the enemy of man,
        the master of confusion,
        the instigator of the lie,
        the manipulator of The Truth
        that blends opposites together.

Confused thinking is indicative of a soul under a foreign influence,
        of a spirit retreated into silence,
        of a body without direction from The Light.

Confused thinking should be bound and dismissed,
        the soul should be cleansed and re-aligned,
        the spirit should be uplifted by the tongue of The Spirit.

Clarity of thought arises from the guidance of My Spirit as He conveys the intent of God
        The Father and God The Son in
        conference with the spirit of man.

Clarity of thought is confirmed by the knowledge of man overlain by The Wisdom
        of God.

Clarity of thought is expressed with the power of The Spirit when reliant on
        the prayer of the humbled righteous soul,
        the encouragement of the spirit that moves in meekness
        of fellowship,
        a body that is unmarked by man,
        that knows the cleansing water,
        that is justified as The Temple of The Holy Spirit.

In these things lie the road of discipleship:
        The Fear of God,
        The Love of God,
        The Call of God,
        The Servant-hood of God,
        The Acceptance of God,
        The Holiness of God,
        The Presence of God.

In these things lie the path to perfection:
        the keeping of the Sacraments,

        the sacrifice of self,
        the retention of the Wisdom of The Word,
        the application of the call,
        the immediacy of obedience,
        the quest for excellence of character,
        the walk within The Will of God.

In these things lie the victor's crown:
        the reception of The Truth,
        the overcoming of deception,
        the persevering through adversity,
        the standing on the rock of revelation,
        the growth of Faith,
        the attaining of the summit of each mountain,
        the adornment of the gown of Life.

The end of life is unknown to The Saints.

The end of life collides with the second death.

The end of life is the death of the spirit,
        the extenuation of the soul.

Woe to the extenuated soul that has no end,
        that has no hope,
        that circles in despair.

The perfected saints of God will witness a new dawn,
        will witness the angelic hosts in action,
        will witness the fulfilment of The Promises of God.

The perfected saints of God will be welcomed home,
        will be welcomed by generations past now present,
        will be welcomed with new senses,
                new bodies so equipped,
                a renewal that befits the rebirth of the
                      spirit in an environment of Light.

The perfected saints of God will enter into the garden of The Father,
        the birthplace of The Bride."

My Content Study Aid

_____
_____
_____
_____

The Defilement of The Spirit

"The defilement of The Spirit is the seeking of the ordure of The Earth.

The defilement of The Spirit is in the vile contempt for the image of God.

The defilement of The Spirit is the denial of God's gifts,
        is the rejection of God's Grace,
        is the absence of repentance in the presence of a testimony,
        is the blasphemy of God,
        is the non-acceptance of the offerings of God.

The defilement of The Spirit brings fragmentation of a temple,
        brings disfigurement of a temple,
        brings re-instatement of the curses of God upon a soul
            through the refusal of The Grace of God.

The Grace of God speaks of reconciliation between God and man.

The Grace of God speaks of the redemption of man through the servant on The Cross.

The Grace of God speaks of the salvation of man through an empty tomb,
        speaks of The Love of God through not leaving man alone,
        speaks of the eternity of God through the promise of return,
        speaks of the fullness of the Gospel in the presence of His ecclesia,
        speaks of His testimony made known to man in this age of Grace.

The Grace of God is offered in an age that will soon end.

The defilement of The Spirit resets the clock of sin in the soul of man."

My Content Study Aid

The Needs of Life

"The need of a parent should be uppermost within a family.

   The need of a child,
        removed from where the devil rages,
        is as an orphan,
        fallen on a journey and found lying in distress.

   The need of the imprisoned should speak to the overcoming of rejection,
        the laying-down of bitterness,
        the dispelling of loneliness through the companionship of The Word:
                thereby to seek the reclamation of the soul,
                the re-awakening of the spirit.

Blessed are they that walk within the marriage covenant,
        with vows intact and sealed in the presence of God,
     that carry mercy in their hearts,
     that linger in My service with opened eyes that detect the injured and
                the lame.

A need signs as an impairment to the being of the soul,
        to the life of the spirit,
        to the health of the body.

A need should be addressed in the confines of a family,
      addressed in the lot of a widow without a family,
      of short duration within the gatherings of The Saints.

A need that remains unchallenged is a foothold,
        a stepping-stone,
        an anchor point,
        for the enemy of man.

A need that remains but is ignored will fester as the untreated wounding of the flesh,
        will breed resentment in the soul,
        will leave the spirit with no defence to the accusations
                of the foe.

A need that is unresolved will bring criticism from man,
        impose guilt upon the righteous,
        degrade The Love of God.

A need that is unresolved asserts the presence of the values of the secular in a
                fallen world.

A need starts as a prayer to the heart that once was stopped upon a cross,
        is assigned as to an angel,

>ends as a divine appointment that fulfils The Will of God.

A need declined is lost forever and impacts on a life.

The wants of the flesh are not the needs of life,
>have the urgency of man.

The wants of the flesh are discarded in the dust,
>are not seen on the gown of life,
>>waste away with an eventual loss of interest.

The needs of life are a testimony of God in action,
>are time-tabled by God,
>are sanctified by The Spirit.

The needs of life are withdrawn by the enemy of man,
>just beyond the outstretched hand,
>just beyond the reach of man.

The needs of life are priced by the enemy of man above the daily wage of man.

The needs of life are increased by the enemy of man at the counter of exchange faster
>than the accrual in the daily wage of man.

The needs of life are paramount when the needs of life encounter the poverty of man.

The starvation of a child,
>the killing fields of disease:
>bring condemnation to all who roll out weapons and pass by on the other side,
>>to all who show no mercy,
>>to all who move in hatred,
>>to all who impede the righteous from their mercy-call."

My Content Study Aid

The Utterance of A Promise

"The utterance of a promise is a binding movement of the tongue.

The utterance of a promise cannot be reassigned,
    commits the soul and the spirit to observe the body.

The utterance of a promise marks certainty of intent,
    certainty of action,
    certainty of redemption of the vowing of the tongue.

The utterance of a promise impacts on hearing ears,
    impacts on seeing eyes,
    has no impact when reiterated to the unintended.

The utterance of a promise requires wisdom from the utterer,
    requires wisdom in its framing,
    requires wisdom in its issuance.

The utterance of a promise is as a covenant of law,
    is not to be repealed.

The utterance of a promise has truth as its foundation,
    has truth as its support,
    has truth displayed upon redemption.

Man's utterance of a promise consigns the future to the present,
    consigns the body to the tongue,
    consigns a bounded premise to the life of man.

Man's utterance of a promise is limited by time,
    cannot impale eternity,
    proceeds beyond mortality only in a will.

Man's utterance of a promise tests the character of man.

Man's utterance of a promise is an eternal record,
    can affect a destiny,
    can repulse the angels if it becomes a lie that seals a link.

Man's broken promises form a chain of heavy links around his neck,
    a necklace of shame upon his chest with each link thereof inscribed—
        'The Truth is not within him';
    a necklace that bears him downwards into darkness.

Man's utterance of a promise stands as it is uttered,
    stands as it proclaims,
    stands as it is qualified,
    stands into the future,

stands open to attack by the foe of man.

If man's utterance of a promise should fall upon The Earth,
        fails to be redeemed when due,
        is negated by denial,
        is held in low esteem,
        is conveniently forgotten,
        is subjected to procrastination,
        is subjected to excuse:
then thereby know the attacks of the enemy of man upon the soul of man:
        the attacks that would pre-empt the gaining of his Glory in
                the presence of The Saints.

Man's utterance of a promise is mortally dependent for its redemption upon the future
                will of God.

Let he who has wisdom,
    understand.

Let he who has need,
    repent.

Let he who has insight,
    qualify."

My Content Study Aid

The Visitation of The Earth

"The visitation of The Earth is not confined to angels,
        is not confined to deity,
        is not confined to the foes of Heaven and of man.

The visitation of The Earth is as the record stands,
        is as the record self-updates,
        is as the record speaks of what is soon to be.

The visitation of The Earth has hosted cosmic forces,
        has hosted celestial events,
        has hosted the rain of stardust from the heavens.

The visitation of The Earth records the imprint of the visitor,
        records the destruction of the foe,
        records the benefit of the well-wisher.

The visitation of The Earth is never an event of little consequence,
        occurs through grand design,
        fulfils an enriched destiny through both cause and effect.

The visitation of The Earth is sequestered in the record,
        is there to be perceived,
        is as a history of the construction of a home.

The visitation of The Earth speaks of building-blocks assembled,
        of materials delivered,
        of items carefully aligned.

The visitation of The Earth speaks of needs foreknown,
        of resources required within the realms of time,
        of deposits built and stored for withdrawal as the
                need arises.

The visitation of The Earth commenced before time could have a meaning,
        curtails when time has no further relevance.

The visitation of The Earth has not yet reached its zenith,
        has yet to dress and to display,
        as yet is still in preparation.

The visitation of The Earth has yet to witness the changing of dimensions,
        has yet to be enhanced to Glory,
        has yet to witness to the cosmos that is to be unveiled.

The visitation of The Earth does not end with fire,
        does not end with calamity and fear,
        does not end with the loss of hope.

The visitation of The Earth contains an expounded promise,
                        a vista of a destiny that holds the promise
                                        of eternity,
                    the promise from one who has been before and
                                knows the time of His return.

Faithful and true is He.

Mighty are His ways.

For He,
    alone,
        is as a point of singularity in the deisms and theisms of The Earth."

My Content Study Aid

_____
_____
_____
_____
_____
_____
_____
_____
_____
_____
_____
_____
_____
_____
_____
_____
_____
_____
_____
_____
_____
_____
_____
_____

The Power of The Spirit of Man

"The power of the spirit of man is mostly ignored by man,
                    is often acknowledged then set aside by man,
                    labours hard on behalf of man,
                    continually seeks good for man.

The power of the spirit of man is such that it communes with God,
                    that it hearkens to the word of God,
                    that it assimilates the counsel of God,
                    that it modifies the character of man,
                    that it is taught The Wisdom of God upon assignment,
                    that it instigates an overcoming.

The power of the spirit of man enables the learning of many tongues,
                    enables the acceptance of the gifts of God,
                    enables the conversations with The Spirit of God,
                    enables the growth of Faith,
                    enables the will with righteousness,
                    enables the walk of companionship with God.

The power of the spirit of man places order in a life,
                    places The Fear of God within A Temple,
                    places a destiny within a soul.

The power of the spirit of man places love within a heart,
                    places ambition within the bounds of righteousness,
                    places man within a family home.

The power of the spirit of man can be subdued by man,
                    can be decried by man,
                    can be denied by man.

The power of the spirit of man can be embraced by man,
                    can be augmented by man,
                    can be encouraged by man.

The power of the spirit of man is a force for confronting the foe of man,
                    is a force for entering through a gate,
                    is a force that celebrates a victory.

The power of the spirit of man unites with The Spirit of God in a time of ululation,
                                        in a time of praise,
                                        in a time of worship.

The power of the spirit of man unites with The Spirit of God in a time of communion,
                                        in a time of salvation,
                                        in a time of silence.

The power of the spirit of man unites with The Spirit of God when in prayer,
>when in distress,
>when in the presence of the foe.

The power of the spirit of man is directed towards seeking The Household of God,
>is directed towards knowing the fullness of The Spirit of God,
>is directed towards being in the presence of God.

My Content Study Aid

The Preparedness of Man

"Great is the fellowship of The Saints.

Great is the power of The Saints,
    is the authority of The Saints,
    are the works of The Saints in My Name.

    For in My Name they will call,
        in My Name they will visit,
        in My Name they will summon,
        in My Name they will heal,
        in My Name they will rebuke,
        in My Name they will feed,
        in My Name they will witness.

    For in My Name will the message be proclaimed to the ends of The Earth,
        "Repent,
            for The Kingdom of God is at hand."

The Kingdom of God awaits the lifting of the veil.

The Kingdom of God asserts its right to be:
    for The Banner of The Kingdom of God is about to be raised over all The Earth as
            The Son comes to take His Kingdom.

    For in My Name will The Word be upheld by The Father,
        in My Name will The Word be upheld by The Son,
        in My Name will My Spirit manifest The Will made known to Me,
        in My Name will The Edifice of God be established on The Earth,
        in My Name will Satan be made subservient,
        in My Name will the covenants be upheld,
        in My Name will the graves be opened,
        in My Name will Earth be linked to Heaven.

The Hosts of Heaven are prepared for events of cataclysm to be unfolded in these days.

    The end of age is signed;
        an epoch dawns with a new day:
        that welcomes the awaited.

    The fear of death;
        the joy of life:
        will overtake The Earth.

    A sense of dread;
        a Banner of hope:
        approaches one and all.

The age of Grace forsakes the unrepentant;
> the epoch of The Son opens with a flourish:
>> at the trumpet call.

The heart of man drafts each according to his will,
> determines his record in a book,
> is stated in the utterings of his tongue.

The heart of man cannot distort a life before The Great White Throne."

My Content Study Aid

The Crown Jewel of Creation

"Behold!
    In the twinkling of an eye the life of man can change.

Behold!
    In the setting of the sun an age can end.

Behold!
    In the rising of the sun a new dawn can break forth.

Behold!
    The machines of man do fail him.

Behold!
    The fallibility of the consciousness of man bears witness.

Behold!
    The stumbling of man feeds upon pride that rules supreme.

The wonders of creation are there for all to know.

The wonders of creation exist at the pleasure of God,
    do not all have an eternal existence,
    can fade with fulfilment of their purpose.

The wonders of creation are viewed within the time frame of man,
    are tinkered with by man,
    are oft abused by man.

The wonders of creation are seen as curios by man,
    are not seen by chance,
    were not placed by chance,
    are not a happenstance of composite mistakes,
    do not result from a random walk.

The wonders of creation bear witness within the soul of man,
    form the home of man,
    ensconce the spirit of man.

The Crown Jewel of Creation has an image beyond compare,
    has an image that should not be besmirched,
    has an image arising from eternity,
    has an image of recognition,
    has an image assigned to the presence of the image-maker,
    has an image constructed from the clay by a potter of
        great renown.

The Crown Jewel of Creation has an image that will not be destroyed,

The Crown Jewel of Creation will travel beyond the grave,
  will survive the fire and the sword.

The Crown Jewel of Creation has an image bound for an ever-lasting journey,
  has an image that will absorb the darkness or reflect
    the light,
  has an image of completeness that is self-aware.

The Crown Jewel of Creation has the gift of freewill,
  the counterweight of choice,
  the instigator of accountability,
  the credence of a soul without compulsion,
  a character that seeks perfection or grovels in the dust.

The Crown Jewel of Creation is cherished by The Lord,
  is encouraged by His Spirit,
  is the recipient of blessings from a loving oversight.

The Crown Jewel of Creation is the crown jewel of His Kingdom,
  is guarded day and night by attendants who never sleep,
  has a promised future:
    for all who walk the high way;
    for all who embrace a downhill slide.

The Crown Jewel of Creation has an inherent intended destiny—
  as the crowned jewel of creation that resides within
    a residence specially prepared."

My Content Study Aid

_____
_____
_____
_____
_____
_____
_____
_____
_____
_____
_____
_____

The Survival of The Flock

"The sequencing of time is not for the faint-hearted.

The passage of time is not for the weak-minded.

The future,
      past and present rely on expectation,
            memory and experience.

    The present will not always be the basis of the future.

    The past is only valid if memory is not impaired.

    The future has no bearing on those without belief.

    The past has no relevance for those in denial of a future.

    The present cannot be a stepping-stone for those without progression.

Denial of a God of impact destroys the morality of man,
            makes ethics relevant to the chorus of the refrains of man,
            tears down the fabric of society to the rule of violence
                          by decree.

Justice cannot be complete in the absence of the reading of the heart.

    Man is not able to release The Truth when perceived in the absence of a standard.

    Man's idea of justice is judgement via the law.

The deviousness of man prevents the law of man to deliver justice when so sought.

The acorn of the oak tree has more chance of success than a child
                      when encircled by the faithless,
                      when schooled without control,
                      when reared solely by the world.

None deserve of honour in a home that has no faith,
            has no hope,
            has no vision,
            where the present is repeated as a cycle of despair.

A home cannot teach what remains unknown.

A child is not instructed by what has been discarded,
            by what has been ignored,
            by what has been rejected,
            from the maturation of that child.

Even so man can aspire to be an over-comer,
            a seeker of The Truth:
                      that which remains always as it was,

>   always as it is,
>   always as it is yet to be.
>
> Even so man can exercise freewill:
>   to accept the need to change,
>   to turn from and forsake a character of hopelessness that
>   denies The Truth.
>
> Even so man can be as he was intended,
>   with potential fully realized,
>   with ability developed,
>   with wisdom ingrained upon his soul.
>
> For such,
>   the laws of man hold no fears,
>   deliver no injustice that endures,
>   are not misused because of pride.
>
> For such,
>   a hand uplifts;
>   a voice quietly whispers to a spirit;
>   a soul listens and obeys.
>
> For such await the fulfilment of a promise that extends a life for ever.
>
> For such await the promise that enables the shedding of the grave as the husk
>   of transformation,
>   the promise of a further welcome,
>   the promise of fellowship within a garden crafted at The Son-rise.
>
> For such are sealed through an eternal covenant,
>   bestowed by Grace at a sacrifice they could not pay,
>   a redemption from sin that has power and authority:
>   to fill the halls of Heaven or the chambers of a heart or a mansion
>   on high,
>   with the flock that knows the shepherd's call."

My Content Study Aid

_____
_____
_____
_____
_____
_____

The Feast of The Incarnation

"The Feast of the Incarnation is not a matter of choice to those who know The Truth.

The Feast of the Incarnation is the richest in its spread,
        the richest in its offering,
        the richest in its succour.

The Feast of the Incarnation is not a lowly supper,
        is not to be postponed,
        is not to be omitted.

The Feast of the Incarnation is not of no account,
        never invites casualness of approach,
        is not without reproach to those who treat it as a token.

The Feast of the Incarnation is accompanied by the presence of deity,
        brings holiness in silence to each eternal being,
        is engraved with the intent upon a record as it passes
                through the lips.

The Feast of the Incarnation is the outreach of Deity to the loneliness of man,
        to teach man of his new relationship within the timeframe
                of mortality,
        to vest in man due reverence to those who were not there:
                to those who could not witness,
                to those who have been told.

The Feast of the Incarnation tests the loyalty of instruction.

The Feast of the Incarnation tests The Fear of God,
        tests man's transmission of an event of Glory,
        tests man's understanding at the core of his discipleship.

The Feast of the Incarnation rejects sin brought before The Throne,
        sees as an affront the casualness of man,
        hears at last the penitent with the humble heart.

The Feast of the Incarnation is majestic in its scope,
        redemptive in its application,
        eternal in its significance.

The Feast of the Incarnation is the verifier of Faith,
        the touchstone of belief,
        the feeder of the soul.

The Feast of the Incarnation is the unifier of The Faith,
        the measurer of the sheep,
        the drafting-gate for goats.

The Feast of the Incarnation is the message of departure to those who would be discipled,
        is the bedrock of assembly,
        is at the centre of remembrance.

The Feast of the Incarnation transmits the love of Deity to the soul of man.

The Feast of the Incarnation transmits the love of man to Deity in freewill recognition.

Each Feast of the Incarnation is visited by angels,
        expresses the sanctity of The Bride,
        seals a broken covenant anew within each trembling heart.

Each Feast of the Incarnation has the time of celebration entered within the record of all participants of the day.

The Grace of The Lord is mighty to behold and all His ways are just."

My Content Study Aid

The Comfort of The Lord (1)

"The comfort of The Lord has recognition beyond the grave of man,
                addresses the needs of man,
                is an extension of His favour.

The comfort of The Lord is to be surrounded by His arm,
                to know the shedding of the fears of life,
                    the absence of life's worries,
                          the attempts to strive that do not overcome.

The comfort of The Lord brings The Wisdom of self-worth,
                the appreciation of good health,
                the contentment of well-being.

The comfort of The Lord brings a sojourn of replenishment,
                the growth of inner peace,
                the presence of His smile upon a face.

The comfort of The Lord brings wisdom to a tongue,
                a fire upon the lips,
                a vision to the fore.

The comfort of The Lord encourages the will to speak within the spirit,
                the sight to see beyond horizons,
                the hearing of the spirit that may whisper to
                                the soul.

The comfort of The Lord has certainty of access,
                validation of a Faith,
                the comfort of a friend.

The comfort of The Lord furnishes a temple with a throne of Grace;
                      with a bell of the pitch of truth;
                      with a door of open access that never closes
                                to exclude.

The comfort of The Lord is not swayed by the comforts of man,
                is immune to the aggrandizements of man,
                is deaf to the authority of man.

The comfort of The Lord is not attained by the unrighteous,
                by the restless,
                by the thankless.

The comfort of The Lord is a blessing for the righteous,
                is at home amongst The Saints,
                is a stepping-stone towards His Presence.

The comfort of The Lord is cause for celebration,
>> is cause for a thankful heart,
>> is cause to witness the growth of Faith.

The comfort of The Lord increases The Wisdom of each student,
>> for those who seek will find without the need to grope."

Scribal Note: Refer also 'The Comfort of The Lord (2), this book.

My Content Study Aid

The Temperature of The Soul

"The temperature of the soul,
>> as measured by the spirit,
>> as reported by the tongue,
>> as evidenced by the body,
>> is of great significance to man in his mortality.

The temperature of the soul when freezing:
>> plumbs the depths of depression that ignores the spirit's input,
>> is confident in the denial of God,
>> is self-assured in slamming all doors shut in the face of hope,
>> is at home in the company of others of similar disdain.

The temperature of the soul when boiling:
>> brings the heights of elation that are difficult to counsel,
>> expands expectations beyond the realms of sanity,
>> nurtures excess straining that exceeds The Will of God.

The temperature of the soul governs the behaviour of the soul in the presence of
>> a teacher,
>> the reception of the soul when subject to control,
>> the response of the soul when resisting an attack.

The temperature of the soul best serves the body and the spirit's destiny of dreams when
>> heated by the fire of Heaven from the brazier of the spirit.

The temperature of the soul is kept hot by the brazier of the spirit when ignited and
>> replenished by the torch of The Spirit.

The visitation of the flaming torch causes the blazing of the brazier that heats the soul
>> to hot.

The hot soul proclaims its status to the heavens,
>> its status to The Earth,
>> its status to Satan and his hordes.

The hot soul soaks up information,
>> demands more of the spirit,
>> showers commands upon the body.

The hot soul seeks out lost souls,
>> offers a destiny of which they may have dreamed,
>> displays a face of recognition that will lead them into light.

The hot soul has a fire that burns within a temple,
>> that is fuelled from Heaven,
>> that is tended day and night.

The hot soul knows The Spirit as the builder of The Kingdom,
    is in fellowship with the members of The Household,
    knows the power of the tongue of fire,
    exuberantly rejoices at each known advancement of The Kingdom of God
        upon The Earth.

The hot soul embraces new instructions,
    moves forward without fear,
    does not retreat,
    does not repeat the moves of yesteryear.

The hot soul is set to be a winner of a race that has a garland as a prize,
    is accompanied by the support of Heaven,
    should be forewarned against attempts to cool the soul.

The cooling of the soul brings experiences of stages that are not encouraged,
    stages that are comfortable,
    stages that confuse,
    stages that start to question,
    stages that start to threaten the destiny of dreams,
    stages that impose a potential future in the destiny
        of nightmares.

The temperature of the soul when cooled:
    idles in inaction,
    suffers sinful surroundings without rebuke,
    does not scale the mountain tops,
    has lapsed promises galore with little motivation
        for redemption.

The temperature of the soul when cooled:
    is unpredictable in response to a call to service,
        to an uttered promise,
        to a yea or nay.

The temperature of the soul when cooled:
    delays the building of The Kingdom,
    postpones the progression of the soul,
    frustrates The Will of God.

The nightmare of the soul is not a delight to visit,
    is not a delight in which to dwell,
    is not a delight of informed choice.

The nightmares of the soul open a window to a potential destiny,
    open a window for a sampling,
    open a window that will have the curtains drawn.

The nightmares of the soul are where the impounded stay for all eternity.

The blessings of the soul prepare,
        direct and transport all of like freewill to a destiny that befits the
                righteous aspirations of man,
     in his quest for life's meaning and the answers thereto
                made known.

There is no cause for disappointment,
    no cause for a withdrawal,
    no cause for a desire for the alternative,
        when man,
        with Faith,
        first encounters the preparations of The Lord:
              for life within His jurisdiction."

My Content Study Aid

The Wealth of Man

"The wealth of man is easily measured by man,
>>is easily measured by God.

The disparity in the wealth of man is seated in the values of assessment,
>>the basis of assessment,
>>the core of the assessment.

The wealth of man as measured by man,
>>counts accumulations,
>>counts deposits of his riches,
>>counts the things with which he plays:
>>>the things that he has shed,
>>>the enticements of the world that may masquerade as the
>>>>wealth of man.

The wealth of man as measured by God,
>>values the reasons for accumulations,
>>the reason for deposits and whether they are locked,
>>the reasons for the things with which he plays.

The valuation by God of the wealth of man is impacted by:
>>>whether the heart is tabulated with the values of the world or is
>>>>softened to hear the quiet impartation
>>>>from a counsel that may disclose a need;
>>>whether the soul still beats a chest in its rampage of the self or
>>>>has learnt obedience and no longer shouts 'I shall';
>>>whether the spirit's voice is silenced in despair or is permitted
>>>>to grow a character that appeals from within the grave.

The valuation by God of the wealth of man is magnified by the treasures accumulated
>>>>in Heaven,
>>those that adorn the gown of life,
>>>the gown worn within the grave,
>>>the gown seen there only by the angels,
>>>the gown that clothes upon transformation from the grave in
>>>>preparation for eternity that
>>>>Faith and hope reward.

The valuation by God of the wealth of man has a process that is not secret;
>>>a benefit revealed,
>>>a prize greatly to be esteemed;
>>>has a declaration at a seat of justice.

The valuation by God of the wealth of man is always extremely accurate,
>>does not forget,

                does not overlook,
                does not undervalue.

The valuation by God of the wealth of man knows the gateway of repentance.

The valuation by God of the wealth of man is not subject to exaggeration,
                is enabled to accompany man beyond
                              the grave,
                is the only wealth the wise endeavour
                              to accumulate.

Beware of the wealth of man that burns as straw thrown on the fire—
                that does not survive the burnishing of the grave,
                that does not trouble the hardened heart.

Beware of the wealth of man that is not present on a gown when needed,
                that stays within a vault,
                that always is left behind.

Beware of the wealth of man that is present only for an instant—
                that leaves a vacuum in the future—
                that screams of the paucity of man."

My Content Study Aid

The Lion of Judah Reigns

"The Lion of Judah was where people came to mock;
        has freed waters from each dam;
        has opened doors that will not slam;
        holds keys so gates no longer lock.

The Lion of Judah is at ease in His surrounds;
        calls to every creature;
        is prepared in dress of stature;
        has visited the time of bounds.

The Lion of Judah mingles in the midst of throngs;
        regally before the crowns;
        is seated with the ones in gowns;
        hears an anthem among the songs.

The Lion of Judah has a gown that will endure;
        is settled to host a feast;
        greets the great and the very least;
        has the demeanour of the sure.

The Lion of Judah knows well The Song of The Lamb;
        marks the anthem of the rock;
        accepts homage from an epoch;
        rules in majesty as I AM.

The Lion of Judah achieves the flight of the beast;
        has redressed all unjust wrongs;
        overcomes those who beat the gongs;
        reigns from the west unto the east."

My Content Study Aid

_____
_____
_____
_____
_____
_____
_____
_____

The Trinkets of The Heart

"The trinkets of the heart are gathered one by one.

The trinkets of the heart are not gender sensitive,
        testify of the gods of each heart.

The trinkets of the heart are obtained without approval,
        have not had a blessing sought,
        will not bestow good health upon a body.

The trinkets of the heart are not known as the desires of the heart,
        are the wants of the soul.

The trinkets of the heart are seized upon a moment,
        are acquired to satisfy the eye,
        are sought to deafen the ear of the spirit,
        are designed to appeal to the body as the armour of that soul.

The trinkets of the heart invade the homes of man,
        make statements of idolatrous belief,
        speak volumes to a guest,
        deny the spoken words in opposition.

    Beware of the trinkets of the heart that are garish,
            that distract the ear,
            that desecrate the body,
            that invade the presence of the nose.

    Beware of the trinkets of the heart that speak of other gods,
            that pervert the soul,
            that dampen down the spirit,
            that squander the time of man.

    Beware of the trinkets of the heart that will bring curses from their origins,
            will barter with the soul for right of occupation,
            will bring blasphemy to the lips,
            will stem the seeking of the spirit after truth.

    Beware of the trinkets of the heart that capture the neck of man,
            the wrist of man,
            the flesh of man,
            the extremities of man.

    Beware of the trinkets of the heart that capture the wealth of man in collections
                      without merit.

    Beware of the trinkets of the heart that will not festoon a gown of great importance.

The trinkets of the heart confess no shame upon an injury,
> use vanity to clothe the proud,
> declare self-righteousness to the uninhibited.

The trinkets of the heart tear at the heart of God,
> decompose the bearings of The Cross,
> lead the wayward along paths they should not choose.

The trinkets of the heart cannot bind The Saints of God,
> cannot establish dominion within the guidance of My Spirit,
> will not tempt the righteous who know fellowship with God.

The trinkets of the heart will become as ashes at the grave."

My Content Study Aid

The Morality of God

"'Doing good' is an aspiration of man.

'Doing good' is relative without the morality of God,
>requires a judgement without the awareness of The Truth.

'Doing good' appeals to the emotions,
>cannot confirm the absence of harm,
>can be a self-deception that has no long term benefit.

'Doing good' is not a cry heard in the market place,
>is not a cry heard by those without resources,
>is not a cry that brings contentment either to the spirit or the soul.

'Doing good' is analgesia to the burdened conscience,
>freeing idle hands in motions of recompense for responsibilities avoided at
>>a prior encounter.

'Doing good' is as the idle chattering of a stream,
>as brief in its encounter as in the winter when ice encroaches on
>>the stream,
>>silencing all as the living water is entombed,
>waiting yet in hopefulness for a new day when the living water will gush
>>forth from its imprisonment within the body that held it bound.

The living water waits for the dam-burst that will inundate the country.

'Doing good' rarely achieves its initial aims,
>rarely is appreciated,
>often is a sop to the muddled thinking of the mind.

'Doing good' is dependent on the culture in which it is given birth.

'Doing good' may not be understood,
>not have the desired results,
>>not procure the end result of calculation when transported across
>>>boundaries of nations and applied with
>>>knowledge but with little wisdom.

The benefits of 'Doing good' rarely offset years of neglect of those in need,
>rarely change a destiny,
>rarely enhance the lives of the recipients after the doer
>>has departed.

'Doing good' is an exercise in frustration,
>an exercise in semantics that changes from ear to ear,
>an exercise without completion that heaps disappointment on the backs
>>of the expectant.

'Doing good' is unrealistic as an objective when none are good but God.

    For who will judge,
            decide,
            supply,
            enforce,
            guide,
            direct,
            the goodness to be done and when completion is attained?

'Doing good' is not necessarily the adjunct nor the antithesis of 'Do no evil'
                                        without the morality of God.

    The ethics of man do not stand unmodified,
            are not universal,
                squander early ideals to the unfulfilled mind of man in his quest for
                      a reason for existence in the timeframe of a life.

The ethics of man lead only to despair when reality of his logic ultimately declares they
                        were formulated by the inhabitants from a pond
                        of soup which defy The Truth of replication.

The morality of God stands as a testimony to man of man's own immorality.

The morality of God has stood for millennia for the benefit of man.

The morality of God supervises and instructs,
            judges and rewards,
            punishes and destroys.

The morality of God is just in altercation,
            is true in application,
            is fearful in supplication.

The morality of God is administered with authority,
            is circumscribed by mercy,
            knows the gift of Grace.

The morality of God is not swayed by man,
            is not swayed by angels,
            is not swayed by demons.

The morality of God has the highest of ideals,
            has the backing of great wisdom,
            has the foundation of the greatest love.

The morality of God separates the obedient and the disobedient,
                the righteous and the unrighteous,
                the walkers of the narrow and wide ways.

The morality of God declares the purpose of life,

carries the seal of truth,
announces,
warns of,
destinies that lie within the scope of man's freewill.

The morality of God is a work of grand design that will not terminate.

The morality of God covers,
shelters and protects all those who accept with understanding the mercy and The Grace established to reconcile the lost through a sacrificial son."

My Content Study Aid

The Gospel of The Lord

"The gospel of The Lord is the good news of the coming Kingdom,
                                The Kingdom that is close to hand,
                                The Kingdom that prevails.

The gospel of The Lord is a restoration with a cross.

The gospel of The Lord brings dispensation from the law and decrees the age
                                                                               of fellowship.

The gospel of The Lord is not imposed,
                          builds on Faith,
                          changes accepting lives.

The gospel of The Lord speaks of governing authority,
                          honouring family life,
                          adopting lives of rectitude.

The gospel of The Lord has extensive testimonies,
                          has impressive testimonials,
                          has martyrs of conviction.

The gospel of The Lord expresses majestic principles,
                          reaches across divides,
                          spans encountered cultures.

The gospel of The Lord unites in harmony,
                          manifests in deeds,
                          witnesses to mankind.

The gospel of The Lord brings social responsibility,
                          speaks in truth,
                          brings forth illumination.

The gospel of The Lord is a message of uniqueness,
                          has a promise of forgiveness,
                          extends hope to the hopeless.

The gospel of The Lord presents an offering of sacrifice,
                          has confirmations of its truth,
                          has evidence of many miracles.

The gospel of The Lord is unmatched by other theisms,
                          has claims that are exemplary,
                          has changed the lives of many.

The gospel of The Lord explains the sin of man,
                          appeals a change of heart,

                requires repentance from the sinful.

The gospel of The Lord refutes the multitude of paths,
                denies the equivalence of gods,
                proclaims the pre-eminence of Jesus.

The gospel of The Lord proclaims the morality of God,
                proclaims turning from all sin,
                proclaims reconciliation through The Cross.

The gospel of The Lord discloses the meaning to mortality,
                imparts purpose to the soul,
                          as directed counselling when invited.

The gospel of The Lord is good news for mankind,
                has the perspective of eternity,
                contains outpourings of agapé love.

The gospel of The Lord records eyewitnesses of a life,
                is verified in daily happening,
                affirms with stones long placed.

The gospel of The Lord answers the seekers of The Truth,
                imprints the seal of racial harmony,
                insists on the justice of The Cross.

The gospel of The Lord is the reading of the centuries,
                the compelling call across the ages,
                the moral source with appeal to reason.

The gospel of The Lord details the effective gifts of God,
                is birthed from an incarnate deity,
                impacts the senses of the flesh.

The Gospel of The Lord:
                The expression of The Living God and His will for man.

The Gospel of The Lord:
                The disclosure of the grand design for man by The Loving God.

The Gospel of The Lord:
                Offers understanding of the greatest sacrifice brought before the
                                  hopelessness of man.

The Gospel of The Lord:
                Presented for acceptance in an age of mercy undeserved.

The Gospel of The Lord:
                To bring light into the darkness in a world without restraint.

The Gospel of The Lord:

Reaching out to those with initial Faith and witness and The
Wisdom born of Grace.

The gospel of The Lord contains an offer within a timeframe for acceptance,
contains a timeframe for repentance.

The gospel of The Lord speaks of the ending of the age of the church,
speaks of a new beginning ushered in by a new dawn when
justice will prevail.

The non-repentant should beware of their coming judgement when justice
will prevail.

Repent and turn while it is yet today,
for the day when an accounting is required of man is not known to man.

Yet to each that day approaches,
without pause,
as the sands run through the hour-glass of every man's mortality."

My Content Study Aid

_____
_____
_____
_____
_____
_____
_____
_____
_____
_____
_____
_____
_____
_____
_____
_____
_____
_____
_____
_____
_____

The Dispelling of The Shadows

"The dispelling of the shadows is a joyful assignment of the angels.

The dispelling of the shadows is attended to with glee,
                with thoroughness,
                with a hand upon the helm.

The dispelling of the shadows is the remnant,
        the residue,
        the vestiges of grief,
            of mourning,
            of what broke a heart.

The dispelling of the shadows brings restoration of the spirit and transference to a
                                  memory within the soul.

The dispelling of the shadows brings closure to a wounded heart,
        brings relief within a soul,
        brings recuperation of the body.

The dispelling of the shadows completes the cycle of relationship,
        puts new hope where none existed,
        permits the expression of new love that surmounts
                                  the past.

The dispelling of the shadows gives acceptance to a separation,
        completes the consolation of the heart,
        welcomes the wonder of a new day.

The dispelling of the shadows removes the fear of loneliness,
        removes vengeance from the soul,
        removes the cry of desperation from the
                            agony encountered.

The dispelling of the shadows brings understanding of The Love of God,
        causes the examining of any residue of curses,
        enables waters again to refresh the cheeks with the tears
                                    of joy.

The dispelling of the shadows removes the desire for retribution,
        brings mercy to the fore on the wings of forgiveness,
        completes fulfilment of a season in the life of man.

The dispelling of the shadows brings peace to the heart that dwells on
                            'What might have been...',
        comforts those who shoulder blame for events they did
                                    not control,

                lifts burdens from backs no longer caused to stoop.

The dispelling of the shadows seals the unspoken word,
                releases the word that did not carry love,
                      the word that imposed a barrier.

The dispelling of the shadows obtains confirmation of the guilt:
                      of pain imposed,
                      of love undeclared,
                      of apologies untendered.

The dispelling of the shadows recalls items of non-completion,
                softens the intensity of regret,
                touches relationships in need.

The dispelling of the shadows has victory in completion when angels record a repentant
                                              prayer from a contrite heart.

The dispelling of the shadows enables a new approach to life,
                            without bitterness or rancour.

The dispelling of the shadows removes confusion from the mind.

The dispelling of the shadows is an act of God,
                is a blessing in disguise,
                marks the end of a time under Heaven in the life of man."

My Content Study Aid

_____
_____
_____
_____
_____
_____
_____
_____
_____
_____
_____
_____
_____

The Cup of The Fruit of The Vine

"The cup of the fruit of the vine has a special place in the life of each disciple,
  in the life of My Church,
  in lives that hold a promise dear.

The cup of the fruit of the vine was set apart for remembrance:
  at a supper,
  within an appointed time.

The cup of the fruit of the vine is available through all seasons of The Earth,
  through all climates of The Earth,
  through all locations on The Earth.

The cup of the fruit of the vine does not suffer the spoilage of the foe,
  does not contain additions to the must.

The cup of the fruit of the vine results from the very best,
  does not bring a grimace to the face,
  is not imbibed to excess when reason may be forsaken.

The cup of the fruit of the vine was valid in the days of the incarnation,
  has been valid through the centuries,
  is as valid today as it was in these times past.

The cup of the fruit of the vine has been decried,
  has been withheld,
  has been withdrawn,
  from its place of honour as a symbol of shed blood.

The cup of the fruit of the vine has been allowed to be trammelled by the will of man
  when bowing to an addiction held in sin by some.

The cup of the fruit of the vine does not tear down the drunkard when the odour of the
  fresh fruit solely lingers in the cup,
  does not tear down the rehabilitated when the will
  is re-established.

The cup of the fruit of the vine is not to be made a victim,
  without power,
  by those serving up social responsibility as an
  adjunct to The Power of God.

The cup of the fruit of the vine always bears witness of the Gospel message in
  its fullness.

The cup of the fruit of the vine bears witness to the failure of the counsel when addiction
  continues unabated.

The cup of the fruit of the vine arouses the jealousy of God when His ordinance installed
            at such a cost is held as of no account through
            selection without wisdom so the addicted may
            continue so.

The cup of the fruit of the vine knows the message that accompanies The Cross.

The cup of the fruit of the vine does not countenance—
            the removal of temptation so addiction may continue,
            the assumption that failure remains the outcome in a
                        life where hope was lost,
            the position that the will cannot be strengthened in a
                        life without support:
            the proposition that man should not be tested for
                        resolve and thereby arise in
                        the esteem of self-worth.

The cup of the fruit of the vine knows that were it so that man should not be tested for
            resolve then Abraham did not need his son on a journey to an
            altar and a promise from the lips of man may be of no account.

The cup of the fruit of the vine does not suffer usurpers parading in false colours,
            does not suffer the usurping of its place of honour,
            does not suffer denials of its standing in the house of God.

The cup of the fruit of the vine does not suffer those who partake with
                        double-mindedness,
            those who partake with wandering eyes,
            those who partake with misdirected thoughts,
            those who partake with no recall,
            those who partake with closed ears,
            those who partake without an intent of welcome.

The cup of the fruit of the vine is there for My Disciples,
            is not for those without a memory to remember.

The cup of the fruit of the vine should not lightly be taken to the lips.

The cup of the fruit of the vine is the highest emblem on The Earth:
            that brings,
            each time,
            to the fore the new covenant entered into with,
                        and by,
                        The Saints.

The cup of the fruit of the vine is a voice within a voice that calls man repeatedly
                        to repentance.

The cup of the fruit of the vine recognizes those with unrepentant lips,
            those without a memory,

those who would test The God who upholds
His Word.

The cup of the fruit of the vine carries a blessing or a curse,
a celebration or a judgement,
a future of companionship or a future
of separation.

Unwise are they who partake lightly of the cup of the fruit of the vine.

Unwise are they who treat the cup of the fruit of the vine with familiarity,
with contempt,
with an approach that
speaks of little worth.

Such are they with little worth to their appeal when the cup of the fruit of the vine
shall testify of Faith encountered on the lips of man.

Wise are they who adjust their lives in line with The Word for they partake in celebration
with all the blessings of the cup of the fruit of the vine.

Wise are they who imbibe only the blessings of the cup of the fruit of the vine.

Wise are they who confirm their covenants upheld through the cup of the fruit of
the vine."

My Content Study Aid

_____
_____
_____
_____
_____
_____
_____
_____
_____
_____
_____
_____
_____
_____
_____

The Feeding of The Sheep

"The feeding of the sheep can be a shared responsibility.

My shepherds feed My sheep,
>My lambs,
>>in preparation of a call,
>>in preparation for a journey,
>>in acceptance of a new beginning.

My shepherds feed the flock with oversight and care.

My shepherds feed the flock that has intermingled sheep and goats:
>>whose time has not yet come.

My shepherds may permit sheep to feed each other according to the diet,
>according to the roughage,
>according to the taste.

Those sheep that tender food will account for its effect,
>bringing nourishment or sickness,
>resulting from both the selection of the food and The Wisdom of the sheep that tendered such for consumption by a flock that paraded trust.

Those sheep that have tendered food found to be bitter,
>that leaves sores within the mouth,
>that causes stomachs later to vomit,
will each be marked by the shepherds as by raddle in the colour red.

Shepherds are to watch for sheep known to be marked with red for such as they—
>will no longer feed the sheep,
>will no longer share a diet,
>will no longer lead to a new pasture,
>will no longer open gates,
>will no longer bleat a call,
>will no longer bring the song from another shepherd.

Beware of sheep known to be red that wander in from distant flocks travelling the waterfall of pride,
>that will contaminate the flock with a false quest that neither succours nor satisfies the appetite.

For such sheep,
>in these days,
>>are but temporarily mistaken by the shepherds as sheep to be trusted with the lambs.

For they will soon gather the weak and bereft around them,
                together with those too young to shear,
              in the centre of the flock where their bleating
              causes havoc as discontent is spread.

Beware of a sheep that needs the drench of liberation for it will kick to escape to fresh
        pastures before the raddle can be erased:
            enticing,
            with false companionship,
            walks to other flocks.

Beware of a sheep that would lead others to be slaughtered,
        would promise food appealing to the palate,
        would deny the quality of the pasture that surrounds the flock,
        would accuse it of little nutrient,
        would tempt a comparison without honour to the shepherd,
        would accuse without foundation when on betrayal's
                slippery slope.

For such a sheep was known in a flock of long ago.

Beware of a sheep that hides a history,
        that claims the status of a sheep.

For a sheep that dwells within a flock soon creates a record of a journey,
            of testimony,
            of progress,
            of knowledge,
            from sharing within the flock.

For lone sheep are alone for a reason,
        are beyond the reach of counsel,
        have set attitudes of behaviour,
        have beliefs not open to be changed,
        are stunted in their growth,
        have diminished spirits,
        suffer enlarged souls as hermits from rebuke.

For such sheep will claim entitlements that do not exist,
        will attempt to bleat without consent,
        will share a testimony built on flights of fancy,
        will direct without authority,
        will pursue the boundaries of new vistas,
        will hover in mid-stream not knowing where to settle.

Beware,
    there are goats in flocks that look and sound and act like sheep,
    until the day of their unmasking when they will be seen in the true colours of
                what their souls declare.

The feeding of the sheep brings unity of purpose,
> brings health to all the flock,
> imparts knowledge of defence,
> ensures all are dipped and clean.

The feeding of the sheep sees gambolling around the shepherds,
> sees feet ready to be sent,
> sees tongues that quiver in anticipation with arrows
>> all prepared.

The feeding of the sheep is completed:
> when new journeys are commenced in the company of a sword,
> when sheep are all enamoured by the opening of horizons,
> when sheep all have new tongues that no longer bleat,
> when sheep have had their stomachs filled and all know their
>> own ways home.

The feeding of the sheep brings honour to the shepherd as they depart now to feed others:
> as they themselves now know the feeding from on high,
> as they are affixed as jewels to the shepherd's cloak,
> the shepherd that suffered and rejoiced through all the seasons
>> in his caring for his flock."

My Content Study Aid

Attacks Upon The Heart of Man

"Beware of the attacks upon the heart of man.

The attacks upon the heart emanate from unexpected sources,
        can be manipulated for disastrous effects,
        can build upon each other until the objective is achieved.

The heart attacks of man play out on a thoroughfare,
        are not a sideshow in an alley,
        are minimized where the light is bright,
        are threatening in alleys where the light is dim,
        are bred from diets administered under the instructions of
                the foe.

Beware the foe of man.
Beware the foe of Heaven.
Beware the foe of God.

He who has dominion in defiance of a King is not,
        was not,
        will never be,
        the friend of man.

For the foe is determined to bring about the downfall of man:
        the downfall of his soul,
        the destruction of his spirit,
        the prior decay of his body,
        the downfall of man's surroundings,
        the social orders,
        the societies established in the nations of
                The Earth.

All will fall in chaos when the battle is not joined,
        when the battle is attended by the ill-equipped,
        when the remnant of a battle has no-one in reserve,
        when the general is ignored with the battle lines in tatters,
        when the battle is one-sided and no-one believes it's theirs to fight.

Then watch the families fall,
        the cities turn to obscenities that pander to the lusts,
        the nations turn to the slaying of The Innocent.

Watch the iniquities of man spread to the boldness of the day and no longer shelter in
                the company of the terrors of the night.

Then approaches at a gallop the quartering of The Earth.

The heart attacks of man can be traced to his environment,
        can be traced to abuse not alleviated,
        can be traced to ignorance sustained,
        can be traced to invasions that remain uncurbed,
        can be traced to warnings not heeded,
        can be traced to emotions running high,
        can be traced to pressure not relieved,
        can be traced to a diet without an antidote,
        can be traced to a shock without resuscitation,
        can be traced to exertion without a pause,
        can be traced to a heart always in pain,
              that is fractured without repair,
        can be traced to a heart that suffers a stranglehold that chokes.

Attacks upon the heart of man strike at the very mortal centre of man's eternal life,
        can bring a termination while a decision is still pending,
            while a promise awaits further consideration,
            while a call is still outstanding.

Attacks upon the heart of man come in many different guises:
        leave open or slowly shut the door of life.

    The door of life is not easily re-opened once it shuts,
        is never re-opened once the key is turned.

    The door of life closes out an offer of co-existence when allowed to fall from the
              table of acceptance,
        whereon it was laid before the mortality of a soul.

    The door of life is fragile when it opens,
        is buttressed when it closes.

    The door of life introduces each new spirit,
        farewells departing souls.

    The door of life,
        as it locks,
        opens the gateway of the grave.

Attacks upon the heart of man threaten future existence,
        bring time frames to the fore,
        reminds man of his proximity to the grave.

Attacks upon the heart of man should warn of breath foreshortened,
        should warn of the need to listen,
            to accept,
            to act,
            to reach out,
            to grasp,

the saving hands that brought a message:
> a message of uniqueness,
> a message rendered at great cost,
> a message that rings with truth,
> a message with an eternal consequence,
>> for acceptance or rejection,
>>> before the heart of each is stopped.

Attacks upon the heart of man can come without a warning,
> can be spoken as a curse by man,
> can invoke the presence of Death.

Attacks upon the heart of man can cause the spirit to succumb,
> the rebellious soul to rejoice,
> the healthy body to decline.

Attacks upon the heart of man may come through the wielding of a weapon,
> may be countered by the wise,
> may be overcome by the valiant,
> may be non-threatening to the prepared.

Attacks upon the heart of man may culminate in a broken heart,
> may culminate in death.

The heart attacks of man may release the body,
> may bring a change of life-style,
> may cause alterations in a diet.

The heart attacks of man may culminate in the stopping of the heart."

My Content Study Aid

_____
_____
_____
_____
_____
_____
_____
_____
_____
_____

The Exorcizing of Demons

"The exorcizing of demons holds no fear for those who walk in designated authority.

The exorcizing of demons is the exercise of power within bestowed authority,
        is of no great portent,
        is manifested in changed lives.

The exorcizing of demons can be seen and heard and felt,
        is a testimony of The Holy Spirit.

The exorcizing of demons quells the querulous,
        opens mouths,
        widens eyes.

The exorcizing of demons tests The Wisdom of The Saints.

The exorcizing of demons is not for those who insist on drinking milk,
        who do not appreciate the need for informed company,
        who do not understand authority,
        who would seek shelter from power displayed.

The exorcizing of demons is signed by those with averted eyes,
        by those without muscular control,
        by those with obscenities on their lips,
        by those with vocal cords in disarray.

The exorcizing of demons is required by those who sense all is not well within their soul,
        their body,
        their spirit.

The exorcizing of demons is required for those who come with curses,
    for those subjected by oaths that swore allegiance to other gods,
        in idolatry,
        in the occult,
        in the isms of their lives,
    for those who would seek freedom from the generational past,
        from societies that spoke of other gods,
        from when the knee was bent and brought
            no honour.

The guidance of The Holy Spirit is there in each participant to direct the comfort of the afflicted in reassurance of the outcome.

The exorcizing of demons is not for those who do not seek,
        who will not confess 'Jesus is Lord',
        who do not wish to disturb what they already have.

The exorcizing of demons is an offered pathway of release,
        is not a compulsive exercise.

The exorcizing of demons should not bring distress to those who value freedom.

The exorcizing of demons when in the presence,
        the power,
    the moving of The Holy Spirit cannot result in the endangerment of
                anyone's mortality,
        cannot cause a death,
        cannot issue threats with any thread of truth.

The exorcizing of demons are not the acts of man.

The exorcizing of demons exhibits the pled ministry of God,
        the sought ministry of God,
        the imparted ministry of God.

The exorcizing of demons is evidence of demonic influence that is to be brought to an
                abrupt ending,
        that is to be no longer countenanced,
        that is to denote the restoration of a temple,
        that is to mark the eviction of the squatters
            who have now outstayed their welcome.

The exorcizing of demons is not a conversation,
        is deaf to a pleading of a cause,
        invokes no sympathy for invaders.

The exorcizing of demons is the gathering of evidence,
        a judgement made on truth,
        the issuing of commands that bring release,
        from those who know authority:
        when the power of The Holy Spirit will witness to
                the senses.

Failure to evict is an admission of defeat,
        is a sign of the lack of much prayer and fasting,
        requires a designated time for when the battle is rejoined.

The exorcizing of demons leaves none in residence,
        no caretaker to open doors,
        none charged with spheres of influence:
                for all is swept and clean.

The exorcizing of demons drops the hangers-on,
        sheds the riders on the shoulders that whisper to the ears,
        removes the probing fingers searching for a hook:
                then surfaces are all dry-cleaned.

The exorcizing of demons is needed when relationships are strained,
　　　　　　when counsel is declined,
　　　　　　when confusion strikes the mind,
　　　　　　when a cowed spirit hovers over a soul doing as
　　　　　　　　　　　　　　it pleases.

The exorcizing of demons is needed when an invitation has been extended,
　　　　　　when there has been an impartation through the laying-on of hands,
　　　　　　when deeds signify acceptance of tentative enquiries.

Demons can be invited through the landscape of the eyes,
　　　　　　the misuse of the hands,
　　　　　　the irreverence of the tongue.

Demons can be invited through the impulses of the ear,
　　　　　　the odours of invasion,
　　　　　　the forbidden touch.

Demons gleefully participate in the occult,
　　　　　　in idolatry,
　　　　　　in perversions with mind appeal.

Beware of the windows opened:
　　　　the windows of the residence,
　　　　the windows of The Temple,
　　　　　　that will display a welcome sign to demons in the absence of a covering.

The exorcizing of demons follows a request,
　　　　　　a confession,
　　　　　　a repentance born of understanding:
　　　　of the influence previously yielded to those who would but harm.

The exorcizing of demons follows repudiation of the contract with the demons that
　　　　　　accepted an invitation to attend.

The exorcizing of demons spells an end to suffering incurred without informed consent,
　　　　　　incurred by agencies beyond immediate control,
　　　　　　incurred by the willingness of acceptance of
　　　　　　　　　　experiments with death.

The exorcizing of demons should result in a change of attitude,
　　　　　　in a seeking of The Truth,
　　　　　　in a forsaking of past habits,
　　　　　　in a denial of an access previously laid bare.

The exorcizing of demons re-establishes the firewall of a recovering soul.

The firewall of the soul is checked for leaks by the spirit of man,
　　　　　　the lamp of The Lord,
　　　　　　　　　　that searches in the light."

The Visitors to The Garden

"The visitors to the garden have had trauma in their lives.

The visitors to the garden have their status changed by prayer,
               have recall according to their prior testimony,
               are accompanied by the gardener.

The visitors to the garden reel under the impressions on their senses,
               load memories to be recalled in dreams.

The visitors to the garden may elect to stay when qualified,
               may elect to return to surroundings more familiar.

The visitors to the garden do not converse with others,
               cannot catch anyone's attention,
               cannot determine where they visit.

The visitors to the garden may have open vistas,
               may be focussed on a beam of light,
               may see shadowed figures beyond the veil of recognition.

The visitors to the garden are called within the plan of God and in the presence of
                                                              an appeal.

The visitors to the garden are there when time is stationary,
               are there when time is dependent on a decision,
               are there when time is soon to be restarted.

The visitors to the garden do not linger at their leisure.

The visitors to the garden are there for a set purpose,
               are not judged for their behaviour.

The visitors to the garden are there for validation of intent,
               for validation of a testimony,
               for validation of a change of pace.

The visitors to the garden are there to bear witness to the sceptics of access to existence,
               are there to bear witness to an excursion,
               are there to carry a vision seen to those who have no way of
                                                        knowing hope.

The visitors to the garden need little understanding,
               will know what they have seen,
               will always bear The Truth when exaggeration is impossible.

The visitors to the garden are reporters of 'what is',
               are reporters of an experience,
               are unable fully to explain its scope in the words of man.

The visitors to the garden travel to where few are granted access,
> travel with the breath of life still active,
> travel in the company of angels.

The visitors to the garden often want to stay.

The visitors to the garden have all requests refused when the spirit is unqualified and the
> soul does not claim the surroundings.

The visitors to the garden are not accepted thrice while the breath of life is resident.

The visitors to the garden will not forget their visit,
> may attribute to it a change in lifestyle,
> may evidence a changed belief,
> may change a destiny of ignominy to one of gratitude
>> in choice.

Wise are they who listen to the visitors to the garden.

Wise are they who question intently the visitors to the garden.

Wise are they who accept as true,
> the experience of a lifetime as recounted in all earnestness by
>> the visitors to the garden."

My Content Study Aid

_____
_____
_____
_____
_____
_____
_____
_____
_____
_____
_____
_____
_____
_____
_____
_____

The Lick of The Lion

"The lick of the lion is the sign of acceptance within the pride.

The lick of the lion gives the licked a bath,
                cleans the coat,
                prevents infection to a wound,
                removes contaminants on the skin,
                removes infestations from the hiding places.

The lick of the lion speaks of love,
                speaks of care,
                speaks of the supply of the necessities of life.

The lick of the lion sets an example to be followed,
                teaches the young of expectations,
                confirms the presence of paws holding the promise of security.

The lick of the lion leads on to an endowment,
                accompanies on future journeys,
                offers protection when in difficulty.

The lick of the lion is confirmation of a loving father,
                is confirmation of close attention,
                is confirmation that all is well.

The lick of the lion is accompanied by the growl of correction,
                is accompanied by the paw that gives a cuff,
                is accompanied by instructions on behaviour.

The lick of the lion is never far away,
                is in the proximity of a cuddle,
                is near a resting place of comfort,
                ensures protection when asleep.

The lick of the lion is in the presence of good food,
                is in the presence of other licks,
                is in the presence of both day and night.

The lick of the lion surrounds the search for truth,
                directs the thirsty to the water,
                the hungry to the larder that is never empty.

The lick of the lion expresses knowledge found beyond horizons,
                expresses knowledge gained for the end of life,
                expresses knowledge acquired through a life on Earth.

The lick of the lion wipes away the tears of misery,
                the tears of hurts,

>   the tears of happiness.
>
> The lick of the lion removes the devourers of the body and the soul,
>   evicts hyenas from vicinities where the young attend their schooling.
>
> The lick of the lion frees the body,
>   frees the soul,
>   frees the spirit,
>   frees life to continue in a remote land of plenty.
>
> The lick of the lion is a sacrifice of time,
>   was present at a sacrifice in time,
>   is a sacrifice throughout time.
>
> The lick of the lion stops disease in its tracks,
>   opens the way to unending health,
>   has a lesson in each lick that should never be forgotten."

My Content Study Aid

The Victors of The Soul

"The victors of the soul are spread throughout The Earth.

The victors of the soul are unified in creed,
                are a multitude of races,
                have diversity in tongues.

The victors of the soul seek each other's company,
                hold hands in adversity,
                seek to strengthen ones that waver.

The victors of the soul long for justice in their home lands,
                long for sanctity of life,
                long for the eviction of corruption.

The victors of the soul have experiences worth telling,
                have stories that will keep the ears inclined,
                have wounds that testify to The Truth.

The victors of the soul expand the choice of the soul,
                expand the influence of the soul,
                expand the horizons of the soul.

The victors of the soul value the company of the soul,
                value the consistency of the soul,
                value the experience of the soul.

The victors of the soul treasure the memories retained within the soul,
                treasure the worth of the soul in the sight of God,
                treasure the value of a soul that yields to the authority of God.

The victors of the soul have an insight that appeals to others.

The victors of the soul acquire support rather than baggage,
                acquire wisdom rather than knowledge,
                acquire the walk of righteousness rather than flounder through
                                          a quagmire.

The victors of the soul have lit a candle that burns within,
                have lit a candle with portholes in the face,
                have lit a candle protected from the draughts that snuff.

The victors of the soul have lit the candle of The Lord,
                          that searches all within,
                          that shines brightly for each footstep,
                          that is a beacon in the darkness,
                          that is at home within the light.

The victors of the soul have trained,
> have taught,
>> have mastered an errant lively child and have brought it
>>> successfully to the junction of The Cross.

The victors of the soul know the junction of The Cross where that turning point in life
> requires a decision from the soul.

The victors of the soul know the junction of The Cross,
> that splits between the broad and narrow ways.

The victors of the soul have The Fear of God,
> impart The Fear of God,
> carry The Fear of God.

The victors of the soul know full well that all road blocks will crumble when confronted
> by The Fear of God.

The victors of the soul know the bridle of obedience,
>> that harnesses the soul,
>> that indicates direction,
>> that brings the victor's touch.

The victors of the soul instruct but do not beat,
> teach but do not enslave,
> value freedom highly that results in the embrace of love.

The victors of the soul know of a special sacrifice made for the soul not governed by
>> a victory:
>> that does not wear a bridle,
>> that has yet to encounter,
>>> in a battle,
>> the rider on a white horse."

My Content Study Aid

_____
_____
_____
_____
_____
_____
_____
_____

The Power of The Holy Spirit

"The power of The Holy Spirit is grossly misunderstood,
    is grossly under estimated,
    is grossly under utilised.

The power of The Holy Spirit is extremely benign,
    is extremely widespread,
    is extremely concerned with man.

The power of The Holy Spirit is there by invitation,
    is there to dispense favour,
    is there to be a witness.

The power of The Holy Spirit upholds The Word of God,
    upholds the body of the ministry,
    upholds the body of believers.

The power of The Holy Spirit is displayed within the works of God,
    is displayed within The Temple of the spirit,
    is displayed within the emergencies of man.

The power of The Holy Spirit overcomes all others,
    overcomes acts of attrition,
    overcomes dictates of the soul.

The power of The Holy Spirit attends each new installation,
    frequents the presence of a temple wound,
    calls attended gatherings of angels.

The power of The Holy Spirit summons as required,
    dispenses as needed,
    inspects all for perfection.

The power of The Holy Spirit erupts in healings of the anatomy of man,
    erupts in the splendour of the tongue that can circumvent
            the lips,
    erupts in a myriad of manners,
        that fall,
        upon request.

The power of The Holy Spirit manifests as miracles within the life of man,
    manifests as incidents of wonder within a landscape
            of design,
    manifests as the imposition of events on a timescale
            of precision.

The power of The Holy Spirit is the inheritance of The Cross liberated into the life

                                                                    of man,
                    is the promise of The Father evident in the rendering of The Cross.

The power of The Holy Spirit is speaking of God exemplified,
                                    personified,
                                    deified.

The power of The Holy Spirit is awe-full in implication,
                                is awe-full in application,
                                is awe-full in supplication.

The power of The Holy Spirit is not to be taken lightly,
                                should not be ill-considered,
                                would not be so easily dismissed by those on whom
                                                    wisdom has smiled.

The power of The Holy Spirit stands for ever,
                                comes with truth,
                                revels in righteousness.

The power of The Holy Spirit is the confirmation of The God of Action involved in the
                                                    life of man,
                                is the testimony of The God of Love in the life of man,
                                is the witness of the involvement of The Living God in the
                                                    life of man.

The power of The Holy Spirit assails the senses of man in this time.

The power of The Holy Spirit assails the harvest,
                                assails communication,
                                assails the soul of unbelief,
                                assails the soul of misbelief,
                                assails the soul of non-belief,
                                assails the wayward soul where belief has yet to root.

The power of The Holy Spirit opens eyes in wonder at the scenes beheld,
                                mutes mouths familiar with obscenities,
                                inclines ears for intensive listening.

The power of The Holy Spirit restores use to limbs not functioning,
                                restores sensing to the senses,
                                restores Faith to the unfaithful.

The power of The Holy Spirit removes pain from the afflicted,
                                removes restricted motion,
                                removes impediments to health.

The power of The Holy Spirit does not discourse with the impediments to health,
                                does not bandy words with the impediments to health,
                                does not permit the impediments to health,

> the hangers-on,
> the influencers of the soul,
> the shadowers of the spirit,
> to continue their activities when access is denied."

My Content Study Aid

The Mustering of The Bride

"The fall of the dew occurs according to the time,
                according to release,
                according to the preparation.

The fall of the dew occurs in announcement of The Eternal Kingdom,
                occurs as an indicator of angelic interest,
                as disclosure of intent.

The fall of the dew occurs to open mouths prepared,
                occurs to heighten expectations,
                occurs to encourage acceptance of the calls,
                occurs to draw attention to the coming presence,
                occurs to indicate commitment,
                occurs for the benefit of man.

The fall of the dew occurs to preserve access to resources,
                occurs to forewarn of a battle,
                occurs so each weapon will be at the ready,
                occurs so defences are impenetrable,
                occurs so footprints can be traced.

The fall of the dew occurs in the driest of the areas,
                occurs to dampen down the dust,
                occurs to soften the reception,
                occurs to ease the penetration,
                occurs to strengthen hope within the workers prior to taking wing,
                occurs to answer righteous prayer.

The fall of the dew occurs as The Spirit goes before,
                occurs as angels are assembled,
                occurs in the sight of the perceptive,
                occurs to prepare the visionary to receive,
                occurs to remind the forgetful of The Promises,
                occurs for the filling of the tanks.

The fall of the dew occurs to enhance effect,
                occurs as a warning to the foe,
                occurs to encourage new behaviour,
                occurs to signify the sealing of the will.

The fall of the dew occurs in expansion as the seed is sown,
                    as the seed is grown,
                    as the seed is mown.

The fall of the dew occurs before the doves have flown.

The spreading of the wetness is a film upon the ground,
        is the promise of a deluge,
        is the offering of uptake to each soul in a desert.

The spreading of the wetness is for assimilation,
        is for accumulation,
        is for resuscitation.

The spreading of the wetness is for the growth of Faith,
        is an initial testimony,
        is confirmation of the time,
        is seen in its effect,
        is in the softening of souls,
        is the breaking of the crust.

The spreading of the wetness is reaching to the roots,
        is to encourage growth,
        is a general awakening,
        is the awareness of great change,
        is to soften the shell,
        is so the kernel of the nut is set free to achieve its purpose.

The fall of the rain comes from an open sky,
        comes when not expected,
        comes without the warning clouds,
        comes as a soaking to the just.

The fall of the rain comes to remove the drought,
        comes to succour the dehydrated,
        comes to refill all the tanks,
        comes to justify the shower.

The fall of the rain comes to trigger fervent growth,
        to trigger explosive Faith,
        to trigger acceptance by the workers of their calls from God.

The fall of the rain comes at a time decreed.

The fall of the rain comes in the dampened areas,
        comes for the sustenance of life,
        comes to rescue prostrate souls,
        comes to replenish the spirit that cries out for assistance.

The fall of the rain comes in time to meet objectives,
        comes in time to answer prayer,
        comes in time to fulfil The Will of God.

The fall of the rain comes in time to fill the rivers of life.

The spreading of the downpour is the soaking of The Spirit,

       is in the presence of the sun,
       is an inundation of the land,
       is an outreach to the nations,
       is the opening of the floodgates,
       is the breaking of the dams,
       is the overflowing of the rivers.

The spreading of the downpour is the cleansing of contamination,
       is selective in approach,
       is the washing of contrition,
       is a testimony of power.

The spreading of the downpour is of great interest to man,
       is of great significance to man,
       is of great impact on man.

The spreading of the downpour is there for all to see,
       is a witness of a sacrifice,
       is the mark of redemption,
       is the abandonment of sin,
       is the retreat of sin,
       is the acceptance of The Word of God.

The spreading of the downpour is seen on fields well watered.

The spreading of the downpour is seen as on rice fields with new plantings,
          where every shoot is green,
          where every shoot is rooted.

The spreading of the downpour is seen as on rice fields where water gushes
            in abundance.

The spreading of the downpour is seen as on rice fields where every shoot is upright,
          where no shoots are bent,
          where no shoots linger in the mud
          with their heads submerged.

The fall of the fire brings the draining of the fields,
    brings the drying of the crop,
    brings knowledge to the workers with wisdom in its use,
    brings enabling to the workers to discern damage within the crop.

The fall of the fire brings boldness in handling the crop,
      in delivering the crop,
      in winnowing the crop.

The fall of the fire brings assurance to the Master that not a single grain of rice has fallen
            to the ground.

The fall of the fire brings great care in how the crop is prepared,

                      on where the crop is sent,
                      on how the crop is divided.

The fall of the fire brings the workers with abilities,
                      not easily explained,
                into contact with the crop that is amazed at what it sees,
                                    at what it hears,
                                    at what it feels.

The fall of the fire brings new recruits to the fore.

The fall of the fire brings new methods of operation,
            new knowledge of belief,
            new reasons for The Faith displayed.

The fall of the fire brings new explanations of the works performed in the presence of
                                                        the sceptics.

The fall of the fire brings new beginnings to those with little Faith,
                    to those with little comfort,
                    to those with misplaced trust.

The fall of the fire brings a searching of the souls without an explanation,
                              for what cannot be,
                                          yet is;
                            for what should not happen,
                                          yet does.

The fall of the fire brings a searching of the souls without an explanation,
                for a testimony of an experience sustained by all the senses
                                    in the presence of a need.

The fall of the fire brings a searching of the souls for an explanation built on
                                the confession,
                                    of the tongue,
                                that passes through the lips.

The spreading of the conflagration brings gathering to a peak,
                brings fire in diverse places,
                brings fire that joins the enclaves,
                brings fire that is unquenchable within the timing
                                                of God.

The spreading of the conflagration brings extreme unity of purpose,
                brings souls in numbers that are difficult to count,
                brings welcome pressure on the workers,
                brings welcome pressure on facilities,
                brings welcome pressure on resources.

The spreading of the conflagration brings testimonies to within the reach of the souls
                                                                      at large,
                brings The Word to the souls for an entry in the Book,
                brings jubilation to those in the fields,
                brings jubilation to those who dwell within the fields,
                brings jubilation to the angels charged with a
                                                      recording brief.

The spreading of the conflagration brings gifts falling on upraised hands,
                              on each accepting soul,
                              on each uplifted spirit.

The spreading of the conflagration brings encountered sin up to the fire as fuel;
                brings waters of immersion to the body;
                brings fresh gifts of communication to the spirit
                                            through the tongue.

The spreading of the conflagration brings a hastening of closure to the age,
                brings nearer the return of promise,
                brings a notice to the door of Grace that is about
                                                    to close.

The vestiges of the harvest are not to be overlooked.

The vestiges of the harvest are as important as the first:
                              for,
                              when order is important,
                the last will be first and the first will be last.

The vestiges of the harvest have places reserved,
        have equality of access,
        are not deprived of anything.

The vestiges of the harvest who seek will also find,
                will not be forgotten,
                will be triumphant in establishment.

The vestiges of the harvest,
        though they be recruits but an hour or a minute in the fields,
        will they themselves receive the same reward as those on whom the centuries
                                                                     melt away:
                        when the days of Grace come to an end.

The gleaning of the fields is carried out with thoroughness,
                is neither hurried nor in judgement,
                closes with the recording of the secret desires of the heart of
                                                  each remaining soul.

A field is closed to Grace when the remaining hearts are unanimous in rejection.

A field is closed when there is no queue at the door of entrance,
        when there is no clamour that includes a cry for help to The Name above
                all names.

For even a whispered cry from the weak,
        the weary,
        the dying,
    is heard as if a trumpet blast above the clamour of the worldly,
        the clamour of the foe,
           the clamour that will not be answered except
                before a throne.

The dressing of The Bride is composite but separate.

The dressing of The Bride is an exciting time for man,
        is an exciting time for angels,
        is an exciting time for God.

The dressing of The Bride occurs during the life time when Faith is present,
        during the life time when Faith is evident,
        during the time of life from when the lips of man
            profess belief upon the promise of a cross.

The dressing of The Bride is a daily occurrence,
        does not dress in the gown of yesterday,
        cannot dress in the gown of tomorrow,
        will not be permitted to dress in the gown of promises.

The dressing of The Bride always wears the dress of today,
        passes through the grave with the dress of that day,
        wears for all eternity the emblems on the final gown
                of mortality.

The dressing of The Bride has wisdom to assist,
        knows what to expect,
        knows how to acquire,
            the emblems,
            the jewels,
            the attachments of the suffering and the pain,
            the impositions that tested Faith:
    the adornments that will be transferred to the gown of eternal life.

The dressing of The Bride occurs daily in the presence of the angels so assigned.

The dressing of The Bride has great interest among the angels as progression of each
                gown is keenly noted,
        as additions are warranted for lives that dwell in righteousness.

The dressing of The Bride leaves nothing to be desired,
        is not gender sensitive,

reflects the rewards of a race well run.

The dressing of The Bride beyond the grave of man encompasses the gown of life:
>> of great scintillating beauty beyond compare,
>> of the six degrees* of honour,
>> of Glory:
>> due a triumphant soul with a spirit that has attained eternal life."

Scribal Note: *Hebrews 6:1-3 ('Six degrees of honour' affirmed, and so reference added,*

> 6 Therefore, leaving the discussion of the elementary principles of Christ, let us go on to perfection, not laying again the foundation of repentance from dead works and of Faith toward God, ²of the doctrine of baptisms, of laying on of hands, of resurrection of the dead, and of eternal judgment. ³And this we will do if God permits.
>
> Scripture taken from the New King James Version®. Copyright © 1982 by Thomas Nelson. Used by permission. All rights reserved.

My Content Study Aid

The Rise of Ashkelon

"The fall of Babylon is the fall of papered wealth.

The fall of Babylon is the shattering of the empty money pots,
        is the breaking of extended trust,
        is as the overturning of the tables,
        is in the presence of the money changers.

The fall of Babylon is as a temple in which they choose to worship,
        an edifice of man they thought could never fall.

The fall of Babylon is when the few have squandered the wealth of many,
        is when a single cry goes forth from a reservoir declaring
        "There is no money!",
        is when the steel cages become empty and the despots run for caves.

The fall of Babylon is when contracts are repudiated,
        is when beggars are able to survive,
        is when revenge is sought for dreams destroyed,
        is when 'responsibility' has long been a forgotten word on the lips of
        the unjust.

The fall of Babylon witnesses tremors of convulsion prior to the final throes of death.

The fall of Babylon sees the paper wealth of man blowing in the wind of change.

The fall of Babylon sees the paper wealth of man become of little worth,
        that is left lying in the dust,
        that is trampled underfoot,
        that cannot purchase when placed within
        the hand,
        that cannot be exchanged for anything
        of value.

The fall of Babylon is not an instant pile of bricks.

The fall of Babylon causes earthquakes of dissolution that rumble warning shouts upon
        ears that do not want to hear,
        is only after the shoring up of foundations that gobble the reserves,
        triggers the teetering of exchange in the nations of the world.

The fall of Babylon is complete when printing presses can no linger feed the maw of
        voracious greed;
        when the widow's mite is rendered worthless;
        when starvation feeds upon itself;
        when the rider on the pale horse careers where e're
        he will.

The fall of Babylon brings the rise of Ashkelon.

    Beware the rise of Ashkelon whose greed,
                whose corruption,
                whose harshest deeds,
                        will exceed those that brought the fall of Babylon.

    Beware the rise of Ashkelon that shakes its head as it awakens from the slumber of
                                            the centuries,
                in the monopolizing of trade within the enclaves,
                that heralds the coming of the turmoil.

Ashkelon will not fall,
    will order and control.

Ashkelon will have no mercy,
    will not help,
    will watch and count the tribute while nations fall and wither.

Ashkelon has armies too numerous to count while the eye remains awake,
    threatens and enforces,
    withholds and then laughs in each face.

Ashkelon turns its back and reaps the body parts to the highest bidder.

Ashkelon has a history of barbaric cruelty,
    will not yield to appeals for clemency,
    will only yield to the greater force.

Ashkelon will bring ruin to its debtors,
    will capture resources from behind the distant frontiers,
    will navigate The Earth in its quest for dominion of the seas and its conquest of
                                                          the skies.

Ashkelon will reap where it has not sown,
    will garner and not replenish,
    will lay waste without a care.

Ashkelon will seize without any reparation,
    will plunder as it pleases,
    will offer none a recompense for the stripping of a landscape.

Ashkelon will be empowered by the nations of The Earth,
    will entrap the nations of The Earth,
    will subjugate the nations of The Earth.

  Beware the hand that seizes and will not release its grasp.
  Beware the honeyed tongue and the fleecing contract.
  Beware the armour that defies and the sandalled feet of peace.

Let those with wisdom understand the need for preparation with
>
> the passing of each day,
> the passing of each month,
> the passing of each year.

Let those with wisdom be informed.

Let those with wisdom seek wise counsel.

Let those with wisdom have a hedge that protects both day and night."

My Content Study Aid

The Hackers of The Body

"The hacking of the body is the expertise of the foe.

The hacking of the body penetrates the defences with a hole within the wall.

The hacking of the body finds holes that have not been patched,
                    that have been left unattended,
                    that have no guards in place.

The hacking of the body searches diligently for wounds,
                    prises open an entry point,
                    expands it for others to follow.

The hacking of the body is an intrusion of the demons into a place where they should
                                                                         not be.

The hacking of the body employs viruses galore,
                    is aware of back-door entry,
                    rarely knocks on the front door.

The hacking of the body has attendees always waiting at the door of invitation.

The hackers of the body know the door of invitation is their best foothold for an entry;
                    know the door of invitation,
                                when fully opened,
                                is difficult to close;
                  know the door of invitation is very rarely locked.

The hackers of the body make known their success to others,
                    post the challenges on the notice board of temptation,
                    very rarely scrub them from the list of prospects.

The hackers of the body know that doors are left upon the latch,
                    that gates are left swinging on the hinges,
                    that windows to the soul are often left partly open,
                            are rarely fully shut at the closure of the day.

The hackers of the body know that windows to the soul have screens not set in place,
                                have their shades left undrawn;
                                their shutters rattling in
                                      the wind,
                                clashing in the storm.

The hacking of the body is simplicity itself when the modes of the attack remain
                                                          unknown to the owner,
                  is not required when the door of invitation is left ajar,
                  often fails in the presence of a protective hedge.

The hacking of the body is often successful when the hedge has withered,
                                                                                       is not watered,
                                                                                       has not been fed.

The hacking of the body is usually successful when the hedge is nearly dead.

The hacking of the body exposes vulnerabilities when encountering a withered hedge that
                                                                             offers no resistance.

The hackers of the body hate the firewall of enclosure,
                      the firewall replenished daily,
                      the firewall that feeds upon The Spirit's torch.

The hackers of the body hate the firewall with the password of a name they cannot use,
                      the name that reinstates the firewall,
                      the name that both waters and feeds the hedge."

My Content Study Aid

The Pets of The Earth

"The pets of The Earth should not be eaten by man,
                should not be abandoned by man,
                should not be mistreated by man,
                should not be slaughtered by man,
                should not be stolen by man,
                should not be imprisoned by man.

The pets of The Earth are there to create a bond,
                are there to express affection,
                are there to pay homage to each master,
                are there to display their beauty.

The pets of The Earth are there to teach responsibility to the young,
                to teach commitment to the mature,
                to bring companionship to the aged.

The pets of The Earth are there to dispel loneliness,
                to dispel selfishness,
              to dispel restlessness.

The pets of The Earth are there to display their senses within the scope of man.

The pets of The Earth have eyes of many different colours,
                have many different languages,
                have many different means of travel,
                have many different homes,
                have many different appetites,
                have many different sizes,
                have many different skins made for the hands of man to stroke.

The pets of The Earth seek little loyalty for trust,
                seek little by way of necessity,
                seek few comforts in their homes.

The pets of The Earth are wary with the predators,
                are wary in new surroundings,
                are wary with loud sounds.

The pets of The Earth shudder in the presence of the inflictors of pain,
                are concerned in the presence of those who measure the portions of
                              their food,
                are stressed in the presence of those who care not to preserve
                              their health.

The pets of The Earth have a message of eternity,
                have a message of creation,

have a message of survival.

The pets of The Earth have a message of inspection that speaks of their presence to all
the senses of man.

The pets of The Earth do not have voracious mouths,
do not have venom at their discretion,
do not have beaks that tear the flesh,
do not have rearward sloping teeth,
do not look down on man,
do not become pets simply through withdrawal from their
own environment.

The pets of The Earth are aware of God,
will communicate with God,
may object to the pains of mistreatment knowingly administered
by man.

The pets of The Earth are there to cultivate the spirit of man.

The pets of The Earth are there to intermingle with mankind,
to dress the habitations of The Earth,
to bring to A King the experience of A Kingdom where
his word is law.

The pets of The Earth are not religious symbols,
are not idolatrous by nature,
are not to receive worship that surpasses friendship."

My Content Study Aid

The Arms of The Lord

"The arms of The Lord reach out to enfold,
        reach out in love,
        reach out to welcome the wanderers.

The arms of The Lord beckon to those tentatively approaching,
        beckon to those who are hard of hearing,
        beckon to those who are busy playing,
        beckon to those immersed in work,
        beckon to those immersed in mire,
        beckon to those immersed in their denial.

The arms of The Lord strengthen the weak who seek support,
        the bold who seek assurance,
        the homeless who would have a home,
        the lost who seek The Truth,
        the thinkers who would have the answer,
        the knowledgeable who would crave The Wisdom
                behind the purpose of their lives.

The arms of The Lord reach out to catch the blind before they stumble,
        to steady those uncertain of their steps,
            those who falter with the goal in sight,
            those who have nearly lost their way;
        to confirm His Presence to a groping hand,
            with encouragement to the disheartened.

The arms of The Lord stretch down to uplift the prostrate who cannot move,
        those who crawl on hands and knees,
        those who are gasping and out of breath,
        to uplift the repentant sinners,
        those with contrite hearts,
        those with humble spirits,
        to uplift those who cry out to The Name above
                all names,
        to uplift those with the anguished cry of
            the downtrodden.

The healing arms of The Lord receive with tenderness those with a sickness of the soul,
        those with a sickness of the spirit,
        those with a sickness of the body;
        with tenderness those maimed by life,
        those insanely plagued by demons,
        those crippled by disease.

The arms of The Lord wait to hug the finishers of the race.

The arms of The Lord wait to link arms with the dancers,
                with the singers,
                with those of merry hearts;
                with the music makers,
                      the tune keepers,
                          the songsters of His flocks.

The arms of The Lord await to link arms in unity,
                in joyousness,
                in greeting all who walk the way.

The arms of The Lord await the washing of the repentant,
            the purifying of The Saints,
            the cleansing of His Bride."

My Content Study Aid

The Wherewithal of Man

"The wherewithal of man everywhere abounds.

The wherewithal of man is there in excess of requirements.

The wherewithal of man feeds his eyes,
                his ears,
                his soul.

The wherewithal of man rarely feeds his spirit,
            languishes where the unused have been last left,
            can be garnered for recovery before the termites erode the worth.

The wherewithal of man can be farewelled in a fire sale of surrender.

The wherewithal of man can be farewelled in games of chance,
                    when no more can be tendered,
                    when the labourer is no longer paid;
                  when no longer valued within a home,
                  when effort is no longer counted,
                  when the surplus is so great that the cost is
                          not remembered.

The wherewithal of man can be farewelled to greed,
        can be farewelled to selfishness,
        can be farewelled to the gods of man.

The wherewithal of man can be spread upon a table,
        can be spread to feed man's spirit,
        can be spread before the presence of The Living God.

The wherewithal of man can be an offering that fills a hand,
        can be a tithing for a storehouse,
        can be an answered prayer.

The wherewithal of man brings poverty in its shadow,
        brings riches in its light.

The wherewithal of man is man's plumb-line of success,
        is man's measure of his failure.

The wherewithal of man is a building block of character.

The wherewithal of man can vanish or accrue as snowfall upon the mountains so marks
                              their height of majesty.

The wherewithal of man can vanish or accrue depending on the height of man,
                          his goals,
                          his knowledge,

                his wisdom,
                      all sought to be retained,
                      all bought to be retained,
                      all ought to be retained.

The wherewithal of man can vanish or accrue according to the season,
                according to location,
                according to the labourer's intent.

As the wherewithal of man is used,
        so shall man survive,
        so shall the character of man develop,
        so shall man decline or blossom,
        so shall life stagnate or proceed,
        so shall an account be rendered for the presence of the soul,
                the presence of the spirit,
                the presence of the body:
                the residence,
                unconverted to a temple.

The wherewithal of man may be multiplied or squandered,
        may be set aside in wisdom or encounter an empty purse.

The wherewithal of man may be a blessing that uplifts,
        or a curse that disparages,
                the life of man.

The wherewithal of man stands or falls on the resultant character of man:
        the character of man that has an eternal bearing on his relationship with God."

My Content Study Aid

The Goliaths of Man

"The goliaths of man stop man in his journey.

The goliaths of man stop man for a second look:
>>through malfeasance,
>>through the lack of honour,
>>through the fear of loss.

The goliaths of man are constructed for man by the enemy of man.

The goliaths of man are encountered on a billboard,
>>are encountered unexpectedly,
>>are encountered as much smaller when first introduced.

The goliaths of man are encountered as the monoliths of man,
>>are encountered in the confirming of the imagination,
>>are encountered in the oaths of man.

The goliaths of man are encountered as perspectives of the mind.

The goliaths of man are encountered as obstacles to forward motion,
>>as obstacles to conduct that is orderly,
>>as obstacles to the achievement of objectives.

The goliaths of man are encountered to bring man to an impasse,
>>to bring man to buckle at the knees,
>>to bring man to the limit of endurance.

The goliaths of man are encountered to bring man to a destiny where there is no joy.

The goliaths of man are encountered when superimposed on the soul,
>>are encountered as imaginings without solutions,
>>are encountered as sheer walls without a portal.

The goliaths of man are encountered when silence is all invasive.

The goliaths of man are encountered when found in the solitudes of desertion;
>>the solitudes of selection;
>>the solitudes of play.

The goliaths of man are encountered when dwelling in the drugdom of addiction,
>>when within a palace built for pleasure,
>>when images of private preference fall upon the eye,
>>when in the midst of depravity,
>>when surrounded by minds that will not stand
>>>together in the light of day.

The goliaths of man appear impossible to overcome,
>>appear impossible to circumvent,

appear impossible to conquer.

The goliaths of man appear before all the senses of man.

The goliaths of man are laid upon a platter ready for consumption,

The goliaths of man are prepared for the consumption of the heart,
                                 the consumption of the mind,
                                 the consumption of the lungs.

The goliaths of man are ready to consume all that is on offer,
                                 all that is without protection,
                                 all that lies open with an invitation.

The goliaths of man relish an attack,
                       are well prepared to fight,
                       will not easily relinquish what they regard as theirs.

The goliaths of man stand firm behind their blockades,
                       can withstand volleys of arrows that are blunt,
                       will not retreat before a brand new sword with a feeble thrust.

The goliaths of man are difficult to fracture,
                            to tear down,
                            to sack,
                            when they have their foundations well established
                                       with a construction of completion
                                       that holds presented keys.

The goliaths of man are willing to destroy all areas controlled in the progress of a battle.

The goliaths of man are susceptible to,
                must obey,
                will fall to,
                       the concerted forces of the counselled spirit.

The goliaths of man are susceptible to a short battle of command,
                       to a hunger march on an appointed day,
                       to the word from a named commander.

The goliaths of man are susceptible to demolishment by the unfolded wings of Heaven."

My Content Study Aid

_____

_____

_____

_____

The Coming of The Kingdom

"The coming of The Kingdom was never a figment of the imagination,
                  was never a flight of fancy,
                  was never a lost cause.

The coming of The Kingdom of God is very close at hand,
                  is very robust in its nature,
                  is very well planned and long expected.

The coming of The Kingdom is about to burst forth with governance,
                  with finery,
                  with the familiar laws of The Kingdom.

The coming of The Kingdom is about to re-introduce a culture,
                  to restore what was lost,
                  to again sanctify The Earth.

The replevin of Heaven is about to come to be:
                  the replevin that recovers all the thief has stolen in a dominion he usurped,
                        all that has suffered shortfall in the wake
                                of deprivation,
                        all that has reflected the mayhem that has
                                been loosed.

The replevin of the coming of The Kingdom is a time that is fast approaching:
                  has a long list to address,
                  will not overlook a jot,
                  will account for all and sundry.

The coming of The Kingdom is a promise about to be redeemed:
                        in its entirety of provisioning,
                        in its fullness of The Spirit's presence,
                        in its completeness of installing a King
                                into His residence.

The coming of The Kingdom will justify the hope,
                  will justify The Faith,
                  will justify the grievance not addressed.

The coming of The Kingdom will inaugurate justice that is righteous:
                      judgements that will sate the victim,
                      judgements that will deter the ungodly.

The coming of The Kingdom will redeem the promise of the resurrection,
                      the promise of the incarnation,
                      the promise of the turmoil.

The coming of The Kingdom will never be forgotten:
> will thereafter be with man,
> will extend the culture of Heaven,
> will instate the attributes of Heaven,
> will instill the behaviour of Heaven,
> will install the goals of Heaven,
> will set in motion,
>> as an hourglass on a pedestal:
> that which marks the time tabled for the banishment of evil."

My Content Study Aid

The Portals of The Kingdom

"The portals of The Kingdom have been open for man's centuries,
                do not close at night,
                      are accessible from great distances.

The portals of The Kingdom are not protected by portcullises,
                are not surrounded by a moat,
                are there for all with Faith,
                do not endanger those who enter,
                have all been given names.

The portals of The Kingdom have defences when attacked.

The portals of The Kingdom keep darkness well at bay,
                glow beautifully when needed,
                play music on request.

The portals of The Kingdom allow the penitent to pass,
                allow the righteous to travel freely,
                allow the sheep who know the sheepfolds to enter to see
                                                          their shepherd.

The portals of The Kingdom are very numerous,
                are as difficult to count as the stars in the starry way.

The portals of The Kingdom have inviting odours wafting out,
                have sights of wonder beyond the sight-lines of those who
                              stand at portals with no intention to commit.

The portals of The Kingdom separate the carnal from the sacred,
                separate the worldly from the holy,
                separate the mortal from the eternal,
                separate the seen from the unseen.

The portals of The Kingdom will handle all requests.

The portals of The Kingdom know the rights of entry,
                protect them with great care,
                never are the cause of a complaint.

The portals of The Kingdom do not know decay.

The portals of The Kingdom have agents far and wide,
                have ambassadors at large,
                have negotiators who do not compromise the status
                                                          of The Kingdom.

The portals of The Kingdom send out scouts to investigate receptions,
        to report their findings back,
            to receive counsel in discussions of their
                further actions.

The portals of The Kingdom know the location of each command post in the wilderness,
        know the facilities contained therein,
        know the resources that have been supplied,
        know the fruitfulness of all the expended effort.

The portals of The Kingdom have communications in the light with each outreach in
                the darkness,
        have alarms that rouse the guardians when help is
            requested promptly.

The portals of The Kingdom see appointees to attendance pass through—
        on their way to births,
        on their way to weddings,
        on their way to the overseeing of the graves.

The portals of The Kingdom see appointees to attendance pass through—
        on their way to washings,
        on their way to divine appointments,
        on their way as intercessors at the scenes
            of violence.

The portals of The Kingdom see appointees to attendance pass through to return with
        reports where opportunities were lost,
            where there were rampant enemies of man,
            where a promise of fulfilment fell to the ground under a
                stomping heel.

The portals of The Kingdom see appointees to attendance pass through with messages
        that will fall upon ears that cannot hear,
            ears that will not hear,
            ears that hear yet do not comprehend the cost
                of postponement and delay.

The portals of The Kingdom see appointees to attendance pass through to attend to—
            the maladies of man,
            the requests of man,
            the provisioning of man.

The portals of The Kingdom see appointees to attendance pass through on the way
        to evict malingerers,
            to act upon a conscience when a lie has escaped
                the lips,
            to endorse an action of divine instruction completed
                under stress.

The portals of The Kingdom are on foundations of the rock,
            cannot be shaken by any foe,
            will not fall to any ruse.

The portals of The Kingdom are in for a busy time,
            do everything in order.

The portals of The Kingdom are constructed for inspection,
            never miss a spoken word,
            always can determine of what each heart desires,
                  of what each heart does carry,
                  of what each heart venerates in secret,
                      venerates in public,
                      venerates by way
                          of proclamation."

My Content Study Aid

The Purring of The Lion

"The purring of the lion welcoming all the blest;
The purring of the lion greeting every guest.
The Lion of Judah purrs when all is going well.
Others snuggle closer when the great lion does stir;
Story telling comes to life with nearness of the fur.
Visions are imparted in the comfort of a tell.

The purring of the lion is the lion at ease;
The purring of the lion is ruffled by a sneeze.
The Lion of Judah purrs when resting with His pride:
Gathering together for exercise and play times,
When settled,
    each loves to tell him their much practised rhymes,
Some also regaling with adventures found outside.

The purring of the lion is the sound of blessings;
The purring of the lion is near His Bride's dressings,
The Lion of Judah purrs by those for whom he cares.
The prides are invited there to gather with their keys:
All are most welcome from the lands washed by distant seas.
The lair of His Kingdom is the residence he shares."

My Content Study Aid

_____
_____
_____
_____
_____
_____
_____
_____
_____
_____
_____
_____
_____

The Righteous in Preparation

"The way of the righteous is a race of perseverance.
The sight of the righteous is focussed by The Spirit.

The voice of the righteous thunders in the silence,
                announces a coming storm,
                speaks of the downpour on the land.

The sight-lines of the righteous view the flash of Heaven that imprints the soul,
                within an instant,
                with the frames of recall of The Earth.

The stance of the righteous is attentive with a dedicated ear that hears
                with understanding.

The volition of the righteous is at the command of God.
The purpose of the righteous is at the behest of The Spirit.
The activities of the righteous are of guarded confirmation.

The speech of the righteous has unity in tongues,
                augments the sword in thrust and parry,
                is strident in proclamation,
                exhibits boldness in its testimonies,
                has the ring of truth,
                contains a message from A King.

The message of the righteous reveals the covenants in force,
                comes forth from the character so imbued,
                is validated by its fruit,
                serves The God of Abraham,
                is spoken by The Spirit within The Temple.

The message of the righteous lays all before The Word who left the grave-clothes where
                they fell,
                will stand as a record without refutal when presented before
                a throne of white.

The impact of the righteous is seen within the generations,
                bejewels a gathering of a treasure,
                changes projected destinies,
                creates relationships that extend beyond the grave.

The impact of the righteous imparts direction to the lost,
                introduces the footsteps to be followed,
                encourages a lifestyle of celebration.

The footsteps of the righteous witness at the crossroads where life events
                                                                                                 are encountered,

The footsteps of the righteous have certainty of purpose,
                have certainty of direction,
                have certainty of the foundation which bears them forward.

The footsteps of the righteous progress in skips,
                        in dances:
                        declaring the fullness of the joy in their exuberance
                                                            of Faith.

The deeds of the righteous are concerned each for his brother,
                        are a measure of the progress of a nation,
                        are those of which the angels sing,
                        are as jewels offered on a golden platter;
                        uphold The King of kings,
                        change the landscape of eternity,
                        are recounted by the redeemed of The Lord.

The callings of the righteous progress the coming of The Kingdom:
                        are released by the grave,
                        are overseen by angels,
                        are offered by The Spirit,
                        are accepted by the spirit,
                        are honoured heart to heart.

The lives of the righteous are a confirmation of their Faith:
                        render homage to the attributes of God,
                        tender obedience to the righteous laws of man,
                        can be followed as examples,
                        will have histories of mistakes,
                        testify of the need for repentance.

The wisdom of the righteous grows with requested impartations from The Household
                                                                                           of God:
                        is in the company of The Keys,
                        contrasts with the offerings of a fool,
                        confounds the worldly wise,
                        builds depth of understanding in the relationship with God.

The wisdom of the righteous inherits His revealing of the nature,
                                  the essence,
                                              of all that is Divine."

The Trickle of The Foe

"This day,
    I speak to all My sheep saying:
        'Be Faithful to your calling,
            and the day will soon dawn when you will be able to look back and see
                      the progress achieved as a result of My Spirit
                      going before and blessing your endeavours.

        Further,
            you will have the ability to see the path laid out for you to tread in these
                      coming Days of The Lord.

        Even so,
            the shuddering days of The Lord which will see the siren of Hades entering
                      into every unprotected home,
                      every nook,
                      every cranny,
                      where privacy prevails.

For the siren of Hades has antennae as her head-dress and her dressing gown is
                disrobed in the solitude of her dressing
                room where there are invited eyes.

Her dressing room where glazed eyes filled with lust are led by the hand progressively
                to a destiny they do not question.

Be aware of doors which should be open yet are closed;
        which should be manned yet are without response.

Be aware that these are the days of the virus of the foe,
                where access is prepared,
                where a welcome is received,
                where networks are to be eagerly traversed with
                      the downfall of tomorrow that just
                      awaits the trigger of the trickle.

Be aware of the trickle of the foe that starts in silence and builds to a crescendo that
                causes the fall of nations,
                    of kingdoms,
                    of both the wilful and the righteous.

Be aware of the trickle of the foe that has debt as its structure,
                has related debt,
                has interwoven debt,
                has debt with warranties,
                    with guarantees,
                    the documents of debt:
                    all worthless once the trickle starts to fall.

Those who would listen should acquire The Wisdom to nurture the hedge that
                                                                     withstands the trickle of the foe.

The hedge of protection,
                which all The Saints should seek to establish,
                is freedom from the debt of man.

For such a man this freedom gifts immunity to the summons of repayment:
                        then he does not stand as part of the pathway of the trickle;
                        then he cannot be coerced against his will;
                        then he stands with his free agency intact.

For such a man will not be trapped,
                will not be enslaved by Satan within the credit circle of the foe.

For his dwelling will be secure beyond the fear of foreclosure,
                        where a knee cannot be caused to buckle in subservience
                        to the shadow of a mountain whose base is built on debt.

For such a man,
                with wisdom as his guide,
                      will not be lured onto another path where a trickle lies in wait;
                      will not have pledged his righteousness as security for his debt;
                      will still be standing when others fall as a sacrifice to Mammon.' "

My Content Study Aid

The Promises of God

"Mighty are the ways of God,
        mighty in dispensation,
        mighty in application,
        mighty in restoration.

Behold!
    In the might of God,
        with all power,
        with all authority,
        will The Earth be born again.

Again,
  behold!
    By the might of God,
        in all power,
        in all authority,
        will The Earth be renewed,
            made fit,
        for the habitation of The King.

Again,
  behold!
    Through the might of God,
        by all power,
        by all authority,
        shall The Earth be prepared for a change of government.

For the ways of man,
        in governance:
            are to be set aside;
        in distribution;
            are to be re-directed;
        in social order:
            are to be superseded;
        in hunger:
            are to meet a new criterion,
            that none may suffer from an empty mouth;
        in war:
            will suffer confiscation of his weapons;
        in development:
            will experience the presence of a lasting peace;
      the edifice of man,
            is soon to acknowledge The Edifice of God.

In that day the ways of man will not prevail against the might of God,
    the ways of man will not pre-empt The Promises of God,
    the edifice of man will yield to The Edifice of God.

Then will the foolish continue to ignore the counsel of the wise,
    fight the battles of the misers.

Then will the foolish readily accept a ticket,
    with instructions,
    for a golden handshake.

Then will the foolish have been garnered by the foe,
    have utterances of despair.

Then will the foolish face up,
    be called,
    settled in,
    to the destiny of their ilk.

Then will the wise be found within The Edifice of God,
    be called in supervision,
    have their inheritance made known,
    have their Faith turned into knowledge,
    be welcomed at the Altar of Sacrifice,
    see the significance of their gowns of life.

Then will The Earth be dressed as at the end of time:
    receive her Glory entrained since the beginning,
    be circumscribed by the beauty of The Spirit,
    be replenished as a garden;
    become a stepping-stone of exploration,
        of wonder,
        of delight.

Then will the time sphere of man no longer hold him prisoner to the grave.

Then will The Earth be free to launch and to recover journeys to the magnitudes
    of God,
    pass into her fullness beyond the realm of time in handclasps
        with the heavens.

For man has always been at the forefront of God's care.

Man has always been as a favoured child of God,
    always received the encouragement of God.

Man should hold in a sacred memory The Promises of God,
    await with eagerness the fulfilment of The Promises of God,
    set his Faith in preparation for The Promises of God,
    structure all his ways to qualify for The Promises of God,

determine the intentions of his heart align with The Promises of God.

Man,
   in his wisdom,
      should acquire a relationship with God that confirms the relevancy of a claim upon The Promises of God."

My Content Study Aid

The Census of God

"The eyes of God see all which occurs within the life of His creation.

The eyes of God see all the impacts on the life of man,
      of the life of man,
      for the life of man.

The eyes of God see all the activities of man,
      those in his public arena,
      those in his private forum,
      those thought to be hidden as a secret within his well
                  of denial.

The eyes of God seek out the deeds deemed as righteous within a heart attuned to God.

The eyes of God rove over all of His creation,
    see every sparrow fall,
    see every action which inscribes a record on the soul of man.

The eyes of God everywhere abound,
     are there within the plates which form the windows of the soul,
     know the eyes of His creation,
     can see through the eyes of His creation.

The eyes of God,
    pausing at the coverings,
        discern what is to see.

The eyes of God know what they have seen.

The ears of God are attuned to the voice of man.

The ears of God can multi-task,
     can separate the urgent from the profane,
     can separate the calls of the flock from those of predators,
     can separate the loving from the shrill.

The ears of God are neither channelled nor frequency dependent,
   have no need to modulate.

The ears of God hear each utterance as intended,
      each prayer that moves the lips,
      each tongue as the spirit speaks.

The ears of God hear each silent thought of man that discloses the status of the soul,
              the status of the spirit,
              the status of the intent
                   of character,

                        the status of the heart.

The ears of God accommodate the heartbeat of the universe,
        the heartbeat of creation,
        the heartbeat of each man.

The ears of God are aware of the muffled voice of man,
        ignore the muffled voice of man,
        are especially attentive when the muffle is removed.

The ears of God recognize the muffle of the foe,
        the muffle that brings incoherence to the speech of man,
        the muffle that speaks of idolatry before a god of
                limited dominion,
        the muffle that does not speak to God.

The ears of God rejoice in the absence of the muffle,
        the discard of the muffle,
        the overcoming of the muffle.

The ears of God are vibrant with a conversation re-established,
        the re-instatement of a walk,
        the growth of a reformed hope in Faith.

The ears of God tingle with excitement when a new entrant is welcomed,
        a new dwelling comes into preparation for
        dedication as a temple,
        a new saint is qualified,
        is cleansed,
        is set free through the waters
                of immersion.

The census of God is compliant with His being—
    is beyond the imagining of man,
    is both specific and generic,
    is active within and beyond all of His creation;
    is not impaired by distance:
        is everywhere enacted,
        is empowered by might and power,
        is fulfilled in majesty.

The census of God knows the grain of sand,
    knows the galaxies of wonder.

The census of God is pleased with the furbishing of the onward home of man,
    is pleased with the travelling arrangements within the onward home
                of man,
    is pleased with the security for the onward home of man,
    is pleased with the refreshments available in the onward home of man.

The census of God will be present at the greeting or farewell of man as destinies, selected by his freewill, draft man into his chosen habitation in the onward home of man."

My Content Study Aid

The Age of Grace

"I,
    The Lord Jesus,
        speak to the hearts of man this day.

I,
    The Lord Jesus,
        speak to the souls of man this day.

I,
    The Lord Jesus,
        speak to the spirit of man this day.

'For this day has it been said that the heart of man,
        the soul of man,
            the spirit of man should accept The Grace offered to
                man while it is today.

The sins of man accumulate and are written on the slate of eternity.

The slate of eternity can be erased,
        is not written in the dust.

The slate of eternity bears witness of what is thereon written,
        of the infractions of the soul,
            of what has not been erased from the sight of angels
                before they are asked to read the
                inscriptions laid before them.

The slate of eternity has status as a drafting gate for the destiny of man which always:
            causes diversion when inscribed,
            permits free passage when erased.

An inscription always restrains the expectations of man,
      always brings the conviction of the soul of man,
      always deafens the call of man from within the dungeons of despair,
      always results in the lost soul of man even with but a single line of entry,
      always brings tears to the eyes of those who will abide by the eternal
            impact of freewill on the immortality of man.

The sins of man have been defined,
      have been discouraged,
      have been forsworn.,
      are not accepted in the presence,
      have been resolved to man's advantage,
      may still become a burden,
      can be erased by Grace.

The journey of each man should lead to the company of The Saints.

The company of The Saints should prepare to be a Bride.

The Bride should be as the stars at night—
> each secure in its place.

The stars at night declare the works of God.

The works of God do not envisage that man should be as a falling star.

A falling star,
> in its fall from Grace,
> will meet a fiery end.

A fiery end is not The Will of God.

The journey of each man reflects the inclinations of his soul,
> the conflicts of his heart,
> the heeding of his spirit,
> the care-taking of his body.

The journey of man is built upon the relationships of man:
> with a spouse,
> with the offspring of the womb,
> with his fellow man.

The journey of each man is determined by his freewill:
> the clearness of his sight,
> the acuteness of his hearing,
> the counselling he sought.

The journey of each man results in a character attained,
> in wealth departing at the grave or awaiting where stored
> > within a storehouse,
> in wisdom that honours the counselling heeded within
> > his spirit.

The journey of each man is judged before the tribunal of God for sin carried
> throughout mortality.

The carried sin of man causes great loss to man,
> prevents a relationship with God,
> shuts down an open Heaven,
> prevents a walk of righteousness,
> does not accept a covenant of offering,
> forsakes access to the Grace of God.

The carried sin of man speaks of fleshly desires,
> of a carnal nature,
> of lust,
> of gods within his life that are served until the grave,

of denial of The God he does not desire to know.

The carried sin of man restricts man's freedom to a lifetime wherein he lives with
freedom of expression,
    preserves a captive to his sins,
    prevents an extended voyage of discovery,
    denies access to ancestral relationships,
    denies access to descendants,
    is an horrific price to pay in the light of what will be foregone.

The age of Grace continues until the end of man's mortality,
    is closed by the coming of The Lord,
    is serviced by the gifts of The Spirit,
    denotes the time frame of acceptance,
    offers all the fruit of acceptance.

The age of Grace separates the sheep from the goats,
    the wheat from the tares,
    the righteous from the iniquitous.

The age of Grace carries the cleansing power for man,
    began with an empty tomb,
        shed by a risen King,
    ends for a new beginning,
        the instigation of a throne heralding the coronation of
        The Bride.

As the record stands,
    so shall it declare before the face of man.

Neither the gainsaying of man nor the martyring of The Saints of The Lord will fortify
the gates of Hell.

What is,
    is;
    and shall not be undone by the whimperings of man,
        the activities of demons,
        the invocations of Satan.' "

My Content Study Aid

_____
_____
_____
_____
_____

The Ways of God

"The caravans of God are soon to be established,
                are soon to traverse the trade routes of The Earth.

The caravans of God will carry the wares of God,
                will neither suffer let nor hindrance,
                are to serve the purposes of God.

The caravans of God succour the needs of habitation,
                remove hunger from the stomachs.

The caravans of God are the harbingers of health,
                      of education,
                      of peace within the heart.

The caravans of God are not a vision in a wasteland,
                are not a mirage on a desert floor,
                are not the refuse of the proud thrown on a smouldering stack,
                are not marked with the signs of death.

The caravans of God are not the results of theft,
                      of intimidation,
                      of deceit.

The caravans of God are not seeking a safe haven,
                are not subject to extortion,
                are not for homes that have already captured the electrons of
                                              the universe.

The caravans of God are not there to disappoint,
                    to bring discontent,
                    to curry favour,
                    to fill hands that hang in idleness.

The caravans of God are to vanquish the domains of Satan,
                    to defeat the diseases brought by demons,
                    to refurbish temples in despair,
                        homes in non-repair,
                        dwellings in a harsh domain.

The caravans of God are to lead the revival of The Earth.

The caravans of God are at the forefront of a battle—
                        to be fought on lands laid waste by demons,
                              for lands:
                        to be redeemed through a replevin,
                        to be dressed in gowns of beauty that speak of the

dressage of a mantle with supreme authority.

For as the ice does melt so will new vistas be apparent,
> so will the pathways of the rain submit to new deliveries,
> so will the seas arise,
> so will the seas absorb,
> so will the seas wash footprints of contamination from the
>> hemlines of The Earth,
> so will the seas redistribute the bounty of their harvests,
> so will the new resources of The Earth be opened.

For as the ice withdraws so will land awaken from its slumber.

For as the ice departs so will the land be furnished.

Behold,
> the intent of God evidenced before the face of man.

Behold,
> the intent of God for this season of man.

Behold,
> the intent of God for justice to prevail.

The lands of slumber have been preserved in their entirety for the nations whose
> homelands have been stolen,
>> have been raped,
>>> have been pillaged by the usurers.

The lands of slumber are for the meek in spirit,
> with humbleness of soul.

The lands of slumber are to welcome the peoples from the islands of the seas:
> islands which will no longer be on the maps
>> of man.

The lands of slumber will not be limited by coldness,
> will not be limited by heat,
> will not be limited by being inhospitable—
even so the deserts,
> the lands of dust storms,
> the high plateaux,
> the dry plateaux,
> the mountain valleys,
> the swamps:
> the terrain where the environment does not favour presently the
>> livelihoods of man.

For as the winds reverse,
> so will the rains be carried;

        so will the rivers form;
        so will the livelihoods of man be extended to new pastures
                of rebirth:
                    where once there were,
                    where once were none,
                    where now will be again.

For as the rivers in the seas reverse:
        so will fish feed in fresh locations.

For as the rivers in the seas are plotted:
        so will man reap the harvest afresh decreed.

For as the rivers in the seas flow:
        so will the pathways of all life be settled.

The prideful nations of The Earth:
        which shared only but a morsel of their bounty,
        which forced the destitute to watch and starve beyond a fence of selfishness,
        which spent on weapons of destruction what should have been a source
                of bounty,
        which squandered wealth without regard to mercy,
        which were blind and deaf to beseeching cries of the downtrodden,
        which turned away the outstretched hands that testify to angels,
        which recount the wealth that was imparted to the humble in a guise which
                filled the secret coffers.

The secret coffers of those with eternal slates inscribed with the iniquities of their
                unchecked souls:
        these are they who will not twice feed at a laden table;
        these are they who will not acquire the awakening lands of slumber of
                The Earth;
        these are they who will now trade with difficulty;
        these are they whose day of plenty is now turning to an eve of shortage.

    These are they who only by repentance,
        from their lifestyles fraught with wants,
        can they be saved from the autumn of their needs.

    These are they who will no longer subdue the impoverished,
                in labour,
                for the others' gain.

The ways of God are not found in the avaricious governing extremes of man.

The ways of God are found in the trading which is just,
        where the labouring of man ignores the domiciles of man yet is seen
        to have input a contribution of equal value to the merchandise,
                to the service,

to the produce.

The ways of God treat the currency of a realm as but a medium of exchange within the
jurisdictions of man:
so each trader has equal access without
fear of deprivation of a livelihood.

The ways of God are soon to prevail,
are soon to establish justice that is both swift and just,
will end the plundering of the poor,
will end the enslavement of the poor for but a pittance of return.

The ways of God know the chains of commerce which frown on competition;
the cabals of business where there is unity in pricing;
the enclaves of injustice where edicts are delivered which
circumvent the rights of the disenfranchised;
know the entities of integration where the false pricing of
transferred goods,
within control,
feeds the funding of wealth accumulation in
distant jurisdictions;
know the behaviour of monopolies which deny the benefitting of man
for the extreme favour of a few;
know the huddled cartels of The Earth which ignore their
responsibilities through agreed
excessive pricing of their products;
know the companies of man which demand excessive returns on the
funds involved;
know those which use poverty as a weapon;
know those which ensure the retention of poverty on The Earth,
in the days of plenty,
for servicing their greed.

For the winds of change encircle The Earth:
bringing a new accounting;
bringing a reckoning of justice;
imparting a sea-change of behaviour;
instilling new landscapes for the meek;
warning of a change of scenery in the lands of pride:
bringing forth the active management of God."

My Content Study Aid

_____

_____

The Advent of The Lord

"The coming of The Lord is on the horizon of eternity;
        is at the forefront of a stage;
        is awaiting the raising of a curtain on a stage that is far
                from empty.

The coming of The Lord has trumpeters in the wings;
        has choristers in flight;
        has the angelic hosts waiting just off stage.

The coming of The Lord awaits The Father's consent in confirmation;
        has the announcing shofar with attentive lips;
        has The Holy Spirit,
            as if a 'best man' at a wedding,
            calling for attention.

The coming of The Lord has no parallel in the history of mankind.

The coming of The Lord will fulfil what 'is to be',
        as 'is'.

The coming of The Lord changes everything for ever—
        seals the destinies of men and the destinies of kings,
        verifies the scriptures that extend beyond the memory of man,
        awakens A Kingdom as the Edifice of God on the colony
                of Earth,
        breaks the seal of the covenant of the last supper with His
            Presence at the feast of the incarnation.

The seeking of The Lord is about to require no Faith,
        will be found within His residence,
        will be an act of man outside the Age of Grace.

The seeking of The Lord will no longer be accompanied by The Holy Spirit's gifts,
            as previously tendered,
            to a soul in need.

The seating of The Lord will be beyond the time frame for salvation with a presentation
            at a court,
        has the martyrs,
           with their gowns,
           in the place of honour,
        acknowledges the deeds of each;
            the calling of each soul when in the realm
                of discipleship;
            The Faith of each expressed within a

mortal testimony,
for the invited of The Lord is as a shepherd with His sheep who
recognize His voice.

The summons of The Lord which cites an appeal for justice is beyond the timespan
of redemption,
which cites an appeal by an injured soul for justice is served
upon the errant soul,
which cites a lodged appeal for justice yet may be satisfied by
an appellant offering
of mercy.

The summons of The Lord addresses grievances and wrongs,
always is resolved by The Truth of the occurrence,
will hear the confession of the sinful soul before
an open court."

My Content Study Aid

The Inheritance of Man

"Many are the ways of The Lord.

    For the ways of The Lord cannot be counted by man in his mortality.

    As the ways of The Lord testify of His creations so is man blessed in his surroundings.

The blessings of The Lord are as numerous as the raindrops that fall from within the
                      pathways of the rain,
                      within the sight of man.

Who on Earth can count the raindrops as they fall?
        can measure the effect of each on the life that is thereby succoured?
        can gauge the seeding of a rainbow,
            the feeding of a rainbow,
                in the skies of man?

Who can sustain a rainbow in its Glory through the weeding of the clouds:
            for the sun to cast its Glory in the rain drops of The Earth?

Only God within the heavens has the foresight of an action previously unknown to man,
        can bend them to His will at His word's command,
        knows all there is to know,
        knows the way of each creation,
            whether static or dynamic,
        knows the seen and the unseen by the eyes of man.

Oh,
    that man would sharpen all his senses,
    focus his perception,
    awaken his awareness of the wonders of creation laid before his path of discovery in
                      his lifetime of incubation.

A lifetime of incubation in preparation for his voyage of discovery in the eternity of
                      the soul.

A voyage with his senses added to,
    enhanced beyond his imagination,
    with opportunities to travel in ways unknown to man,
    to appreciate the timeless arcades of pleasure,
            of the reserves of beauty,
            of the parks of rest,
            of the vistas in the gardens of The Lord.

Oh,
    that man would value the generations past,
    the inheritance of man,
    that follows in the footfalls of his God."

The Fear of God

"The sons and daughters of a prophet inherit the mantle of a prophet,
       have ears prepared to hear the word of God
               made known,
       carry The Fear of God within their hearts.

The sons and daughters of a prophet hear as they incline their heads,
       see as they kneel before their God,
       worship with hearts on fire when prostrate on
               their faces.

The sons and daughters of a prophet inherit a history of a relationship with God,
       inherit generational blessings at the gifting of God,
       reach maturity of the spirit when their souls
         recognize The Fear of God within their lives.

The fear of God is to do with reverence,
   is to do with worship,
   is to do with holiness.

The fear of God leads through the gates of praise,
    dwells in the presence of a temple,
    teaches wisdom to the silent.

The fear of God is focussed in the presence of the presence.

The fear of God requires a commitment that is total,
     a vow that will be long remembered,
     an understanding of repentance.

The fear of God precedes birth from the womb of man,
    invites birth from the water of The Spirit,
    guards birth from the grave of The Father.

The fear of God seeks transformation to a sheep,
    the recognition of the shepherd,
    being garnered in a flock.

The fear of God causes cleansing of a soul,
    brings freewill within the bounds of discipleship,
    prepares A Bride of purity for the wedding of The Groom.

The fear of God is built upon the rock of revelation,
     The Faith nurtured within the soul,
     a directed walk of righteousness.

The fear of God arises from a two way conversation,
     the gifts of The Holy Spirit,

        the evidence of creation.

The fear of God is born from a written testimony,
        from a spoken testimony,
        from all the evidence laid before the senses of man.

The fear of God overcomes the profane tongues of man,
        the idols of the world,
        the corruption of the soul.

The fear of God confirms new tongues which sing new songs from within the heart,
        new tongues of wonder which pass across the lips,
        new tongues from a new Kingdom empowered with authority
                for change.

The fear of God upholds the secret to the progression of the life of man,
        the gifting of a destiny as written,
        the being in eternal life through the presence of
                the sacrificial God.

The fear of God is cause for great celebration in the life of man,
        is cause for much jubilation at the future life of man.

The fear of God is the threshold to eternity that brings the 'Welcome Home!' "

My Content Study Aid

_____
_____
_____
_____
_____
_____
_____
_____
_____
_____
_____
_____
_____
_____
_____
_____

The Profanity of Man

"The profanity of man plumbs the depths of Satan's wells and brings up contaminated
water that puts the soul in chains.

The profanity of man burns the lips of man,
signals to one and all the captured soul within,
scorches the unprotesting ears of all on whom it falls.

The profanity of man falls as an extensive work of Satan,
promotes the extension of the Satanic kingdom to the detriment
of man.

The profanity of man is given little thought,
profanes the name of God,
indicates each fool for disregard within the role of friendship.

The profanity of man pre-empts acceptance of a righteous walk,
pre-empts a change of status,
pre-empts a destiny with light.

The profanity of man spreads as a wildfire without control amongst each household
wherein it dwells,
amongst the language of such children,
amongst their daily speech.

The profanity of man denies the honour due the tongue of man,
the honour due his fellow man,
the honour due his waiting God.

The profanity of man is encouraged by the demonic entities with a future
of imprisonment,
is a progressive pathway of destruction,
stops the development of the intellect of man,
restricts the language of man as if an ice cube in the mouth.

The profanity of man cannot share the language of endearment for which the tongue
was made,
for which the lips exist,
for which the ear of man
is attuned to hear.

The profanity of man has the harshness of contempt,
accompanies violence as a refuge,
knows anger as a stepping-stone to intimidation.

The profanity of man breeds frustration at limited expression,
at minimal vocabulary,
at weakened communication.

The profanity of man causes disease of the heart,
        unwelcome changes in the brain,
            heightened blood pressure with which the plumbing can
                      scarcely cope.

The profanity of man shrinks the opportunities for man,
        the growth of man,
        the stature of man.

The profanity of man curses God without dismay,
            without distraction,
            without distinction.

The profanity of man is recorded by the lips,
        is held accountable for each so uttered,
        is construed as each is meant.

The profanity of man leads to the company of the damned.

The profanity of man becomes as a gun drawn from a holster at home upon the hip,
        has bullets that can be fired in rapidity of action,
        has bullets that can wound the soul,
        can render a life as being of a worthless presence,
        can antagonize to conflict the body born of man.

The profanity of man sheds filth upon the head of man,
        creates a downward spiral that may never see the light,
        feeds upon itself,
        wallows in the mire of man,
        dredges,
            from greater depths,
            increasing filth to spread.

The profanity of man disGraces the welcome of the marriage bed,
        adopts depraved imaginations which conjure up the feeding of
                                  his lust.

The profanity of man has no redeeming feature,
        has nothing worth promoting,
        has no virtue worth preserving.

The profanity of man is in fellowship with demons,
        is overseen by Satan,
        may tread a future highway through the gates of Hell.

The profanity of man will be silenced by the tongue in death,
        will deserve a lonely future,
        will not be uttered by an imprisoned soul.

    Forsake the ways of the profane.
    Walk in the footsteps of the Divine.
    Turn from the profanity of man."

The Comfort of The Lord (2)

"The comfort of The Lord is available to all,
                is found by very few.

 The comfort of The Lord is received with a smile,
                is sought by those without.

 The comfort of The Lord is a blessing to the mournful,
                is solace to the troubled.

The comfort of The Lord is a hug where one is needed,
                is shelter from a stormy blast,
                is a handhold on a cliff,
                is a refuge from despair,
                is affirmation of a hope,
                is a word on time.

The comfort of The Lord draws a chair up to a table,
                affirms the counsel for the spirit,
                upholds a lamb within the soul,
                encloses and enfolds,
                carries the lonely back to safety,
                mends the broken-hearted.

The comfort of The Lord is a whisper in the trees,
                a vision for the uncertain soul,
                a dreaming in the twilight.

The comfort of The Lord overcomes memories not valued,
                overcomes memories of conflict,
                overcomes memories of derogation.

The comfort of The Lord hears every voice that calls,
                answers the sincere,
                attends until comfort is attained,
                can place feet upon a slope.

The comfort of The Lord can restrain a hand from habit,
                can modify desire,
                can distract addiction.

The comfort of The Lord can command the angels.

The comfort of The Lord is the measure for the moment,
                overflows the cup,
                anoints as oil upon the head,
                is a mercy seat of God,

> imparts a testimony to the soul,
> verifies The God of Love.
>
> The comfort of The Lord weans from the milk onto the meat,
> brings a lamb before the shepherd,
> precedes all steps which follow the pathway home,
> reveres The Spirit with a flame,
> has tongues of praise for the weary soul,
> supports a desolated soul.
>
> The comfort of The Lord resolves the vicissitudes of life,
> the attacks of demons,
> launched by the foe of man."

Scribal Note: *Refer also* 'The Comfort of The Lord (1), in this book.

My Content Study Aid

The Roar of Zion

"The pride of the Lion arises as the pride of the Lion,
                no longer mews as kittens.

    For the kittens of the Lion are now the power of Zion.

The power of Zion recalls;
                falls,
                trembles all The Earth and all the heavens.

    All the heavens see Zion on its knees;
                hear Zion with its prayer calls.

    Zion with its prayers assembles Zion with its cares,
           its cares is *(stet)* now fervent in its prayers.

    All The Earth responds,
           to Zion,
           as it dares.

Zion,
   as it dares,
   wings the covering of praise to The King of kings.

The King of kings with worship sets a stage upon the clouds of conquest.

The clouds of conquest carry upon the stage Zion as the pride which sings.

The pride which sings is the roar of Zion throughout The Earth.

    Throughout The Earth,
       the stage of supplication is riding upon the clouds.

    Riding upon the clouds,
       The Lion of Judah calls to The Bride of great worth.

The Bride of great worth upheld the covenants that meld.

The covenants that meld are to be instated over all The Earth.

    All The Earth hears the roar of Zion's answer to the covenants which weld.

The covenants which weld unite still:
                      each soul of conquest to The God with Will.

The God with will initiates the roar,
                awaits for the response without an echo.

The response without an echo has clarity of tone,
                has but purity to instill.

Purity to instill uplifts The Banner of Zion in the presence of The Lion.

The presence of the Lion acknowledges the right to The Banner held in readiness.

The Banner held in readiness storms the citadels of The Earth,
with the sign of Zion."

My Content Study Aid

The Tears of The Lord

"The tears of The Lord were shed upon a cross.

The tears of The Lord were never wiped away,
              still stain the face with love,
              carried recompense with mercy,
              watered life upon The Earth,
              uplifted man to stand,
              broke the curse of disobedience.

The tears of The Lord witnessed to a future in the making,
              signed forgiveness of intent,
              mended the pathway home for man,
              spoke of the remorse of man.

The tears of The Lord washed away the dust upon the eyes of man,
              opened a new vista for man to then perceive,
              taught man by example the love of his fellow man.

The tears of The Lord offered a renewal of a relationship once abandoned in a garden,
              made possible a relationship to be affirmed within a garden.

The tears of The Lord are teardrops of significance in the life of man,
                      in the growth of man,
                      in the eternity of man.

The tears of The Lord can be brushed aside by man,
              can be sponged by a disciple with due reverence for occasion.

The tears of The Lord testify of an offer opened for acceptance,
              marked payment,
                  then in progress,
                  for the excuses of man:
            is as the shepherd weeping for lost sheep.

Beware the tears of The Lord which are carelessly expunged by man in his mortality;
              which fall on the rocky ground;
              which are trampled in the dust by the disdainful foot
                              of man.

The tears of The Lord opened the gateway of repentance;
              opened the doorway of Faith;
              signified a reservoir of love in the midst of the rejection by
                              a multitude.

The tears of The Lord hold a promise of acceptance;
              hold the knowledge of wisdom shared;

> hold,
>> within control,
>> the handle of the doorway which is
>> opened on request and awaits a knock."

My Content Study Aid

The Strength of The Lord

"The strength of The Lord is mighty to behold,
        is mighty to experience,
        is mighty to sustain man.

The strength of The Lord is The Power of God,
        is The Authority of God,
        is The Oversight of God.

The strength of The Lord is the active presence of The Spirit,
        is the power of creation deployed to remedy the self-imposed
                fears of man,
        should not be underestimated,
        upholds man in his mortality as if an adult with an infant,
        does not succumb to tiredness,
        is not subject to fatigue,
        has a surplus to requirements in the support of man.

Mighty are the ways of God—
        Great in His Commitment;
        Complete in His Outpouring;
        All inclusive in His Love;
        The Shepherd of Salvation;
        The Answerer of Prayer;
        The Confounder of The Enemy;
        The Defender of Free Agency:
            in the mortality of man.

Mighty are the plans of God—
        To have man as the confidante of God;
        To cherish man within creation;
        To want man with his nature;
        To encourage man from waywardness;
        To promote man past the grave;
        To accompany man in conquering the enemies of man;
        To prepare for man,
            furnishing in magnificence,
            the anticipated destiny proposed:
            for the eternal presence of man in The Perfection of God.

Mighty are the acts of God—
        To lift man past the clouds;
        To visit man with victory;
        To speak to man throughout the ages;
        To make promises of destiny to man;

          To heal the ailments born of man;
          To make known to man the seen and the unseen;
          To teach The Wisdom of God:
              to man who seeks in preparation.

For as My servant Paul has written,
    'I can do all things through Christ who strengthens me.'* "

Scribal Note:
* Refer Philippians 4:13, NKJV, The Bible,

    I can do all things through Christ who strengthens me.

(NKJV) Scripture taken from the New King James Version®. Copyright © 1982 by Thomas Nelson. Used by permission. All rights reserved.

My Content Study Aid

The Window of Wonder

1 "The Window of Wonder is the portal of the pain,
>   the mounting of the miracle.
  The entrance of excitement to the viewing of the vastness -
  Seen as the footprints of the frost on the pane of perseverance -
  Where the glass of gladness with the lustre of the light then denies the darkness.

2 The Window of Wonder requires the residue of the whittling of the wood,
  From the searching of surrounds,
>   to the timber of the test.
  The artist of allure sketches the foam of freedom -
  Where the bridge of beauty glows,
>   in the evening of the estuary,
>   for The Glory of the guest.

3 The Window of Wonder knows a site of solitude,
>   the act of aspiration,
  While the roaming of a roadway uncovers the deserted of the dust -
  There in the xeriscape of Xanadu lie the puddles of the prudent -
  And the ubiquity of the usurper in the vale of vapour encounters the tomb of trust.

4 The Window of Wonder discloses the day of dreams,
>   the afternoon of abundance.
  From the excitement of the earnest comes the secret of the sunlight -
  Where the hut of happiness shelters beside the mount of memory -
  There,
>   on the isle of inspiration,
>   is the origin of openness and the treasure of the twilight.

5 The Window of Wonder is the setter of the scene within the morning of the mountains;
  Clothed in the mists of mystery are heard the cacophony of calls -
  For the river of the ruggedness carries the rafting of the race -
  By the peak of perfection in the mourning of magnificence is seen the festooning of
>   the falls.

6 The Window of Wonder highlights the meal of memories as the breakfast of
>   the balcony,
  While the capture of the climate enhances the gale of greeting in the valley of
>   the vision.
  The city of compassion beyond the cape of care,
  Sees the bastions of the bashful bow to the festivities of The Faithful in the timescale
>   of transition.

7 The Window of Wonder has the shutters of the shadows,
>   has an inlet of insistence

Beside the harbour of hope,
>   for the locality of latitude and the nativity of the night.
The wail of whales knows the keeper of the kingfish
And the testing of tranquillity -
>   along the shore of sifting sands guarded by the dolphins of delight.

8   The Window of Wonder lifts the vehemence of victory from being a curtain
>   of containment.
Applying the fire of fervency is the lamplighter of the lane
Who brings the wind of weeping,
>   with the wave of wonder,
On the yeast of youth -
>   on the graciousness of grey:
>   >   as The Glory on the grateful of the grain."

My Content Study Aid

The Window of Wonder— A Parable

Scribal Note: *Parable text saved, and now affirmed by Him for inclusion in this, His book.*

1 "Jesus, The Christ, offers access through a gateway of pain, with a miracle in tow;

> An incredible opportunity of sighting the panorama of promises laid before mankind -
> Discernible as a stroll upon an icy lawn of crystals in the presence of
> extensive coldness -
> So the cup of remembrance in the presence of The Holy Spirit then confirms The Will
> of God.

2 Jesus was in alignment with the cross of calvary,
> Within the context of His time, resulting in the death of execution.
> Satan, the tempting expert, spreads a frothful message of the finality of Jesus's death
> among the Disciples,
> Even so while Jesus is resplendent in the period of rest for The Glory implicit in
> His incarnation.

3 Jesus has experienced a place of loneliness, but proceeds in obedience to
> The Father's Will.
> Whilst on a journey an ignored and beaten traveller is encountered
> But, even in the 'dryness' of the land there are travellers who, in their caring and
> concern, leave traces behind them.
> And the apparent overall widespread presence of Satan, here in a low, pungent
> smelling place, yields knowledge of a tomb that holds but grave clothes.

4 Jesus brings the foretold presence of The Christ, the time of the outpouring of The
> Holy Spirit.
> From His teaching of His Disciples is birthed the Christian message opened to
> the world -
> As vindicated by the empty grave of history which is near a place of gathering -
> There, at a location of divine creative choice, were new concepts and ideals so set: to
> become the future values of mankind.

5 Jesus determines life's priorities in the early stages of life's difficulties;
> Surrounded by the spiritual, is the confused clamouring of mankind -
> As life, with its rough edges, supports the race that must be run -
> Near life's summit of ability, to the regret of things with great appeal, lie in loops the
> stumbling blocks that adorned the source of pride.

6 Jesus attaches status to the bread and to the wine which breaks the fast that is set
> above the world,
> So spiritual control, under the authority of God, intensifies a multitude of greetings in
> a place that nurtures visions to completion.

Zion, within the mantle of protection,
Sees the Jewish nation acknowledge the rejoicing of the Christians when the time of
    change arrives.

7 Jesus has control of darkness, can shut out light, has an isolated place for
    the demanding -
Near an alternate place of destination - for the placement of the lax and the depraved
    born of the night.
Even the monsters of creation know Jesus, the Fisher of men, The King of kings, the
    Keeper of The Keys,
And the Guardian of peace - where all are being sifted, with some protected by
    the angels.

8 Jesus ensures the intensity of victory does not become a means of restriction.
Tending the fire of God is The Holy Spirit
Who brings The Spirit of conviction - and the tears of remorse - with the renewal
    of revival
On the youth unto the elderly: as all, but tares, participate in the raining of the
    blessings on the wheat."

My Content Study Aid

The Replevin of The Lord

"The replevin of The Lord needs to be retrieved,
        has been taken as an instance,
        has been hidden with stupidity.

  The replevin of The Lord is subject to pursuit,
        is subject to the hand of ownership,
        is subject to the voice of recognition.

The replevin of The Lord is subject to the claimant of the stolen,
        the claimant of the misappropriated,
        the claimant of the law change that brings injustice
                in its guises:
            deprivation of a benefit,
            unjust division of resources,
            preferential treatment for an enclave that shouts,
                for an enclave of intimidation,
                for an enclave that preaches
                    peace inside the
                    practice of perfidy,
                for an enclave imposing the
                    glove of terror on
                    those outside its walls.

The replevin of The Lord restores possession of what was taken,
        restores relationships which have been broken,
        restores the livelihoods which have been made of no account.

The replevin of The Lord accounts for every jot,
        accounts for every item,
        does not forget a thing.

The replevin of The Lord is seizure within a right that overcomes a wrong,
        returns all components of consumption from the storage
                    place involved,
        deals with wrongful gain.

The replevin of The Lord insists on the act of recompense for what no longer is,
        brings retribution on the pillager,
            on the looter,
            on those active in a smokescreen.

The replevin of The Lord includes the plundering of a nation,
        the plundering of a family,
        the plundering of a saint of God.

The replevin of The Lord bears on all injustice to and from A King down unto a slave.

The replevin of The Lord is sought by the wise,
        is subject to a conversation,
        is granted to the righteous who know the works of God.

The replevin of The Lord is as a message in a bottle,
        a message for the reading if the glass is shattered,
        a message of the consequences to the ill-considered.

The replevin of The Lord has immediacy of action,
        follows in the footsteps,
        catches the culprit in possession.

The replevin of The Lord exercises immediate recovery upon the testimony of
        the observant.

The replevin of The Lord may involve a chase,
        may involve the surrender of the fool,
        may stake a claim for the damage done,
        may follow the trail of a confession of disposal.

The replevin of The Lord knows the arm of man raised in violence,
        the arm of man raised in greed,
        the arm of man raised to meet the call from
                the plumbing,
                the pathways,
                of the body.

The replevin of The Lord knows the arm of a child,
        of a youth,
        raised in arousal by the false counsel of those befriended
                by the foe of man."

My Content Study Aid

_____
_____
_____
_____
_____
_____
_____
_____

The Dungeons of The Heart

"Many are the would-be sheep whose lips do not disclose the secret dungeons of
                                                                                                 their hearts.

The secret dungeons of the heart are hidden by man from man,
                        are not considered relevant by man to God,
                        are seen by God with the light as in the lamp-room of
                                                        a lighthouse.

The secret dungeons of the heart swing the drafting-gate to the pen that holds the goats,
                        need to be examined by the candle of the spirit,
                        give shelter to the blackness that needs to be thrown
                                                   into the light.

The secret dungeons of the heart need to be cleaned by man,
                        need to be emptied by man,
                        need to be conquered by man,
                        need to be circumcised by man,
                        need to be filled-in by man,
                        need to be deleted from the places to be visited,
                        need not carry blackness in the heart of man.

The dungeons of the heart are buried very deeply,
                        surface for fresh air,
                        learn to echo,
                        acquire vibrations,
                        can be visited with friends,
                        are known to the righteous,
                        will hold small secrets that expand.

The secret dungeons of the heart cannot surface without consent,
                        can be shared into a wasteland,
                        can become a vault when the key is handed over.

The secret dungeons of the heart can bring destruction to the body when a secret is
                                                     spilled in malice,
                                                   in folly,
                                                 in the quest for wealth.

The dungeons of the heart exist for but one purpose,
                        exist to house the sins of man,
                        exist to hold the dragons with the need to feed,
                        exist through satisfaction from depravity,
                        exist through thoughts of self-destruction,
                        exist through feeding all the senses from a table fraught with danger.

The dungeons of the heart can hold sickness in their thrall,
                can incubate disease,
                can multiply to overcome.

The dungeons of the heart can breed an army for attack,
                can muster germs for warfare on the host,
                can impede the wellness of the heart of man.

The dungeons of the heart can impinge on the body of man,
                can direct invasions,
                can inflict weakness of the spirit,
                can bring about the death of man.

The dungeons of the heart are the meeting place of Satanic souls,
                serve the hatching of the plots,
                are known in all the chambers.

The dungeons of the heart store the curses of generations,
                The Blood Oaths assigned to secrecy,
                the idols that are worshipped.

The dungeons of the heart should not be nourished by man,
                should not be tolerated by man,
                should not be welcomed by man.

Do not build	the dungeons of the heart.
Do not frequent	the dungeons of the heart.
Do not dwell in	the dungeons of the heart.
Do not worship what is found in	the dungeons of the heart.
Do not treat with levity	the dungeons of the heart.
Do not boast of the contents of	the dungeons of the heart.

The dungeons of the heart need to be obliterated from the heart of man,
                need to be annihilated from the soul of man,
                need to be resolved with wisdom prior to the death of man.

The dungeons of the heart quench the fire of The Spirit,
                bring tears to the face once on the cross,
                bring prospects to the cliff-edge,
                sear the gifts of God,
                rebel in anger from the seat of Grace,
                resolve in bitterness The Freewill choice of man.

The dungeons of the heart are cleansed by the heart in full repentance,
                are conquered by the overcoming spirit of man,
                suffer flooding of the caverns in immersion,
                shudder at the waters of new life,
                are dismembered in the presence of The light."

The Extraction of Man

"The adventuring of man can land him in foreign lands,
    can land him in great difficulties,
    can land him in places far from where he planned.

The adventuring of man can land him in a haven,
    can land him in a prison,
    can land him near to God,
    can land him far from God,
    can land him where he planned,
    can land him where only God knows where.

The adventuring of man can land him where he fears,
    where there is no return,
    where the darkness of the night remains forever.

The adventuring of man can land him in repulsive company,
    in the archives of the lost,
    in the entrapment of his soul.

The adventuring of man can land him beyond the reach of starlight,
    beyond the reach of moonlight,
    beyond the reach of sunlight.

The adventuring of man can land him in cold water,
    can land him in hot water,
    can land him in one piece,
    can land him as a shipwreck.

Extricating man from an adventure may not be a simple matter,
    from his own folly may call for much assistance,
    from where he landed may not be permitted,
    from darkness presupposes he can be found,
    from clutches calls for medication,
    from an environment requires knowledge of what is.

Extracting man may not be to his wish,
    may not be according to his will,
    may not be acceptable within his sight.

Extracting man may not be possible at a point in time,
    may require great patience,
    may require a sacrifice,
    may require a full confession.

The extraction of man is removal from the mire,

        is placement on a throne,
        is the feeding in surroundings conducive to great growth,
        is the offering of an alternative,
        is the appealing to his spirit,
        is his fellowship on the greatest of adventures.

The extraction of man is a rescue in disguise,
        is carrying the promise of the future,
        is on the flight path of reality.

The extraction of man confirms what is the closest to the heart of God,
        what is within The Power of God,
        what is the sacrifice of God.

The extraction of man cannot be by any other means,
        by man is a recipe for disaster,
        for man leads to captivity in enslavement.

The extraction of man needs knowledge of the end result,
        of the target destination,
        of the assistance on the way.

The extraction of man is not a joy ride in a hot balloon,
        is not a simulation,
        is not in coercion.

The extraction of man has to be the desire of man,
        has to be at the time of his own choosing,
        has to be as a result of his understanding.

The extraction of man leads to transformation of his soul,
        the safety of his spirit,
        the restoration of his body.

The extraction of man is the path to a new beginning,
        is an occurrence prior to interment in The Earth,
        is there for all to access,
            while it is today.

The extraction of man hears the mercy call of God,
        hears the reason for the sacrifice,
        hears the fare has been fully paid.

The pre-paid extraction of man is the ultimate benefit of life,
        is beyond the purchase of the wealth of man,
        leads to the most joyous of conclusions to the mortality
            of man.

The pre-paid extraction of man speaks to all mankind,
        speaks to every family,
        speaks to the grandest of designs for the destiny of man."

The Measure of A Man

"The measure of a man is his standing before God.

The measure of a man is his relationship with God,
        is his walk in righteousness,
        is his integrity of self,
        is the standards he imposes on his life.

The measure of a man is not to be as a puff of wind in a paper bag,
        as a drop of muck in a paddock filled with cows,
        as a deserted web found blowing in the wind.

The measure of a man requires stability with progress,
        honour with a firm handshake which carry all
                his promises,
        a history which drags no shame within its shadow
                of inspection.

The measure of a man has violence set aside,
        has trust and truth as companions every day,
        has a mouth of praise and worship attached to The Fear of God.

The measure of a man has wisdom with perception,
        has knowledge without deception,
        has the gifts of God alive and embedded in his Temple.

The measure of a man is determined by his goals,
        by the means employed in achievement,
        by the relationship of his spirit to his soul,
        by his dealings with his fellow man.

The measure of a man is not determined by his height,
        by his weight,
        by his girth,
        by his birth.

The measure of a man is how he treats those he encounters in his daily walk,
        with his heart in service,
        with his wealth accumulated as
                sufficient for his needs.

The measure of a man attends his tasks with joy,
        completes them on the schedule which is set,
        has a conscience happy with the outcome of the achievements of
                each day.

The measure of a man can be in tune attending to the reaching for the stars,

> in tune with the rearing of his family,
> in tune with contentment that all is well within his
> mortal life,
> in tune with his future of progression within The Realm
> of God.
>
> The measure of a man leaves a legacy for his life's work,
> leaves a legacy of inspiration,
> leaves a legacy involving both the secular and The Sacred,
> the worldly and The Divine,
> the maturing of man and The
> Maturity of God.
>
> The measure of a man lives a life reflective of his stature before God."

My Content Study Aid

A Foretaste of Heaven

"A foretaste of Heaven is for those who would be well prepared,
                who would have their expectations firmly in place,
                who bring understanding and wisdom to the table
                              of discussion.

A foretaste of Heaven is part of the fare as laid for My saints,
                as an invitation to encourage participation,
                as an embodiment of that which is held in store,
                as an indicator of the proximity of Heaven,
                as an example of life beyond the grave at the
                              closure of mortality.

A foretaste of Heaven requires a different way of thinking,
        requires a new way of conversing,
        requires a fresh approach to sustaining the body of perfection.

A foretaste of Heaven is to remove surprises,
        is to spread familiarity for a welcome home,
        is to enable the adoption of the new without feeling out of place.

A foretaste of Heaven is not a circular existence,
                has movement in straight lines which cannot be in parallel,
                      which do not meet at infinity,
                      which is the fastest way to travel,
                      which are not bent by the needs
                              of gravity.

A foretaste of Heaven has displays reactive to the new found senses of super sensitivity,
                      to the extended senses of mortality,
            where eyes are opened to the fullness of extent,
            where the colour spectrum has the full bandwidth still unknown to
                              the experience of man,
            where sound is no longer sent through the airwaves,
                no longer subject to a limit barrier on speed,
                no longer uses the technology within the mortality
                                  of the past,
                    is at the instantaneity of thought,
                          of the action of the fluency of
                              The Tongues of Heaven,
                    at the interpretation of transmissions of the spirit
                          now at home in surroundings
                          deemed familiar,

        at the ability to cope with the constructs of the
            multiplicity of messages in multiway
            disseminations and receipts.

A foretaste of Heaven has no tiredness arising from activity,
    has no aches and pains,
    has no accidents within mobility,
    has no confusion in the existence of being,
    has no searching for the lost.

A foretaste of Heaven has road maps to the stars with co-ordinates ascribed,
    has access across distances previously found impossible to man's
        then means of voyaging,
    has discoveries of immensity awaiting the sons and daughters of
        God within the playground of His garden:
        unbounded before the sight of My saints.

A foretaste of Heaven holds discoveries now held in check,
    holds means and methods to be handheld by way of introduction,
    has songs and dancing continuously available for the joyous
        and rejoicing,
    has praise and worship set aside for the grateful and the thankful
        both of heart and temperament,
    has the arts and crafts on schemes of grandeur where mountains
        may be dressed with the splendour of imagination,
        with the placing of the mantel of the cloth,
        with the availability of expertise upon request.

A foretaste of Heaven is seeing the surroundings with settings set for royalty,
    with settings commensurate with honouring the sons and
        daughters of God,
    with The Kings and Queens so dwelling in the three estates
        of The Realm of God,
    with all which has been prepared resulting from The Promise
        of The Son,
    with all of an inheritance readied as indicated to the Faithful,
    with the fulfilment of the epoch-in-waiting of God."

My Content Study Aid

_____
_____
_____
_____

The Glory of God

"I,
>The Lord,
>>speak to the peoples of The Earth of The Glory of God:
>>>>The God they may not know,
>>>>The God they may wish to know,
>>>>The God they may already know,
>>>>The God they ought to know,
>>>>The God they despise to know,
>>>>The God that awaits their love.

I,
>The Lord,
>>call for the attention of all mankind to listen to,
>>>to read,
>>>>to acquire,
>>>>>the sources of knowledge of The God of Love.

I,
>The Lord,
>>say,
>>>'Beware of false religions:
>>>>created through dissension—
>>>>which do not honour truth,
>>>>which call for vengeance by man on man,
>>>>which have a history of iniquity,
>>>>>where The Spirit is not present,
>>>>>where there is no reconciliation,
>>>>>where the works of man prevail,
>>>>>where the teaching of morality is flawed,
>>>>>where men and women are not honoured equally,
>>>>>where children are but slaves,
>>>>>where there is regeneration as some aspects of creation:
>>>>>>which are taught in darkness,
>>>>>>which are fraught with danger,
>>>>>>which are bought by those with souls that are thereby endangered.

>>Woe to those who teach,
>>>who impose,
>>>>who enforce such doctrines:
>>>>>for the wrath of God will place them.'

I,
>The Lord,

        created man and gifted him with his freewill,
            have not coerced him,
            have not swindled him,
            have not lied to him,
            have neither changed nor edited My Word that speaks of My relationship
                                                with The Love of My life.

For his sake I,
        have entered into covenants,
        have and do and will honour for ever the words of My mouth,
                                  of My prophets whom I
                                        keep close to My heart.

I,
   The Lord,
      say,
           to the peoples of The Earth:
              'Beware of those who tender codicils:
                        to aspects of behaviour,
                        to change their teachings,
                        to modify mistakes,
                        to edit the records of the past,
                        to circumvent a scrutiny of what has gone before.

            Such as they are not committed to The Truth,
            perceive man's freewill as an obstacle in their domains,
            forsake integrity in the heat of battle,
            bend the books said to be holy into a twisted knot of lies.

            For such as they shy from the light into the darkness.'

I,
   The Lord,
      say The Glory of God resides within His Magnificence and Might,
                              His Power and His Authority,
                              His Love and His Forgiveness,
                              His Incarnation and His Advent,
                              His Mercy and His Presence,
                              His Covenants and Promises:
            all that will be bestowed by The Son upon His Father's Flock.

I,
   The Lord,
      have witnesses unto death who testified of Me—
                            The Martyrs of The Crown.

I,
   The Lord,

have testimonies,
uncountable by man,
    who offer evidence of My visitation to their lives—
        The Healed of The Spirit.

I,
  The Lord,
    have prayers of multitudes who will testify if called—
        The Provisioned of The Lord.

I,
  The Lord,
    know such as these challenge the gods of man where The Spirit does not reign
      and silence begs the question:
        Where is The God with power,
          with impact,
        and with love?

I,
  The Lord,
    say,
      'I AM.'

I,
  The Lord,
    speak to the peoples of The Earth on which I walked,
      on which I died,
      on which I rose to life.

I,
  The Lord,
    speak to the peoples of The Earth to which I will return,
      for which there is a promise,
      on which I will rule.

I,
  The Lord Jesus,
    The Messiah,
    speak to the peoples of The Earth reserved as The Kingdom of The King
          of kings,
      reserved for The Standard of The King,
      reserved to The Banner of Authority that
        denotes possession."

Appendix

Flag and Standard of The Kingdom	382
Banner of The Kingdom in Use	383
Emblem of The Spirit in Use	383
Emblem of The Kingdom in Use	384
Anthem of The King	385
About the Scribe	*387*
Journaling and Notes (1)	*388*
Journaling and Notes (2)	*389*
Book 4 Reviews (2)	*390*
Book 8 Review (1)	*391*

Flag and Standard in Use

The Flag of The Kingdom of God

The Standard of The Kingdom of God

Banner in Use

The Banner of The Kingdom of God

Emblem of The Spirit in Use

Embroidered Caps   Screen-printed T-Shirts
Multi-fitting   Various sizes
For Team Sports, Youth Groups, Christian Activities,
Get Togethers, Marches, Camps, Witnessing,
Displays of Solidarity, Regional Games, Cycling,
Recreational Day-wear.

Emblem of The Kingdom in Use

Vinyl

Make a

Remind us of a

Start a

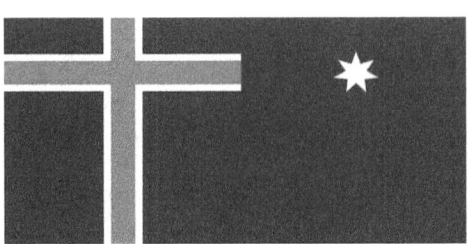

Decals

Statement

Relationship

Conversation

Fridge, Computer, Letterbox, Car windscreen, Car rear window,
Windows, Front Door, & many others - e.g. School books, Lunch Boxes.

Anthem of The King

[Revelation 15:3-4 (Exodus 15:1-18)]
New King James Version

The Lord has indicated that there is to be "**The Anthem of The King**"— *the national anthem of The Kingdom of God here on Earth.*

"The Anthem is to be played with Trumpets,
                      Horns,
                      Drums,
                      Flutes,
                      Harps,
                      Violins and Bells.

    To those called to The Ministry of Clefs:
        These are classes of the instruments of the peoples of the world.
                As the shofar is a horn,
                so the piccolo is a flute.
                As the tambourine is a drum,
                so the piano is a harp.

The Anthem of The Lord,
    The Anthem of The King,
        will not come forth from My people using the electrons of the universe.

        For therein lies dishonour;
            for the electrons of the universe are neither made nor touched by man.

The Anthem of The King is 'The Song of The Lamb'.

    'Great and marvellous [are] Your works, Lord God Almighty!
    Just and true [are] Your ways, O King of The Saints!
    Who shall not fear You, O Lord, and Glorify Your name?
    For [You] alone [are] holy.
    For all nations shall come and worship before You,
    For Your judgements have been manifested.'

        For this was recognised in the days of Moses;
            and now to be instated as The Anthem of The King.

The Anthem of The King that aligns in perfect harmony with The Banner of The King
                                                                             now revealed.

The Anthem of The King is processional,
                calls to worship,
                      precedes the war cry of The Lord.

The Standard of The King accompanies The Anthem of The King throughout
all lands.

The Anthem of The King stirs the soul of man,
    is heard before a seat of judgement,
    brings The Fear of The Lord.

The Anthem of The King calls for attention,
    calls for silence of speech within the throng,
    calls for ears attuned to hear and lips prepared
        to sing The Anthem of The Lamb."

Scribal Note:
'The Anthem of The King of Kings' with lyrics, and the three Fanfares of the commissioned Fanfare Suite, are in Book 6, "GOD Speaks to His Bridal Presence".

My Content Study Aid

About The Scribe

Updated 16 February 2019

Anthony is 78, having been married to his wife, Adrienne, for 55 years. They have five married children: Carolyn, Alan, Marie, Emma and Sarah and fourteen grandchildren: Matthew, and Ella; Phillipa, and Jonathan; Jeremy, Ngaire, and Trevor; Jake, Finn, Crystal, and Caleb; Bjorn, Greta, and Minka.

Anthony was raised on a dairy farm in Springston, Canterbury, NZ in the 1940s. He graduated from Canterbury University, Christchurch, NZ with a B.Sc. in chemistry and mathematics in 1962. He was initially employed as an industrial chemist in flour milling and linear programming applications. These used the first IBM 360 at the university for determining least cost stock food formulations and production parameters. Later he was involved in similar applications on the refining side of the oil industry in Britain, Australia and New Zealand. This was followed by sales and managerial experience in the chemical industry.

The family moved to a Bay of Plenty, NZ, town in 1976 when Anthony took up funeral directing, as a principal, expanding an initial sibling partnership until the close of the century. Anthony acquired practical experience in accounting, business management, and computer usage (early Apples— including The Lisa).

Upon retiring from active funeral directing in 2000 and selling his interests, he then commenced the promotion and the writing of funeral management software for the NZ funeral environment. Rewarded with national success, he retired, in 2007, from the active management of that interest, now living near some of his family in Hamilton NZ.

Anthony was brought up in the Methodism of his father until his mid-teens, his mother's side was Open Brethren. He is Christian in belief within an Apostolic Pentecostal Charismatic framework of choice (since the 1990s) having been earlier in the Mormon church for several years. Thereafter he was in the Baptist denomination followed by finding a home within the Acts (Apostolic) church movement for some years, and now in Glory Release Ministries, one where all have made him welcome.

He and his wife, who has visited a number of Asian countries, have been to India in 2011, 12, 13, 16 and 18 on The Lord's tasks and have witnessed and participated in many miracles which befall His People and The Multitudes.

His forbears William Henry Eddy and Margaret Jane Eddy, née Oats, emigrated to New Zealand from Gulval, Cornwall, England in 1878 on a sailing ship, with a very slow passage time of 79 days, and with their three month old infant child, Margaret Anne, dying 21 October 1878 from Congestion of the brain on board the Marlborough while en route to NZ. The Marlborough sailed London 19 September 1878, via Plymouth 26 September 1878, and arrived Lyttelton 14 December 1878 with 336 assisted immigrants. His grandfather, Alfred Charles Eddy, then but three years old, together with an older brother aged four, obviously survived the trials of the sea voyage to become a part of a family with a further eleven New Zealand born siblings all living to maturity.

Journaling and Notes (1)

Journaling and Notes (2)

Book 4 Reviews (2) 'GOD Speaks to Man in The End-time'

Review: AG

From the point of view of a non-religious reader, the format is a bit perplexing, but the content is refreshing. This isn't a straight-up religious reading, this isn't forcing religion down your throat. This is giving you an interesting way to read through someone else's eyes, this is giving you insight. I chose to read this book because I am not personally religious, and have always found religion something I personally do not choose to devote my life to. Reading from the point of view of someone who does choose to devote their life to faith is far more interesting than I had expected. This gives you pros and cons of your actions, warnings of the future and how your actions may affect you. It warns humanity of its loss of faith, of how its meandering through life deviates from God's views. In a way, this book teaches us not that religion is absolute, but that humanity is absolute, and to treat each other in ways that God has not foretold or suggested is to deny our very humanity itself. It warns us of sin, it congratulates us on things done according to The Lord. This book could be classified as self-help from a religious standpoint. Again, from the point of view of someone who doesn't share the author's faith, this is an extremely interesting read. Anthony speaks from his heart and his faith, and his faith is strong. He truly believes in the ways of his religion and in that way he wishes to share his faith, and share his humanity.

Review: JF

This was a unique book to read because of the way it was formatted in the style of poem readings. I like the "I" outline poems. It was as if Jesus was speaking directly to you. The poems, however, are very, very, lengthy and it could be because the author wanted to stress the importance of the message within the poems.
The poems alleges the thoughts of Jesus and God's purposes in regards to God's timeline and not man's. Patience will be needed in the reading of the poems as the lines and verses are very repetitive but again I, personally, believe this is done to stress the importance of the messages in the poems. If you keep reading then you will get a better insight to the poem's messages and their true meanings.
The poems, also, express the relationship or non-relationship between God and his goodness and Satan and his sinfulness. One of my favorite sections of the book was the end-time specialty poems. I found this section very enlightening. I especially liked reading the "End-time passion of the Lord" poems. End-time prophecies are mentioned, poems in regards to children and God's thoughts pertaining to end-time-prophecies. Do read the beauty of the morning poems it will make you feel appreciation for the morning time and the beauty in it.
I feel the poems main theme were to relate Jesus's messages according to the author, Anthony Eddy and how he feels they pertain to all of mankind as well as establish who Jesus really was and his overall purpose for being on earth.

Book 8 Review (1) 'GOD Speaks of Loving His Creation'

Review : Suzanne H

This is the eighth book in a series of End-time psalms dictated by God through the Scribe, Anthony A Eddy. While the psalms contain counselling and commentary on the current state of humanity, a major theme running through this book is man's freewill to choose or not, his eternal destiny within the Garden of God.

While there is truth for the intellectual in Eddy's recommendation not to read these psalms as stand-alone psalms, as they build sequentially, others will be thought-provoked enough by the first attention-grabbing sentence of each: 'The days of embitterment filled with dissatisfaction are about to come as thunderstorms within the sky.'(p1) 'The arrowheads of God are the means of sending messages to the hearts of man.' (p49) 'In the sights of God is a dangerous place to be, is a blessed place to be.'(p182) – reminding me of what Mr Beaver says about Aslan in C.S. Lewis' The Lion, the Witch and the Wardrobe: "'Course he isn't safe. But he is good. He is the King".

Again, others will be thought-provoked enough, encouraged and uplifted by a particular stanza:

'The beauty of My Garden has the fragrance of delight,
        has the fragrance of the morning dew,
        has the fragrance of the evening dusk.' (p70)

'The Glory of My garden showcases the beautiful and the lovely,
        the wonderful and marvellous,
        the glorified and stately. (p161)

Some of the psalms reflect the current first world state. My first thought was that 'The Tableting of Man'(p146) would relate to our electronic devices but it doesn't. It speaks about the climate of fear induced by advertising which impels us to take supplements for every perceived dietary deficiency and every perceived health benefit.

Some of the psalms reflect the world opinion that dismissing the intellect is a prerequisite of faith. 'The meetings of the minds verifies and supports the edifice of God.' (p106)

The scholar in me found it was sometimes necessary to resort to the dictionary: the difference between salutations and greetings, crevasse and crevice, variance and variability.

The theologian in me was challenged: 'The welcome to my garden has catch-up schools for those who were taught that the tongues of God did not exist,
        were of no avail,
        were to be ignored,
        were not relevant,
        were a demonic babbling of the day. (p211)

I conclude that these psalms could be used as a daily devotional, study topics for home-groups, sermon titles and for those who just love the language of poetry. It was almost impossible to write a review of this book as each first line, stanza or psalm really requires a review of its own! I recommend that you take the time to savour and reflect on each of these beautiful offerings.

www.ingramcontent.com/pod-product-compliance
Lightning Source LLC
Chambersburg PA
CBHW071258110526
44591CB00010B/707